"By arguing convincingly that 'bearing witness' is both the central aspect of the church's mission and the identity of God's people, DeVries helps correct a number of mistaken notions about mission and opens up new avenues for embracing our own calling as witnesses. This book is a tremendous resource: careful, clear, confessional, biblical, hopeful, inspiring, and practical. This will be one of the first books—if not *the* first book—on missions that I recommend to pastors, students, and church members."

Kevin DeYoung, Senior Pastor, Christ Covenant Church, Matthews, North Carolina; Associate Professor of Systematic Theology, Reformed Theological Seminary, Charlotte

"In this book, Brian DeVries helps us to see that we as Christians are called to be witnesses of what we have come to know of God's saving purpose in Christ. He shows this across the Bible and across history since the days of the apostles. I love the fact that he wrestles with how we can carry out this task in light of today's challenges. I am grateful for this warm and informative book!"

Conrad Mbewe, Pastor, Kabwata Baptist Church, Lusaka, Zambia; Founding Chancellor, African Christian University

"Brian DeVries has put together a wonderful arching overview of God's redemptive plan throughout history and the role of his people, through the church, in seeing his glory made known among all peoples. The quality of research, historicity, and biblical rooting make this book a must-read for serious students of missions. May its impact be felt by those in the academy but even more by those faithful Christians in the pew, who through persevering witness will see the gospel of Jesus Christ reach the ends of the earth."

Brooks Buser, President, Radius International

"This book is itself a witness. It's a witness to a mature understanding of a discipline refined by years and years of teaching and ministry. A rich confessional depth coupled with crystal clarity and concision will surely make *You Will Be My Witnesses* a standard missiology textbook relevant to both seminaries and local churches around the globe. Highly recommended."

Daniel Strange, Director, Crosslands Forum, United Kingdom; Vice President, The Southgate Fellowship

T0267334

"*You Will Be My Witnesses* should be the default introductory textbook for classes in missions, laying the theological groundwork carefully and thoroughly. But it also deserves to be read by a multitude of pastors and ordinary Christians who will be stimulated and encouraged to pray for and to participate in the task of bringing the gospel to all nations."

Iain M. Duguid, Professor of Old Testament, Westminster Theological Seminary

"*You Will Be My Witnesses* is an essential work for all who long to understand and effectively participate in God's mission. This book not only captures the essence of the divine mission but also translates it into practical terms, solidly grounded in Scripture. DeVries, with erudition and theological depth, guides the reader on a journey that spans from the biblical call for faithful witness to its contemporary application in the local church. This book is a valuable resource that encourages and equips the church to obey Christ's Great Commission."

Augustus Nicodemus Lopes, Pastor, Esperança Bible Presbyterian Church, Orlando, Florida; former Chancellor, Universidade Presbiteriana Mackenzie, Brazil

"For years I have been waiting for a book to recommend that helps Christians think biblically about their place in God's glorious mission today. This is it. Brian DeVries has drawn together in one accessible book an appreciation of the biblical foundations, historical development, and contemporary challenges of Christian witness. This is a book that lifts our gaze, warms our hearts, and provides practical steps that we and our churches can take to be more faithful witnesses wherever we find ourselves in God's world."

Simon Gillham, Vice Principal and Head of Department of Mission, Moore Theological College, Australia

"At its heart, this fresh reflection on witness and mission in the Scriptures, church history, and the world today is a book about the sort of piety that truly honors God. It shows how love for God and obedience to his command to bear witness to the great acts recorded in his holy word results in what DeVries rightly calls 'missional piety': a spirituality marked by passion and intentionality when it comes to sharing one's faith. All in all, an important reminder!"

Michael A. G. Haykin, Professor of Church History and Biblical Spirituality, The Southern Baptist Theological Seminary

"We are not 'building' but 'receiving' a kingdom. Brian DeVries shows from Genesis to Revelation that God's mission in Christ is center stage. Instead of bearing this mission on our shoulders, we get to be ambassadors of this good news! This paradigm-shifting message from a veteran in missions should be at the top of any reading list on the subject."

Michael Horton, J. Gresham Machen Professor of Systematic Theology and Apologetics, Westminster Seminary California

"If you seek to respond faithfully to the redemptive work of Christ, I urge you to read this book. It will embolden you to proclaim the gospel with confidence, recognizing that without mission, there is no church; without evangelism, there is no advancement of Christ's kingdom; and without witness, there is no growth. Brian DeVries's work can add a relatable and impactful dimension to the recommendation for those who have missionary zeal. May the Lord's saving grace permeate our society through our faithful witness."

Changwon Shu, Emeritus Professor, Chongshin Theological Seminary, South Korea

"The author has provided us with a comprehensive, robust biblical theology of what it means to be Christian witnesses within the mission of God. It is a scholarly work of high caliber and should be recommended as an academic textbook, yet it is also a practical resource for all serious Christians who seek to understand their role in God's saving plan."

Mohan Chacko, Principal Emeritus and Professor of Theology and Mission, Presbyterian Theological Seminary, India

"Drawing from years of personal engagement in God's universal mission and enriched by insights from church history, Brian DeVries challenges us to reexamine the local church's role in God's mission. With a balanced blend of biblical theology of mission, historical perspective, and practical wisdom, this book inspires us to move into a deeper, more fervent commitment to Christ's kingdom. It is a call to rediscover the passion for missions within our church communities as we align ourselves in God's sovereign plan for the world. This book is a must-read for anyone seeking to ignite a renewed zeal for God's mission."

Sherif A. Fahim, New Testament Chair, Alexandria School of Theology, Egypt; General Director, El-Soora Ministries

You Will Be My Witnesses

You Will Be My Witnesses

Theology for God's Church
Serving in God's Mission

Brian A. DeVries

CROSSWAY®

WHEATON, ILLINOIS

Cover design: Jordan Singer

Cover image Jordan Eskovitz

First printing 2024

Printed in the United States of America

Scripture quotations are from the ESV® Bible (The Holy Bible, English Standard Version®), © 2001 by Crossway, a publishing ministry of Good News Publishers. Used by permission. All rights reserved. The ESV text may not be quoted in any publication made available to the public by a Creative Commons license. The ESV may not be translated into any other language.

Trade paperback ISBN: 978-1-4335-9138-9
ePub ISBN: 978-1-4335-9140-2
PDF ISBN: 978-1-4335-9139-6

Library of Congress Cataloging-in-Publication Data

Names: DeVries, Brian A., 1974– author.

Title: You will be my witnesses : theology for God's church serving in God's mission / Brian A. DeVries.

Description: Wheaton, Illinois : Crossway, 2024. | Includes bibliographical references and index.

Identifiers: LCCN 2023053506 (print) | LCCN 2023053507 (ebook) | ISBN 9781433591389 (trade paperback) | ISBN 9781433591396 (pdf) | ISBN 9781433591402 (epub)

Subjects: LCSH: Witness bearing (Christianity) | Church work. | Theology, Practical.

Classification: LCC BV4520 .D48 2024 (print) | LCC BV4520 (ebook) | DDC 248/.5—dc23/eng/20240331

LC record available at https://lccn.loc.gov/2023053506

LC ebook record available at https://lccn.loc.gov/2023053507

Crossway is a publishing ministry of Good News Publishers.

To Lanae, a faithful witness and my best friend.

Contents

List of Illustrations   *xiii*

Preface: Your Church Serving in God's Mission   *xv*

Introduction: Witness within God's Mission   *1*

PART 1: THE BIBLICAL STORY OF GOD'S MISSION

1   Mission in the Old Testament   *27*

2   The Mission of Jesus Christ   *49*

3   The Mission of the Holy Spirit   *71*

4   Witness in the New Testament   *93*

PART 2: CONCISE HISTORY OF CHRISTIAN WITNESS

5   The Church's Witness after Pentecost   *113*

6   Historical Themes in Christian Witness   *131*

PART 3: OUR WITNESS IN AN UN-CHRISTIAN WORLD

7   Christian Witness as Gospel Presence   *155*

8   Christian Witness by Gospel Message   *179*

9   Christian Witness by Gospel Response   *201*

10   Christian Witness in Gospel Community   *223*

Conclusion: Motivating Christian Witness   *243*

General Index   *267*

Scripture Index   *277*

Illustrations

Figures

1   The mission of God the Father   *7*

2   Witness in God's mission in world history   *13*

3   Mission and witness in the Old Testament   *45*

4   Four lenses for viewing Christ's mission   *50*

5   The Spirit's ministry in the world   *80*

6   The mission of the triune God   *88*

7   Mission and witness in the New Testament   *115*

8   Historical themes in Christian witness   *150*

9   Christ's threefold office and our witness   *175*

10   The evangelistic trialogue   *187*

11   God's ancillary witnesses   *216*

12   The church's posture in the world   *236*

13   Actions and features of missional reform   *263*

Tables

1   Parallel passages of the Great Commission   *63*

2   Bearing witness to Christ   *96*

3   Ten aspects of witness in Scripture   *122*

4   Biblical and historical aspects of witness   *156*

5   Heidelberg Catechism, Lord's Day 12   *161*

6   Church witness assessment scorecard   *259*

Preface

Your Church Serving in God's Mission

HOW IS YOUR OWN LOCAL CHURCH a part of God's universal mission? Most of our churches are involved in some form of witnessing activity. Perhaps your church is faithfully sending out and supporting missionaries, either internationally or for other good causes locally. Perhaps some members of your church participate regularly in local ministries: speaking with inmates at a prison, helping the homeless at a shelter, or counseling at a crisis pregnancy center. Perhaps other activities of your church could be grouped into the larger category of outward-facing ministries: leading short-term mission trips to needy areas in your region, donating money to global relief organizations, engaging publicly with political and cultural leaders, or participating in local campus evangelism or even open-air street preaching. These all are often wonderful ways to do our part, to share our time and resources for a good cause around us and across the world.

Many of us, however, wish our churches were more faithful in Christian witness. Our church is the community of God's people in our locality with whom we gather weekly for worship. We love our church and know the community well, and so we are in a position to ask probing questions about ourselves: Are the majority of our members filled with the Spirit of mission, a holy passion for the cause of Christ and his kingdom around the globe? Are we praying fervently for a revival of true religious affections in our community, and for the salvation of our unsaved neighbors next door? Are the majority of our fellow church members participating in at least one form of local witness? Are we living consciously as witnesses of Christ, commissioned to "make disciples" in our local region "and to the end of the earth" (Matt. 28:19; Acts 1:8)? Is our church truly zealous for God's mission, in soul and passion, or are we only associated with several outward-facing ministry projects from time to time?

Some of us may admit that our churches are not yet where they ought to be in this area. We admit that we have been distracted by other things—good things, perhaps, but still diversions from faithful Christian witness. It is a good church, we might say, but this is not our area of strength. Or perhaps we are praying fervently that the Holy Spirit would stir up more of this zeal within our church. We desire to see the witness of Christ become the driving heart-passion of God's people in our church community.

My Prayer and Purpose

My prayer is that this book will help you motivate your church to more faithful participation in God's mission. In his sovereign wisdom, God has appointed his church to be his witness in the world, especially in the present age following the Spirit's outpouring at Pentecost (Isa. 43:8–12; 44:8; Acts 1:8). The collective witness of God's people has always been his primary human agency within the history of his mission. For this reason, we will reflect in later chapters on the empowered witness of all believers and the public witness of the communion of saints. We desire to reform our churches so that they will be more faithful witnesses of Christ. This book is designed to be a resource for Christians who are prayerfully working to stir up their church communities for increased participation in God's mission.

Our motivation for mission, however, must be built on biblical knowledge and vision. Often the weakness of a church's witness is due to an incomplete understanding of God's mission and the best way to participate in it. We do not have a rich and robust biblical theology of mission. We have not reflected biblically on contemporary issues in Christian witness. We have not yet been inspired with biblical hope and passionate desire to see Christ's kingdom filling the earth as the waters cover the sea (Isa. 11:9). We are still distracted by the church's growing ministry challenges in a world that is increasingly hostile to our gospel. Like Christ's disciples experiencing the demonic storm in Matthew 8:23–27, we are distracted by the fearsome winds and waves, forgetting that the Lord of glory is with us in the boat. Christ must first refocus our vision and strengthen our faith before rebuking the circumstantial distractions.

What will motivate us to more faithfulness in Christian witness? We do not want another five-point pep talk about how to be successful witnesses. We also do not want more nebulous dreams built on un-grounded hopes. Instead, we need a biblical theology of God's mission, and especially a robust theology of Reformed experiential witness that is grounded in Trinitarian missiology. We need to see the vision of God's glorious plan that will soon be consummated.

Mission is *God's work within the world to save sinners* for the praise of his glory.[1] He planned this work from eternity, and his mission is now being accomplished in the world. God's mission of redemption started in time when he first came to the world to evangelize fallen sinners (Gen. 3:9–15). Jesus Christ, the sent one, is the center of this mission. God's mission will end when the last of God's elect have been gathered. The Holy Spirit continues this mission today by gathering God's people and empowering them to be his witnesses. God's people have always been called to serve in God's mission by bearing witness to God's Son among all nations.

---

1   We will further explain and expand this preliminary definition of mission in the chapters that follow. Theologians speak of God's external works of creation, providence, and redemption. In this classification, we consider God's mission as parallel with his work of redemption. As with all his works, the purpose of God's salvific mission is to the praise of his glory (Eph. 1:3–14).

Bearing witness to Christ is the work of the church in the world today. Our role, as God's people living within this un-Christian world, is to serve in evangelism, apologetics, global gospel partnerships, church planting, compassion ministries, biblical counseling, cultural engagement, gospel worship, gospel suffering, and the many other activities that faithfully bear witness to Christ. Christian witness is the activity of the church serving within God's mission. The many conflicting definitions of mission, however, require us to ground our understanding of the church's task in a biblical theology of God's overarching mission, to illustrate this definition with practical examples from church history, and to reflect theologically on practical activities of Christian witness in the contemporary world.

The goal of this book, therefore, is to precisely define *mission* and *witness* by studying the story of God's mission and the church's participation in it. My primary method is not an exegetical examination of specific biblical passages but a missiological reflection on how Scripture as a whole portrays the grand metanarrative of God's mission and guides our reflection on issues in contemporary Christian witness. We will define and shape our understanding of the church's witness from Scripture in a way that is grounded in and consistent with the bigger picture of God's sovereign plan and purpose. In this way we guard ourselves from the many extremes and deviations in the history of Christian witness. We can also evaluate and correct recent differences among evangelicals about mission, evangelism, apologetics, and related activities. With this in view, let me sketch a quick picture of where we are going together.

This book begins with an introduction that gives preliminary definitions, continues with three parts, and then ends with a conclusion that brings it all together. Part 1, the biblical story of God's mission (chaps. 1–4), concisely explains the triune God's mission, highlighting ten aspects of the church's witness as taught by the Old and New Testaments, with a specific focus on the ministries of both Jesus Christ and the Holy Spirit. My objective is to lay a foundation of biblical theology and identify principles for the contemporary theological reflection that follows.

Part 2, a concise history of Christian witness (chaps. 5–6), further describes the witness of the church in the world, looking at the apostolic age and mission history from God's perspective and highlighting seven major themes of faithful Christian witness throughout the past two thousand years. This section could have been much longer, but space was limited and there are many excellent historical accounts and missionary biographies available today.

Part 3, our witness in an un-Christian world (chaps. 7–10), reflects theologically on the church's contemporary witness, based on the preceding biblical theology and brief historical review. We look specifically at the church's witness in four areas: identity and calling of gospel presence, effectual and effective gospel communication, apologetic response to idolatry and opposition, and the public witness of the community of saints. The conclusion is more practical, ending with a case study of the missional hope that motivates our Reformed experiential witness.

Becoming More Faithful

There is much we can do, by God's grace, to help our own church members become more faithful in Christian witness. Throughout church history God has often used the following three activities to arouse and encourage the missional zeal of his people.

First, we can *strive together in prayer* for our churches to be filled with the Spirit of mission. As William Carey writes, we "must be men [and women] of great piety, prudence, courage, forbearance; of orthodoxy in [our] sentiments . . . and, above all, must be instant in prayer for the effusion of the Holy Spirit upon the people of [our] charge."[2] Many times in the past our sovereign God has graciously answered the passionate prayers of his people for a fresh outpouring of Christ's Spirit.

---

2 William Carey, *An Enquiry into the Obligations of Christians to Use Means for the Conversion of the Heathens* (Leicester, UK: Ann Ireland, 1792), 75–76. Likewise, Andrew Murray (1828–1917) states, "The man who mobilizes the Christian church to pray will make the greatest contribution to world evangelization in history." Jason Mandryk, *Operation World*, 7th edition (Colorado Springs, CO: Biblica, 2010), 301.

Therefore we continue steadfastly in prayer for the Holy Spirit to fill our church communities afresh, so that our churches will be empowered with boldness and endurance to witness of Christ, and so that Christ's mission will advance both locally and globally (Acts 4:29–31; cf. Rom. 15:30; Col. 4:2–3; 2 Thess. 3:1–5).

Second, we can *remember together* the wonderful works of God in church history, how "the word of God" has "continued to increase" and "multiplied greatly" and prevailed "mightily" around the world (see Acts 6:7; 12:24; 19:20). We must remember these glorious deeds of the Lord; we must not hide them from our children, since forgetting will confuse our vision and kill our zeal for God's mission. The countless biographies of faithful Christian witnesses should be greatly treasured, not only to learn from their strengths and weaknesses but also because God has often used their stories to stir up missional hope and renew missional piety for contemporary Christian witness, as we will consider in the conclusion. Though usually forgotten by the world, the undying testimony of thousands of Christ's faithful witnesses continues to speak (Heb. 11:4).

Third, along with praying and remembering, we must also *carefully study together* God's word to reflect on the mission of God's people, both theologically and practically, in order to learn how our local churches should best participate in God's universal mission. The systematic study of God's people serving in God's mission is the focus of this book. My hope is that this book will help you better understand the significant role of your church within the bigger story of God's redemptive history. Thus we study all of Scripture, both Old and New Testaments, reflecting on how each part of the story relates to Christian witness and considering the many examples in Scripture of how God's people were called and commissioned to serve in his mission.

My primary audiences are faithful Christians, church members and church leaders together, who long to see their own church community more committed to the cause of Christ and his kingdom in this world.

The conclusion's closing section is especially designed for church leaders to use as a template to aid discussion within their own church communities. This book can also be used as a textbook or for supplemental reading at the many faithful Bible schools and seminaries around the world. Additionally, I hope this book will aid your personal reflection and spiritual growth, and especially I desire that this study motivates you to both fervent prayer for the success of God's mission and faithful service in your various activities of Christian witness.[3] This book is especially designed for Bible study groups, with discussion questions at the end of each chapter to stimulate further reflection. It can be used as a fourteen-week study series, starting with an initial discussion and time of prayer, then reading one chapter per session, and concluding with a final review and prayerful reflection on how our churches can be intentional about growing in Christian witness.

Personally, I have taught this material many times over the past twenty years, at various levels of learning, to hundreds of Bible students in both Africa and America. During this time, my academic ministry was never divorced from ministry practice: by God's grace, I planted three churches in Pretoria, South Africa, served as leader of Mukhanyo Theological College, and participated in a number of local and global ministries. Though I do not yet fully understand the mystery of God's mission, and while I certainly do not pretend to have all the answers, I can unreservedly say that I have wrestled personally with all the content in this book. My prayer still is "to comprehend with all the saints what is the breadth and length and height and depth" of this mystery (Eph. 3:18). Along with many other faithful Christians around the world, I am trying to practice the principles of Christian witness and can, by God's grace, share from personal experience a few

---

3 As George Muller (1805–1898) often stated: "This is one of the great secrets in connexion with successful service for the Lord; to work as if everything depended upon our diligence, and yet not to rest in the least upon our exertions, but upon the blessing of the Lord." Mueller, *A Narrative of Some of the Lord's Dealings with George Muller, Written by Himself. Jehovah Magnified. Addresses by George Muller Complete and Unabridged*, 2 vols. (Muskegon, MI: Dust and Ashes, 2003), 2:290.

things that may be helpful to others. My desire is that you will find this format helpful as you prayerfully motivate other people to reflect biblically on God's mission and Christian witness.

I am indebted to the many students at various schools, as well as my ministry coworkers over the past three decades, who have helped me think through this material and test it in various ways. I am also indebted to colleagues who read earlier drafts of this work, including Iain M. Duguid, Simon J. Gilham, Terreth J. Klaver, Ronaldo Lidório, John W. Span, Daniel Strange, Jan H. van Doleweerd, Alistair I. Wilson, and other friends who gave valuable advice along the way. I am especially grateful for my family: my wife and cowitness, Lanae, carried a heavier load so that I could carve out time for writing in the midst of many other ministry commitments. My children also—Krista, Micah, Titus, Andrew, and Mercy—received less attention from me than desired during the past year—but now Daddy's book is finally finished. We as a family continue to pray that the Lord will use this meager contribution as he continues to bless all the families of the earth (Gen. 12:3).

Introduction

Witness within God's Mission

WHAT IS MISSION? Many Christians answer this question by turning to Jesus's familiar words in Matthew 28:19: "Go therefore and make disciples of all nations . . ." Known as the Great Commission, these words are essential for understanding the mission of the church in the world. But using only the Great Commission creates an incomplete picture. There is so much more to the story of God's mission!

I often start by asking my students to make a list of Bible passages that speak about mission. These lists always include Matthew 28 and usually many other verses: Acts 1:8 (witness); 2 Timothy 4:5 (evangelism); Matthew 5:16 and 1 Peter 2:12 (gospel community); 1 Peter 3:15 and 2 Corinthians 10:5 (apologetics); or related activities like Hebrews 13:2 (hospitality). Some students add Old Testament passages, like Genesis 12:1–3, Exodus 19:5–6, and Psalm 67, or even Isaiah 45:22 and 61:1–3.

The deeper concern, however, is how these (and similar) passages fit together to form a comprehensive theology of mission. We know instinctively that faithful mission practice must be grounded in a biblically-based theology, but we often struggle to present a clear and concise—yet also comprehensive—definition of mission. My goal is to help us do just that.

We begin by sketching a preliminary definition of mission in this introduction. It will take several chapters, though, to see how mission fits within the full panorama of Scripture before we can formulate a more comprehensive definition. For now, let's look briefly at two pivotal passages: Genesis 3:1–21 and Acts 1:1–11.

God's Mission in the Garden

In Genesis 3:9, God speaks to Adam for the first time after the fall, asking: "Where are you?" God had spoken the world into existence at creation, but now he speaks within his world for the purpose of re-demption. Now we see God seeking out sinners who are trying to hide from him. This divine activity in Genesis 3 is the beginning of God's mission of redemption. It is the start of the story, a glorious history of redemption that will continue until Christ concludes God's mission when he comes the second time to judge all nations.

Consider the mission activity of the Lord, the first evangelist in the fallen world. First, the Lord *comes* to his world (Gen. 3:8). God's world had been created very good, perfectly displaying his power, wisdom, goodness, and beauty. The whole creation, with Adam and Eve at the pinnacle as God's vice-regents, had unfailingly declared his glory. Adam's sin, however, brought into God's world the reign of death (Rom. 5:12). As a result, the sovereign Creator could have destroyed all nature and created something new in its place. But God acts with sovereign grace, choosing rather to redeem dying sinners from their fallen state in the now sinful world.

The Lord also *calls out* to sinners in hiding (Gen. 3:9). Before the fall, Adam and Eve had enjoyed fellowship with God as their Creator. But after their rebellion against him, they also know God as their Judge and his righteous wrath against sin (Rom. 1:18). Now Adam and Eve experienced fear, guilt, and shame for the first time. They responded in fear by running from God, hiding behind human attempts to cover their sense of guilt and shame. But God, being rich in mercy, chose to seek and to save these lost sinners (Luke 19:10; Eph. 2:4).

The Lord then *convicts* sinners by exposing their lies with probing questions (Gen. 3:9, 11, 13). God already knew where Adam was hiding and what he had done, but he asked these questions so that Adam would be convicted with a sense of his own guilt and shame. God drew Adam out of hiding, unmasking his human attempts to hide from the truth and exposing his fallen condition.

Finally, the Lord *comforts* sinners with the gospel promise. This first promise is the beginning of the story of redemption: another Adam is coming who will carry the curse of sin, crush Satan's head, and remedy the mess that the first Adam had made (Gen. 3:15; cf. 1 Cor. 15:45). The Lord himself is the first evangelist; he himself comes to this sinful world to declare the glorious gospel message of forgiveness and hope.[1]

All three persons of the Trinity are at work already in Genesis 3. The Christ enters his world in his preincarnate form as the Word to evangelize sinners who are running away. The Spirit is also present, working with the Word to expose guilt and shame; he convinces Adam and Eve of sin, righteousness, and coming judgment (John 16:8). In this way, the Father begins to reveal his plan of redemption. This passage introduces mission as, first and foremost, the work of the triune God.

We will return to these themes in later chapters. For now, we may summarize several essential truths about mission already taught in Genesis 3, in the aftermath of the fall. We see *the context of mission*: God's created world, once beautiful and very good but now cursed after sin, having become a mixture of both the truth of God's revelation and the opposition of Satan's lie. We see the *objects of mission*: humans created in God's image to glorify him but now running from God's righteous judgment. We also see the *consequences of sin*: fear, guilt, and shame, which motivate man-made religions and ethical systems as attempts to hide from God's truth. We learn the *wonder of mission*: God has

---

1   J. H. Bavinck uses God's activity in Genesis 3 to lay the foundation for all evangelistic witness. *An Introduction to the Science of Missions*, trans. David H. Freeman (Phillipsburg, NJ: Presbyterian & Reformed, 1960), 270–72.

sovereignly chosen to save sinners who deserve eternal death. We get a glimpse into God's *comprehensive plan of mission* in the first promise of the gospel (Gen. 3:15), though the details are not yet clear. We also realize that there is more to the story than merely the redemption of elect sinners; there are also strong hints of a *coming final judgment*, when Satan will be punished and God's righteousness will be fully vindicated. With these principles in place, let's turn to another crucial passage.

Empowered to Be Witnesses

Acts 1:1–11 is the second pivotal passage for a biblical theology of mission. It comes at the conclusion of Jesus's earthly mission, forty days after his resurrection. It is also ten days before Pentecost, serving as a prelude to mission in the New Testament. Verse 8 is central in this passage and for the entire book of Acts: "But you will receive power when the Holy Spirit has come upon you, and you will be my witnesses in Jerusalem and in all Judea and Samaria, and to the end of the earth." This verse completes the "Great Commission collection" (Matt. 28:18–20; Mark 16:15–18; Luke 24:46–49; John 20:21–22). This passage gives us at least three keys to understand the witness of the church in the world.

First, Jesus's words in Acts 1:8 are rooted in the Old Testament. We do not fully understand this verse until we see it in the light of God's whole story. Many readily acknowledge the clear allusion to Psalm 2:8, the Father's promise to the anointed Son: "Ask of me, and I will make the nations your heritage, and the ends of the earth your possession." But there is more. With these words, Jesus quotes the prophet Isaiah to give us a much grander vision of mission than what could be had by limiting it to its New Testament context. Already in the Old Testament, the Lord described his people as his witnesses among the unbelieving nations: " 'You are my witnesses,' declares the Lord, 'and I am God' " (Isa. 43:12; cf. 44:8; 49:6). They were to worship him alone and declare that he is the only true God.

We will consider the Old Testament foundations of the church's witness in chapter 1. For now, we simply note how Jesus grounds the witness of the New Testament church in the identity and role of God's Old Testament people. As in Isaiah's day, God's people today are called to be his witnesses among the nations. This has not changed. But something very significant has changed, which the disciples realized only after Pentecost.

Second, Jesus's parting words in Acts 1:8 are not news to the disciples. Surely, these words did not surprise them. Bearing witness to Christ was not a new concept for these men; Jesus had already plainly taught them about their task: "But when the Helper comes, whom I will send to you from the Father, the Spirit of truth, who proceeds from the Father, he will bear witness about me. And you also will bear witness, because you have been with me from the beginning" (John 15:26–27).

Furthermore, the followers of Christ had already practiced what they were now commanded to perform. The apostles had been chosen and sent out to proclaim the good news about the coming kingdom of God (Matt. 10:5; Mark 6:7; Luke 9:1). Seventy-two others had also been appointed and sent out to do the same (Luke 10:1).

Although the activity described in Christ's parting words was not new in essence, what followed in his instruction as he left them was very significant. Now they would be filled with his Spirit to accomplish the task for which they had been trained. Now the promise of the Father was to be poured out upon the church, as anticipated by the Old Testament prophets. Now God's people would receive much greater empowerment for this task of bearing witness, preparing them for the much greater scope of the Gentile mission.

Did they fully understand the significance of this truth? Perhaps not immediately, but within days they would experience its reality. Ten days later, they all were filled with the Spirit and empowered to testify to the saving truth of their Lord. This event in Jerusalem on Pentecost was only the beginning of the story of New Testament mission. Soon the apostles went out, joined by an ever-increasing crowd of evangelists, to bear witness of Christ in all Judea, Samaria, North Africa, Asia Minor, and to the ends of the earth.

Third, the truth of Acts 1:1–11 is very important for the church today. In this passage, it is clear that the disciples did not yet fully understand God's larger plan. Jesus gave them final parting instructions not as an afterthought, but as central to God's mission of redemption. But they were only beginning to see the big picture of God's plan.

Our definition and practice of Christian witness today can also be limited if we fail to see the bigger picture of God's plan: his mission of redemption. It is easy to be distracted by details—even important details—while, in practice, we lose sight of what is most important. As a result, the witness of many churches becomes cluttered, if not confused or misguided. So we need to step back to see the whole scope of God's mission of redemption, and then allow Scripture to reform our understanding about our own role and responsibility in the light of it.

These two stories—narrated in Genesis 3:1–21 and Acts 1:1–11—are both pivotal parts of the one story of God's mission in the history of redemption. They help us reflect theologically on God's mission and the church's role in it. We started in the preface with a simple definition of mission as *God's work within the world to save sinners*.[2] But now let's build upon these insights, first by considering briefly the mission activity of the triune God and then by reflecting theologically on the place of the church within this mission.

---

2   This preliminary definition is merely the starting point for our study. Since this book deals with theology for God's church, we will not give attention to the divine missions that theologians have described as part of God's internal works. Likewise, we will deal only implicitly with God's external work of creation, the context of God's mission, and conclude with practical reflection on God's zeal for his own universal glory. While God's nonsaving works also declare his glory faintly (Ps. 19:1), God's salvific work of mission in Christ testifies of his glory to a much greater degree, all to the eternal praise of his glorious grace (Eph. 1:6, 12, 14). Thus our focus in this book is primarily on God's salvific mission, his external work in world history that directly concerns the redemption and witness of his people, the church. As will be described, the church is both an object of this mission and also an agent in God's mission.

The Mission of the Triune God

Each of the triune persons is at work in the history of God's mission. As we already observed from Genesis 3, the three persons of the Godhead have specific roles in the salvation of sinners. While never working inseparably, it is helpful to distinguish these three roles (fig. 1).

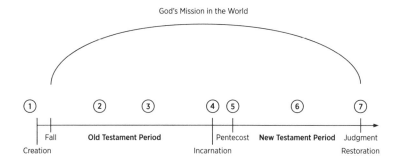

1. God decrees his redemptive mission to save his elect from the nations.
2. God announces and prepares for the Messiah's redemptive mission.
3. God calls his people out of the nations to be witnesses to the nations.
4. God sends his Son for redemption and to inaugurate global mission.
5. God sends his Spirit to empower his church for witness to all nations.
6. God's Son gathers his elect people by means of his Spirit and church.
7. God's Son returns to end mission and usher in the consummated kingdom.

Figure 1. The mission of God the Father.

God the Father decreed the plan of mission before the creation of the world (Ps. 2:7–9). The Father's mission is rooted in his plan from eternity to save sinners (Eph. 1:4–6).[3] He enacts his plan in the history of redemption: the Father prepares for Christ's coming in the Old

---

3   We will give attention to God the Father's missional purpose and plan of redemption throughout the entire book, instead of only one chapter about the mission of the Father. My primary focus in part 1 is a biblical theology of God's redemptive mission, not a systematic theology of Trinitarian missiology. The Father's eternal election, his sending of the Son and Spirit, his ultimate purpose and glory, and the eschatological perspective of his mission will be treated in many places as they relate to our study of Christian witness. The mission of God the Father cannot be adequately covered in one chapter since it is the background and purpose of the whole, a point also made by John Piper in *Let the Nations be Glad: The Supremacy of God in Missions* (Grand Rapids, MI: Baker, 1993).

Testament (Gal. 3:8), sends his Son in the fullness of time to secure redemption (John 3:16), and sends his Spirit to empower his people for witness (Luke 24:48–49). This plan of mission will be fully accomplished when all God's chosen people have been gathered, when every knee bows before Christ, when the rebellious nations are judged with equity, and when God's creation is restored in perfect righteousness. The Father's mission will be completed when all enemies of Christ are punished (Rev. 19:11–21), when Christ's kingdom has fully come (1 Cor. 15:24–28), and when his glory is climactically magnified (Rom. 11:36).[4]

God the Son was sent as the great missionary-apostle (John 20:21; Heb. 3:1). He was commissioned by the Father to display God's truthfulness in this sinful world and to confirm the Old Testament's messianic promises (Rom. 15:8–9; cf. Isa. 42:1–9). Christ came into the world "to seek and to save the lost" (Luke 19:10) and "to give his life as a ransom for many" (Mark 10:45). He also came to institute the messianic kingdom and to inaugurate the Gentile mission (Matt. 24:14; Rom. 15:9–12). Christ now reigns in heaven, gathering God's people from all nations through the gospel witness of his people and Spirit. He will soon return to judge all people and to consummate the kingdom. Christ's work has a unique place in God's mission, which we will consider more fully in chapter 2.

God the Spirit was sent into the world, by the Father and the Son, to bear witness to Christ and to gather God's chosen people from all nations. As the divine evangelist, the Spirit convicts people in the world of sin (John 16:8), he illumines sinners with gospel truth, and he regenerates those dead in trespasses and sins, granting faith (Eph. 2:3, 8–9). As the divine church planter and church revitalizer, he revives

---

4 Thus God's mission of redemption takes place within the context of God's creation, as the remedy of humanity's fall, and with a view to God's re-creation and glorification. "There was no 'mission' in the Garden of Eden and there will be no 'mission' in the new heavens and the new earth (though the results of 'mission' will be evident)." Andreas J. Köstenberger and Peter T. O'Brien, *Salvation to the Ends of the Earth* (Downers Grove, IL: InterVarsity, 2001), 251.

and edifies God's people and he educates and unites all believers (John 16:13; 1 Cor. 12:11; Eph. 4:3). As the divine apologist, he exposes Satan's lie and ensures that the gates of hell will never prevail against the church (2 Cor. 10:4). The mission of the Spirit also includes empowering us to bear witness to Christ, gifting us with spiritual abilities to make us competent gospel witnesses (2 Cor. 3:4–6), and sovereignly guiding our witness in order to accomplish God's eternal plan (Acts 16:6). In chapter 3, we will consider more fully the Spirit's mission and its implications for us.

Recently there has been a renewed focus on the work of the triune God in mission.[5] The term *missio Dei*, Latin for "the sending of God" or "the mission of God," has become popular in the past century for explaining mission as the work of God.[6] The Great Commission passage in John's Gospel conveys this concept clearly: "As the Father has sent me, even so I am sending you" (John 20:21).

The concept of *missio Dei*, however, is not new. It is rooted in the fourth-century teaching of Augustine of Hippo (354–430) on God's triune sending work in salvation. It was also clearly taught in the seventeenth century by Dutch theologian Gisbertus Voetius (1589–1676), who developed the first comprehensive Protestant theology of mission.[7] For Voetius, the will of God is the primary theological foundation for mission, which includes the eternal decree to save sinners, the gospel promises of Christ's coming and the messianic kingdom of peace, and

5 This return in mission studies to a Trinitarian framework is helpful for many reasons, including defending against unbiblical principles and practices, since many recent errors come with a departure from this foundation. For example, Timothy Tennent uses this framework for his introduction to missiology, *Invitation to World Missions: A Trinitarian Missiology for the Twenty First Century* (Grand Rapids, MI: Kregel, 2010). See also Leslie Newbigin, *Trinitarian Doctrine for Today's Mission* (London: Edinburgh House, 1963).

6 The term was popularized in modern missiology with Georg Vicedom's *The Mission of God* (St. Louis: Concordia, 1965), following Karl Hartenstein who used this term in 1934 to distinguish God's mission activity from the role of the church.

7 Jan A. B. Jongeneel, "The Missiology of Gisbertus Voetius: The First Comprehensive Protestant Theology of Missions," *Calvin Theological Journal* 26, no. 1 (1991): 47–49.

the specific mandate for the church's witness given after Christ's resurrection. Voetius used the term *missio Dei* to distinguish God's activity in mission from all subordinate human activity.[8]

As a popular term today, *missio Dei* is used in many divergent ways. Some define it as "everything God does in relation to the kingdom and everything the church is sent to do on earth."[9] In this view, the church's task in the world is usually seen as collaborating with God as he establishes *shalom* and his reign over all peoples and places on earth. Others go further to define mission as a divine attribute, describing God as missional.[10] Others are more restrained, using *missio Dei* to describe the hermeneutical key that unlocks the Bible's story, and seeing God's mission—and the participation of God's people in it—as a framework for the whole Bible.[11]

Unfortunately, the diverse uses of *missio Dei* have made this term ambiguous.[12] It is important, therefore, to be precise as we define *mission* since slight ambiguity here often results in critical confusion later. In my opinion, *missio Dei* is a helpful concept when used in a limited way to distinguish God's overarching work of redemption from the church's activity. For example, missiologist J. H. Bavinck (1895–1964) continues in the tradition of Voetius by defining mission as God's work

8   Ronaldo Lidorio, *Theology, Piety, and Mission: The Influence of Gisbertus Voetius on Missiology and Church Planting* (Grand Rapids, MI: RHB, 2023), 14–15.

9   A. Scott Moreau, Gary R. Corwin, and Gary B. McGee, *Introducing World Missions* (Grand Rapids MI: Baker, 2004), 73, quoting John A. McIntosh, "Missio Dei," in *Evangelical Dictionary of World Mission* (Grand Rapids, MI: Baker, 2000), 631–33.

10 For example, South African missiologist David Bosch explains how, in this view, "mission is not primarily an activity of the church, but an attribute of God. God is a missionary God." Bosch, *Transforming Mission: Paradigm Shifts in Theology of Mission* (Maryknoll, NY: Orbis, 1991), 390. Many missiologists today, both conciliar and evangelical, follow Bosch and others who take this direction. See Thomas Schirrmacher, *Missio Dei: God's Missional Nature* (Bonn, Ger.: Verlag für Kultur und Wissenschaft, 2017).

11 Christopher J. H. Wright, *The Mission of God: Unlocking the Bible's Grand Narrative* (Downers Grove, IL: IVP Academic, 2006), 17.

12 As mission historian Stephen Neill complained many years ago, "If everything is mission, then nothing is mission." Neill, *Creative Tension* (London: Edinburgh House, 1959), 81. See also Tennent, *World Missions*, 55–56.

and distinguishing this work from the church's work in mission.[13] It is most helpful to follow Voetius by grounding the study of mission in God's will and eternal decree, and by framing all that Christians think and do in mission as only part of the mission of the triune God.

For our present study, therefore, I use the term *God's mission* simply to draw attention to the triune God's overarching work of redemption, and to distinguish between the mission activities of the triune God and of his people in both Old and New Testaments. To avoid misunderstanding, however, we must be careful to affirm the following. First, God's mission activity in the world flows out of but must be distinguished from his gracious character.[14] Second, Christ our mediator has a unique and central role in the history of God's mission. Third, God's people, in both Old and New Testaments, have specific roles and responsibilities within God's mission. Fourth, to be considered in later chapters, God's church has a subordinate role within God's mission, participating in it with many activities of Christian witness. Hence we consider next the place of God's people, the church, within the different periods of God's mission.

My Church in God's Mission

Your local church has an important place in the bigger story of God's mission as part of God's plan for his church worldwide. We confess this fact as true. It is crucial, though, to define clearly how the church—and specifically, each of our local churches—fits within this bigger story.

---

13 Bavinck, *Introduction*, 57. Likewise, George Peters affirmed the use of the term as promoted by Vicedom but was careful to insist on a Christological mission and the distinct place of the church, while also affirming God's ultimate purpose: "The end result of such missio Dei is the glorification of the Father, Son, and Holy Spirit." Peters, *A Biblical Theology of Missions* (Chicago: Moody Press, 1972), 9.

14 There was a time before God's mission began in world history, and there will be a time after his mission has ended, yet God himself is eternal and unchanging. My focus in this book, however, is on God's external work in redemptive history, not on intra-Trinitarian relations (the Son eternally begotten and the Spirit eternally proceeding), the divine sendings of the Son and the Spirit (John 14:24, 26; 15:26), or God's eternal decree (Ps. 2:6–9).

Three distinctions help us better understand the place of God's church within God's mission.

First, as considered above, the church's witness must be distinguished from the mission of the triune God. The mission of the church is only part of God's bigger plan. This fact is both humbling and liberating. My local church's witness is only a small part of what God is doing in the world. We trust God to use our local churches in a way that advances his mission and brings him greater glory.

The witness of the church is also different than the mission of Christ. Our activity cannot duplicate or repeat the unique place of Jesus Christ in God's mission. Rather, our primary role is to proclaim the gospel of Christ as we bear witness to what he has done.[15] Furthermore, the church's witness is guided by the sovereign mission of Christ's Spirit. Since the Holy Spirit is the primary agent of mission, the spiritual success of the church's witness is dependent upon him.

Second, the witness of God's people has progressed and expanded within the history of God's mission. The Old Testament, as the start of God's story of mission, lays the foundation for a comprehensive biblical theology of mission. It was the textbook for the apostle Paul's Gentile mission, which he quotes at crucial points to explain his mission theology and practice (Acts 13:41, 47; 28:26–28; Rom. 15:8–13).

Mission in the New Testament is a continuation of what was started in the Old Testament. Already in the Old Testament, God's people were called to be separate from the nations (Gen. 12:1) and to declare God's glory among them (Ps. 96:3). They were called to be a "light for the nations" (Isa. 49:6), though not to the same extent as we see in the New Testament after Pentecost (Acts 13:47). The witness of God's people

---

15 For example, there has been much discussion on the relationship of word and deed in mission. The starting point for answering these questions is located here as we distinguish Christ's unique mission from the mission of the New Testament church. How should the church follow Christ who is both our mediator in salvation as well as our leader and exemplar in mission? More attention will be given to this and related questions later.

started in the Old Testament before the flood (2 Pet. 2:5); it continued and was greatly expanded in the New Testament after Christ's coming and the Spirit's empowerment.

Yet witness in the Old Testament was not identical to witness in the New Testament. God's people in the Old Testament were not commanded by Christ to make disciples of all nations. They were not equally empowered by the Spirit of Christ for this enlarged task, though the Old Testament saints were certainly led by the Spirit of Christ to proclaim the gospel (Gal. 3:8; 1 Pet. 1:10–11) and to anticipate the enlargement of its scope (Isa. 54:2–3; Mal. 1:11). It is helpful, therefore, to compare and contrast God's mission in both Testaments, and to trace the progression of the church's witness within the bigger story of God's mission (fig. 2).

Figure 2. Witness in God's mission in world history.

Third, the church as God's people is both the object of God's mission and an agent in it. We must keep this distinction in mind, not only as we interpret the biblical story of God's mission, but also as we seek to better understand our own role and responsibilities within it. We are the objects of God's mission. God came to this world to seek and to save us, so we bear witness to what God has done for us, in us, and through us.

God has also, in his sovereign wisdom, chosen to use his people as agents to further the cause of his mission. God could have evangelized sinners without any human agency, as he did in Genesis 3. He could have used angels as his messengers. But instead, he chose to use fallen sons and daughters of Adam to proclaim the message of Christ to lost sinners and to declare his glory among the nations. Thus, as agents of God's mission, we bear witness to Christ through our lifestyle and with our words.

These three distinctions help to define the place of our church in God's mission. We will continue to expand our understanding of God's mission in chapters 1–4 (part 1), then develop it further with examples from church history in chapters 5–6 (part 2), and finally add more detail with theological reflection on the church's witness in chapters 7–10 (part 3).

Our Witness in the World

We started our study with a simple definition of *mission*, but it should be obvious by now that this subject area has many nuances and complexities. One word alone is unable to capture the richness and intricacy of this concept. In fact, a whole cluster of words is needed, each in relation with the others, to understand the story of God's mission and our participation in it. Let's now consider several of these words to further introduce this subject.

The word *mission* is most popular today, though it has become ambiguous due to many divergent definitions and uses.[16] This English word is derived in part from the Latin *mittere* and *misso*, meaning to send or sending. It corresponds with several Greek words: a noun, *apostolos*, meaning one who is sent to represent with authority, and two verbs, *pempo* and *apostello*, meaning to send a message or a person for a particular purpose. Hence the concept conveyed by the English word *mission* is associated with the activity of sending or being commissioned

---

16 It is telling to see that even the titles of recent books on mission contain a question about how it should be defined. For example, see J. Andrew Kirk, *What Is Mission?: Theological Explorations* (Minneapolis: Fortress Press, 2000). For a helpful discussion about the need for clarity in defining this term, see Kevin DeYoung and Greg Gilbert, *What Is the Mission of the Church?* (Wheaton, IL: Crossway, 2011), 15–27.

(Matt. 11:10; 28:19; John 20:21; Rom. 10:15; 1 John 4:14) and the apostolic ministry of gospel proclamation (Rom. 1:5; Eph. 4:11; Gal. 2:8; Heb. 3:1).

From this word *mission* are derived other related words: *missionary*, a person who is called and sent to serve in the ministry of mission; *missiology*, the study of the theology, history, integration, and practice of mission; *missions* (plural), the activities we do to accomplish the goal of mission;[17] and *missional*, an adjective for mission that has taken on a diversity of connotations.[18]

In addition to its ambiguity, the word *mission* also has unhelpful baggage.[19] For example, in the minds of many today, Christian mission is often linked inseparably with geographic expansion and Western colonialism.[20] Some who equate mission with geographic expansion even accuse the Protestant church after the European Reformation of being very slow to engage in mission since the church's witness at that time was focused locally with much less attention on distant regions.[21] Others

---

17 Evangelical missiology often distinguishes mission (singular) from missions (plural). For example, Moreau makes three categories: *missio Dei* is "all that God does to build the kingdom"; mission is "what the church does for God in the world"; and missions, as a subset of mission, is "evangelism, discipleship, and church planting." Moreau, Corwin, and McGee, *Introducing World Missions*, 72–73. The same distinction can be made by defining *mission* as everything God is doing in redemption and *witness* as all the activities of the church's participation within God's mission.

18 Being *missional* often means thinking, behaving, and serving like a missionary in order to reach others with the message of the gospel. Like the term *missio Dei,* however, this word has a range of meanings, even among evangelicals, some using it simply as an adjective for mission and others arguing it is the central principle that defines the church, consequently redefining ecclesiology around their conception of what it means to be "missional." DeYoung and Gilbert characterize *missional* as "a big trunk that can smuggle a great deal of unwanted baggage," *What Is the Mission?*, 21.

19 Michael W. Stroope argues that the word *mission* should be replaced since it has become ambiguous and since it is a term derived mostly from Roman Catholic expansionist ambitions patterned in many ways after the Crusades. See his *Transcending Mission: The Eclipse of a Modern Tradition* (Downers Grove, IL: IVP Academic, 2017).

20 Michael W. Goheen complains about this perception as he defines the subject: "Mission is considered to be a unidirectional activity that proceeds from the West to other parts of the world. . . ." Goheen, *Introducing Christian Mission Today* (Downers Grove, IL: IVP Academic, 2014), 15.

21 This unfair critique has been repeatedly refuted. See Michael A. G. Haykin and C. Jeffery Robinson Sr., *To the Ends of the Earth: Calvin's Missional Vision and Legacy* (Wheaton, IL: Crossway,

unintentionally bifurcate mission and evangelism, limiting mission to ministry activity that is geographically removed from the local church.[22]

Therefore, I suggest that the biblical word *witness* is a much better term to comprehensively describe the church's participation in God's mission.[23] This term is central to the book of Acts and a key concept in the entire New Testament (Acts 1:8; John 15:26–27; 16:16).[24] In this book, therefore, I use the term *witness* to describe all the various ways in which God's people participate in God's mission.

There are two Greek root words for witness, the noun *martus* and the verb *martureo*. These root words are used with at least four overlapping areas of meaning: the identity, character, and conduct of the church in the world (Acts 1:8; 1 Pet. 2:12); the verbal proclamation of the gospel of Christ (Acts 23:11; John 1:34; 1 John 1:2); testifying to the truth of Christ despite opposition (Acts 28:23; Rev. 11:3); and suffering persecution for the sake of Christ (Rev. 2:13; 17:6).

As a noun, *witness* (often translated as "testimony") denotes the identity of God's people as those who bear witness to Christ. As a verb, *witness* (often translated as "testify" or "testifying") denotes the activity of God's people as those who communicate the gospel message about Christ. This holistic concept of witness permeates two terms, used throughout this book somewhat interchangeably: *Christian witness* is

---

2014) and Kenneth J. Stewart, "Calvinism Is Largely Antimissionary" in *Ten Myths About Calvinism* (Downers Grove, IL: InterVarsity, 2011), 123–50.

22 The eighteenth-century Western church usually defined mission as being sent away to distant lands in order to teach the gospel in un-Christian nations (Rom. 15:22–23) with less attention given to the local witness of the church, in part because Western society at that time was mostly populated by people with a Christian worldview. As a result, the organizational structures of many churches and denominations today still bifurcate foreign mission and local ministry.

23 The title of this book, taken from Isaiah 43:10, 44:8 and Acts 1:8, reflects my opinion that the biblical term *witness* best captures the essence of the church's participation within God's mission. Michael Green regards *witness*, along with evangelism and preaching, to be "singularly appropriate" for describing the church's mission in *Evangelism in the Early Church* (Grand Rapids, MI: Eerdmans, 1970), 70–76.

24 See James M. Boice, *Witness and Revelation in the Gospel of John* (Grand Rapids, MI: Zondervan, 1970); and Allison A. Trites, *The New Testament Concept of Witness* (Cambridge, UK: Cambridge University Press, 1977).

the personal practice of all believers by which they testify to the gospel of Christ; and *the witness of the church* is the corporate testimony of God's people by means of their gospel presence, evangelistic message, apologetic response, and loving community within society.

The word *witness* is also used in Scripture to describe divine activity in the world (1 John 5:6–12). God witnesses about himself through general revelation (Ps. 19:1–6; Acts 14:17) and special revelation (Deut. 31:19, 26; cf. Isa. 44:8). Christ made an exemplary confession in his witness before Pilate (1 Tim. 6:13). The Holy Spirit bears witness to Christ, and he witnesses within our hearts (Acts 15:8; Rom. 8:16). Thus the word *witness* can be used to speak of both divine and human agency in mission.

Related terms in Scripture are also helpful. For example, the apostles were eyewitnesses of Christ, so likewise, we who have personally experienced Christ's truth and love are sent out to bear witness of him. Other related concepts include testifying (Acts 20:24), making defense (1 Pet. 3:15), living as examples (Matt. 5:14–16), and suffering for the sake of Christ (1 Pet. 4:1).

Therefore, we will structure our study of the church's witness in the world around the overlapping nuances of the word *witness*: the witness of gospel presence as the identity and calling of the church to display Christ's truth in the world (chap. 7); the witness of gospel message in the preaching, teaching, writing, and other modes of evangelistic communication (chap. 8); the witness of gospel response in the church's apologetic ministry within the context of false teachings and ideologies (chap. 9); the witness of gospel community by faithful churches within un-Christian and even hostile societies (chap. 10).

In addition to the terms *mission* and *witness*, many other biblical concepts pertain to our present study. We will unpack these in later chapters; here I only give several short definitions, for the sake of clarity, of various activities included in Christian witness.

Gospel communication is central to the witness of the church. Evangelism is sharing the gospel by public preaching or personal witness.

Preaching is the public proclamation and application of God's word. An impressive range of terms is used in Scripture to describe various communication modes: speaking, teaching, proclaiming, exhorting, reasoning, appealing, urging, convicting, testifying, and so on.

Discipleship ministries are also central to the church's witness in the world, following Christ's example and in obedience to his command (Matt. 28:20). Discipleship is the process of training believers with God's word, in Christian relationship and for ministry, so that they will grow in their spiritual walk and mature in their witness of Christ (1 Cor. 11:1). It includes theological education, an advanced form of training church leaders (Acts 18:24–28; 2 Tim. 2:2).

Apologetics and its related activities have an important role in the church's witness "to make a defense to anyone" who questions or opposes God's truth (1 Pet. 3:13–17; 2 Cor. 10:4–6). All apologetic ministries serve to promote the witness of God's church, though various ministries often specialize in specific areas to witness more effectively to targeted audiences.

Church planting and church revitalization are also important. Church planting is the activity of establishing a spiritually mature church in a new area. Church revitalization is the activity of leading an unhealthy church back toward a state of spiritual maturity. With God's blessing, these ministries of gospel witness lead to the upbuilding and multiplication of local churches.

Gospel partnerships, both local and global, often assist the church's witness (Phil. 1:5). Many other related ministries also find their origin in the witness of the New Testament church, such as hospitality (Heb. 13:1–3), the witness of good works (1 Pet. 2:12), and gospel suffering (2 Tim. 1:8). We will consider many of these ministries in later chapters.

Reformed Experiential Witness

What is your personal confession and witness? This question requires attention before we go deeper into our study of mission. It is here that our study becomes personal, as the contemplation of God's word always should be. Witness is not simply a topic for academic study; it is a calling for every true believer. As Paul wrote to Timothy shortly before his death: "Therefore do not be ashamed of the [witness] about our Lord, nor of me his prisoner, but share in suffering for the gospel by the power of God, who saved us and called us to a holy calling . . ." (2 Tim. 1:8–9). Or as a long-forgotten missionary in southern Africa wrote: "We must remember that it was not by interceding for the world in glory that Jesus saved it. He gave himself. Our prayers for the evangelization of the world are but a bitter irony so long as we only give of our superfluity, and draw back before the sacrifice of ourselves."[25] So we conclude this chapter with a brief review of the church's confessions and our own spirituality, both of which are undergirding themes essential for all faithful witnesses of Christ.

First, the true church since Pentecost has always confessed the importance of gospel witness. We will review some of this rich history in part 2. For now, consider briefly how the historic confessional statements promote the church's witness.[26] For example, mission is implicitly described as Christ gathering his church "out of the entire human race" by means of his word and Spirit.[27] The Canons of Dort, which some have unfairly said is opposed to mission, makes a very strong statement

25 Written by François Coillard who served as a missionary in southern Africa under the Paris Evangelical Mission for almost fifty years. Quoted by Amy Carmichael, *Things as They Are* (London: Morgan and Scott, 1903), 41.

26 See Samuel H. Larsen, "Global Kingdom Vision and the Westminster Confession of Faith" in *The Hope Fulfilled: Essays in Honor of O. Palmer Robertson* (Philipsburg, NJ: P&R, 2008), 317–24; and Wes Bredenhof, *To Win Our Neighbors for Christ: The Missiology of the Three Forms of Unity* (Grand Rapids, MI: RHB, 2015).

27 Heidelberg Catechism, q. 54. See also the Westminster Confession of Faith, 25.3, and the Belgic Confession of Faith, art. 27: "And so this holy church is not confined, bound, or limited to a certain place or to certain persons. But it is spread and dispersed throughout the entire world, though still joined and united in heart and will, in one and the same Spirit, by the power of faith," in *Creeds, Confessions, and Catechisms: A Reader's Edition*, ed. Chad Van Dixhoorn (Wheaton, IL: Crossway, 2022), 101 (hereafter cited as *CCC*).

for gospel proclamation to all nations without reserve.[28] Several confessions also link mission to the second petition of the Lord's Prayer.[29]

More recently, the doctrine of Christian witness has been given more explicit attention in the official statements of various groups. For example, many modern confessions echo similar biblical truths.[30] Other related statements include the Lausanne Covenant and the Southgate Fellowship.[31] Further reflection on and affirmation of the church's public witness is still needed, especially due to the rapidly shifting ideologies at present in the postmodern world.

Second, bearing witness to Christ in the world is very personal for every true believer. If God has mercifully chosen us, if Christ has graciously atoned for our sins, if the Holy Spirit now graces us and empowers us to be witnesses in our world, then how can we not be passionate about this task? So let me conclude this introduction by briefly noting the importance for witness of missionary doxology and biography, and by leaving you with a few personal questions for reflection.

Christian witness is not simply a doctrinal theme in our church's confession, expressed either implicitly or explicitly. Witness is a central part of our personal confession, our personal doxology (Pss. 67:3; 107:2). The

---

28 Canons of Dort, head 2, art. 5: "The promise of the gospel . . . together with the command to repent and believe, ought to be announced and declared without differentiation or discrimination to all nations and people, to whom God in his good pleasure sends the gospel" (*CCC* 150).

29 See the Heidelberg Catechism, q. 123, and the Westminster Larger Catechism, q. 53 and 191.

30 The Baptist Faith and Message (2000), art. 11, states, "It is the duty and privilege of every follower of Christ and of every church of the Lord Jesus Christ to endeavor to make disciples of all nations. The new birth of man's spirit by God's Holy Spirit means the birth of love for others. Missionary effort on the part of all rests thus upon a spiritual necessity of the regenerate life, and is expressly and repeatedly commanded in the teachings of Christ. The Lord Jesus Christ has commanded the preaching of the gospel to all nations. It is the duty of every child of God to seek constantly to win the lost to Christ by verbal witness undergirded by a Christian lifestyle, and by other methods in harmony with the gospel of Christ." "The Baptist Faith and Message 2000," https://bfm.sbc.net/bfm2000/. Accessed January 8, 2024.

31 The Lausanne Covenant (1974) and the subsequent Manila Manifesto (1989) give considerable attention to Christian witness, though with a more inclusive theological scope; see https://lausanne.org/content/covenant/lausanne-covenant. The Southgate Fellowship is much more precise and intentionally grounded in Reformed theology; see "Affirmations and Denials Concerning World Mission," *Themelios* 45, no.1 (2020): 108–35.

Psalms celebrate God's mission and anticipate what God will do on earth for the glory of his name. Many Christian hymns do the same, rejoicing in the triumph of the gospel of Christ among the nations. Indeed, these praise songs often become the songs of our own soul as we learn to think God's thoughts after him and to boast of his gracious deeds in all the earth (Jer. 9:23–24; 2 Cor. 10:13–18). Missionary doxology has always had an important place in the spiritual life of God's people.

Witness is also a central part of our corporate confession, the church's public worship. Worship is both the ultimate goal of God's mission and a vital activity of the church's witness to accomplish this glorious end. In fact, as we will consider in chapters 7 and 10, the church's presence in society—particularly evidenced in its public display of faithful worship and good works—is itself the most powerful witness to Christ. The church's doxological witness in biblical worship continues to serve a vital role in the history of God's mission.

Furthermore, we are surrounded by a great cloud of witnesses (Heb. 12:1), not only in Scripture but also in the centuries since Pentecost. These witnesses must not be ignored. Indeed, reading missionary biographies is an excellent way to stir up within us a biblical passion and zeal for Christian witness. This book, however, is not a missionary biography or doxology; it is a systematic summary of the theology of witness. Yet while we stay focused on this task, the experiential dimension of this study must not be minimized or excluded from our applications in each chapter.

We will return to this theme of Reformed experiential witness in the conclusion. For now, we conclude this introduction with a series of personal reflections to highlight the experiential element of our study. I leave you with these questions for your prayerful contemplation:

- Have you experienced the saving truth and power of Jesus Christ yourself? If you don't know Jesus yourself, how can you tell other people about him?

- What is the purpose of learning about Christian witness if you do not want to do it? If you are not following Christ now, why should other people listen to your words?
- Have there been times in your life when the Holy Spirit has stirred up your heart with conviction to witness of Christ in your family or to declare God's glory among the nations?
- Do you weep with Christ as you experience the stubborn unbelief of dying sinners? Is your heart troubled like Paul's when you see your city that is full of idolatry?
- Do you cry out, with the voice of true wisdom, to the masses of humanity who are living in reckless pursuit of vanity while they blindly follow false teachers into eternal hell?
- Do you long to see Christ's will done in all the earth, to see Christ's kingdom come among all nations, and to see Christ's name glorified by the peoples in every land?
- Have you, with Isaiah, seen a vision of God's glory, and is his Spirit stirring up within you a passionate hope to see his glory fill the earth as the waters cover the sea (Isa. 6:8; 11:9)?

Discussion Questions

1. Read again Genesis 3:1–21 and Acts 1:1–11. Make a list of five essential truths about God's mission and Christian witness from these two passages.

2. What has the triune God already done to restore fellowship between himself and sinners? What is God still doing in the world today to restore this fellowship?

3. Compare and contrast God's mission and the witness of the church.

4. Make a list of all the ways in which your church bears witness to Christ in the world. Are any of these endeavors apparently fruitless? Could

your efforts be better focused into some other activity? Could you, in the light of biblical prudence and your limited time and resources, be doing more?

5. Why do you personally feel the desire to learn more about Christian witness? Why is it important for all church leaders to understand the biblical theology of God's mission?

PART 1

THE BIBLICAL STORY
OF GOD'S MISSION

1

Mission in the Old Testament

THE OLD TESTAMENT is usually not studied as a textbook for Christian witness. We read accounts of the destruction of Canaanite culture and harsh judgments carried out upon the nations surrounding Israel. These topics can be shocking, especially in contemporary culture, and they may seem to stand in opposition to the Great Commission in the New Testament. We also learn about the failure of God's covenant people, who chose the worship of false gods instead of declaring God's glory among the nations, and whose disobedience ended in devastation and dispersion among the nations. Additionally, divergent theories about the Old Testament Scriptures and its relation to the New Testament have limited the attention given by Bible scholars to the foundational themes of Old Testament mission.

But digging deeper, past the many divergent theories and what appears to be a harsh crusty surface, we gain a respectful appreciation for the importance of Old Testament themes in a biblical theology of mission.[1] More recently, a number of Bible scholars have helped us

---

1 J. H. Bavinck writes, "Yet, if we investigate the Old Testament more thoroughly, it becomes clear that the future of the nations is a point of the greatest concern. . . . from the first page to the last the Bible has the whole world in view. . . ." Bavinck, *An Introduction to the Science of Missions* (Phillipsburg, NJ: Presbyterian & Reformed, 1960), 11; cf. 11–24. Richard R. DeRidder states,

discover the rich concepts lying just below the Old Testament's surface.[2] In fact, further Old Testament study is yielding beautiful truths and foundational themes for a comprehensive biblical theology of God's mission and the witness of God's people within it.

We must not overlook the value of the Old Testament for Christian witness today. The Old Testament was the textbook for Paul's mission theology (Rom. 15:8–12). It was also prominent in Jesus's instructions about mission (Luke 24:27, 44–49).[3] Mission themes in the Old Testament were significant for James (Acts 15:16–18, quoting Amos 9:11–12 and Isa. 45:21) and Peter (1 Pet. 1:10–12; 2:9–12). Furthermore, Luke's second book draws clear parallels between Old Testament themes of witness and New Testament witness in practice.[4] We should, therefore, carefully study the Old Testament to uncover its themes of mission and witness, and with the New Testament leaders we must ensure that our theology of Christian witness is firmly grounded upon these foundational truths.

Before we begin our study, however, consider this overarching distinction: the biblical theology of mission in the Old Testament is best understood in view of two interrelated motifs. First, the Old Testament is an introduction to the universal story of God's mission. It announces God's purpose for all nations and reveals how God was preparing for the coming of his Son to fulfill Old Testament promises and to inaugurate a mission to all nations. Second, the Old Testament is also an account of the witness of God's people in the world. It is a colorful history of

---

"No student of missions can long escape the necessity of examining the Old Testament antecedents to the Christian mission." DeRidder, *Discipling the Nations* (Grand Rapids, MI: Baker, 1975), 2.

2 For example, Walter C. Kaiser Jr., *Mission in the Old Testament: Israel as a Light to the Nations* (Grand Rapids, MI: Baker, 2000); and Christopher J. H. Wright, "Old Testament Theology of Mission," in *Evangelical Dictionary of World Mission* (Grand Rapids, MI: Baker, 2000), 706–9.

3 Wright notes Jesus's dual Christological (Luke 24:27) and missiological (24:44ff) readings of the Old Testament. See Christopher J. H. Wright, "Old Testament Perspectives on Mission," in *Dictionary of Mission Theology* (Downers Grove, IL: InterVarsity, 2007), 269–73.

4 Compare Acts 2:17–21 with Joel 2:28–32; Acts 3:25 with Genesis 12:3; Acts 4:24–31 with Psalm 2; Acts 13:34 with Isaiah 55:3–5; Acts 13:47 with Isaiah 49:6; and so on.

the successes and failures of witness in the generations before Christ. So with this dual focus on the distinct motifs of God's mission and the church's witness, let's study the Old Testament to discover its many interrelated themes.

The Gospel Preached in Advance

The opening passage for Old Testament mission is God's promise to Abraham in Genesis 12:2–3: "I will make of you a great nation, and I will bless you and make your name great, so that you will be a blessing. . . . and in you all the families of the earth shall be blessed." As we considered in the introduction, mission had already started in Genesis 3 when God himself came to evangelize the first sinners. But Genesis 12 is the start for a theology of mission; here God begins to reveal his gospel plan for all nations.

Much has been said about this passage in relation to mission. We limit ourselves here to four aspects: God's action, God's world, God's purpose, and God's commentary.

God's action in this passage is his gracious selection of a particular people.[5] He began to reveal his plan for mission by calling Abraham out from the idolatrous nations and establishing with him a special covenant relationship.[6] We will give further attention to this special relationship in the next section. For now, we note that the opening action of God's mission is particular and focused narrowly on Abraham and

---

5   I have intentionally used the word *selection* here instead of the word *election* in order to avoid confusing God's selection of Israel as a particular covenant people with the doctrine of God's election and predestination (Eph. 1:4; Rom. 8:28–30, 9:6ff). While closely related, the selection of a corporate community for a privileged responsibility and the election of individual sinners unto salvation in Christ are different biblical truths. With this distinction in view, there are a number of helpful discussions about Israel's selection for mission; for example, see Lesslie Newbigin, *The Open Secret: An Introduction to the Theology of Mission* (Grand Rapids, MI: Eerdmans, 1995), 67–77; and Christopher Wright, *The Mission of God* (Downers Grove, IL: InterVarsity, 2006), 191–221.

6   The Old Testament often draws attention to the separateness and uniqueness of this special relationship, also making clear that this privileged place was a gracious calling and not due to any merit or superiority (Deut. 7:6–8; Amos 3:2).

his descendants, the people of Israel. God choose one particular family, blessing them in special ways as the possessors of his covenant promises, even while preparing, through them, to bless all families of the earth.

The context of this passage introduces the tale of two globalisms in *God's world*. The first globalism is humanity's ambitious plan at Babel to be mighty and make a name for themselves (Gen. 11:4; cf. 10:8–10). These sinful ambitions are described as defiance against God's repeated command to fill the earth (Gen. 1:28; 8:17; 9:1). This humanistic globalism is still alive and well in the world today, often promoting unity in rebellion against God's truth (Ps. 2:2; Acts 4:27).

It is important to see how God's action in Genesis 12 is intentionally revealed against the background of the Table of Nations (Gen. 10) and the Tower of Babel account (Gen. 11:1–9). Humanistic globalism is the background context for the unfolding story of God's bigger and better plan for all families of the earth. The story of the second globalism—God's overarching universal plan of redemption—is the history of how God makes a name for himself by forming one nation in order to bless all nations (2 Sam. 7:23); it is a story that will culminate in the global dominance of his Son (Phil. 2:9–11) and a perfected, multiethnic community of worship (Rev. 7:9–10).

God's purpose in Genesis 12:1–3 is universal in scope. The covenant promise was not only for the blessing of a particular people but also and especially for the blessing of all nations. God's blessing of Abraham had a much wider focus: in this way, he was preparing to bless all families of the earth. Though God did promise to graciously bless Abraham individually, the grander promise in this passage is not for Abraham only, but also for everyone "who shares the faith of Abraham" (Rom. 4:16).

God's commentary about this passage has already helped us understand his opening act of Old Testament mission: God himself was preaching the gospel in advance (Gal. 3:8), not only to Abraham but especially to all the spiritual children of Abraham who would by faith become keepers of this precious gospel promise. In this way, God makes a name for himself by selecting a particular nation, through whom he prepared to bless all nations.

Thus the basic contour of God's mission is clearly evident in Genesis 12. God himself takes action in the opening story of his bigger plan. In fact, two complementary truths are revealed in this passage: God's purpose and God's means.[7] God's universal purpose is his global plan for the redemption of sinners from all nations. God's particular means is his particular selection of the Old Testament church—the graciously selected covenant family—as his instrument through whom and by which he will bless all peoples.

These complementary truths are interrelated throughout the entire Old Testament narrative. We usually see God's particular people on the foreground: the storyline of Abraham's ethnic descendants and the sociopolitical nation of Israel. Yet, often in the background, we see glimpses of God's grander purpose. For example, when Israel's repeated sins in the wilderness have again brought God's judgment upon them, God, as it were, opens the curtains briefly to show a glimpse of what is happening backstage: "But truly, as I live, and as all the earth shall be filled with the glory of the LORD, none of the men who have seen my glory . . . and yet have put me to the test these ten times . . . shall see the land that I swore to give to their fathers" (Num. 14:21–23; cf. Hab. 2:14; Isa. 56:7; Mal. 1:11).

In addition to the motif of God's mission, the witness of God's people is also clearly evident in Genesis 12. From the opening story, God's plan to display his grace and glory before all nations is achieved,

7 It is important to see these truths as complementary aspects of God's mission rather than as competing aspects in the Old Testament Scriptures. We give considerable attention in this study to the universal aspect of God's purpose and the continuity of God's church across all of redemptive history in order to draw applications for Christian witness from God's people in the Old Testament. Yet we must not overlook God's particular means in each stage of redemptive history and the progressive development of the people of God concept in Scripture. See Johannes Blauw, *The Missionary Nature of the Church* (New York: McGraw-Hill, 1962), 24; Kaiser, *Mission in the Old Testament*, 28; and David Filbeck, *Yes, God of the Gentiles, Too: The Missionary Message of the Old Testament* (Wheaton, IL: Billy Graham Center, 1994).

in part, by means of the public witness of his covenant people. Though not to the same extent as in the New Testament, God's Old Testament people were selected to participate in his mission as his witnesses in at least three ways: as a showcase community, by loving confrontation, and in expectant worship.

Witness as Showcase Community

God's Old Testament people participated in God's mission by living among the nations as a showcase community. They were called to be a living, public display of God's grace and glory among the nations. God introduced this special calling at Mount Sinai when he constituted the nation: "You yourselves have seen what I did to the Egyptians, and how I bore you on eagles' wings and brought you to myself. Now therefore . . . you shall be my treasured possession among all peoples, for all the earth is mine; and you shall be to me a kingdom of priests and a holy nation" (Ex. 19:4–6).

As God's covenant people, they were set apart from the nations as his treasured possession, his trophy of grace (1 Pet. 2:9; cf. Eph. 1:14; Titus 2:14). God had redeemed them from slavery, displaying his power over the gods of Egypt. At Mount Sinai, he consecrated them as a priestly kingdom and holy nation. They were called to live in this special relationship, holy and separate from the nations as God's redeemed people.[8]

Their covenant relationship, however, did not contradict their calling to participate as witnesses in God's mission. On the contrary, their witness to the nations depended on and was reinforced by their covenant separateness from the nations.[9] This holy nation was set apart as

---

8   The showcase community concept is parallel to the concept of church as God's temple; see G. K. Beale, *The Temple and the Church's Mission* (Downers Grove, IL: InterVarsity, 2004), 402.

9   J. H. Bavinck writes, "The work of missions is possible only within the concept a covenant." Bavinck, *Introduction*, 14. Regarding the importance of the covenant for mission, see also D. T. Niles, *Upon the Earth: The Mission of God and the Missionary Enterprise of the Churches* (New York, NY: McGraw-Hill, 1962), 250; and Paul Wells, Peter A. Lillback, and Henk Stoker, *A Covenantal Vision for Global Mission* (Phillipsburg, NJ: P&R, 2020).

God's "treasured possession" to give evidence "among all peoples" of his special grace (Ex. 19:5; cf. Deut. 26:18–19).

God intentionally put his trophy of grace on display in the sight of all nations. The Old Testament church was a special showcase community, an assembly called out of the world and into covenant fellowship with God in order to proclaim his praise globally (Deut. 4:5–8; cf. 1 Pet. 2:9–12). He set them apart as an international exhibition of his power over all so-called gods and as a public demonstration of his redeeming grace. Furthermore, as a continuation of his covenant promises to Abraham, God selected and consecrated this kingdom of priests to be the particular means by which he would make known his plans for the salvation of all nations.

God's showcase community was called to live as a light among the nations. Their witness, however, was not predominantly about them going out to the nations. It is true that God's Old Testament people functioned as witnesses to prove that he is the only true God (Isa. 43:8–12), as we will consider in the next section. It is also true that Isaiah anticipated the mission of the Lord's Servant (Isa. 42:6; 49:6; Luke 2:32) and the Gentile mission in the New Testament (Acts 13:47), as we will study in later chapters. But the witness of God's Old Testament people was predominantly as a living display of God's grace and the ethical implications of keeping God's covenant. Their very existence was a witness to the surrounding nations of God's mighty power and great goodness (Deut. 3:24; 2 Sam. 7:22–23). Their faithful worship included the declaration of God's glory among the nations (Ps. 96:3).

As God's showcase community, God's Old Testament people were called to participate in God's mission by living according to his law in the sight of the nations. Their holiness was of utmost importance: God commanded them to "obey [his] voice and keep [his] covenant" as a holy nation which was consecrated for priestly service (Ex. 19:4–6). The apostle Peter, quoting these words, draws the same conclusion for the New Testament church: God's people have an ethical responsibility in the world to abstain from sin and to keep their conduct honorable among the nations (1 Pet. 2:9–12).

When God's people worshiped him only, living according to his law and remaining separate from idolatry, they were strong witnesses of God's promise and grace. But their witness was hindered—even inverted—when they failed to keep God's covenant and worshiped gods of the surrounding nations. God's name was profaned by his people's unfaithful witness (Ezek. 20), so that God had to act in order to vindicate his own name (Isa. 48:9–11; Ezek. 36:22–24). Thus we need to distinguish between God's intentions for his showcase community and the actual practice of Old Testament witness.

God's Old Testament people often failed to live holy lives among the nations. We must not overlook the high points that reveal Israel's awareness of and faithfulness in their witness among the nations. For example, read Solomon's temple dedication prayer (1 Kings 8:41–43) or recall the Israelite slave girl who witnessed about the powerful God in Israel (2 Kings 5). But most of the Old Testament narrative is about Israel's repeated apostasy from God's law, accommodation of sinful cultures, and spiritual adultery with other gods. Israel's unfaithfulness and disobedience brought God's just judgments upon his own people (Ezek. 5:5–8; Amos 3:2). Many of the later prophets lamented how Israel had become an object of international derision and that God's judgment would soon lead to dispersion among the nations. Indeed, Old Testament history is largely an account of the Old Testament church's failure to participate faithfully in God's mission (Acts 7:1–53).

We must not judge God's Old Testament people by New Testament obligations. They were not guilty of disobeying the Great Commission, because Christ's mission was not yet fulfilled and the Gentile mission had not yet been inaugurated. Yet God's Old Testament people often failed to live as a holy showcase community. The sad commentary of 2 Kings 17:7–23 proves this point implicitly. Here Israel's failures are outlined succinctly at the fall of Samaria when the ten tribes were scattered in exile. Instead of being a showcase community, they feared other gods and followed the customs of the rebellious nations. God's prophets needed to confront his own people for their stubborn refusal to live according to his teaching that kept them from being a light to the nations. Instead of declaring God's glory among the nations, the people provoked God to jealousy by selling themselves to do evil. Thus Israel failed to live as God's faithful witnesses among the nations.

Yet God's mission was not derailed by the failure of God's Old Testament people. God's grander plan cannot be thwarted by his people's unbelief (Rom. 9:6; cf. Heb. 3–4). Though many died in unbelief, God continued to preserve a faithful Old Testament remnant (Mal. 3:17). Despite his people's weakness and failure, God still used their witness, and he was glorified in the process. Many of the prophets called the people back to covenant faithfulness and encouraged them with promises of the better day that was coming when the good news would be fully revealed to all nations.

Witness as Loving Confrontation

What do the Old Testament prophets teach about God's mission and Christian witness? At first, we may be tempted to page quickly through the Prophetic Literature, assuming its message for mission is very limited. Should we copy Elijah's methods on Mount Carmel when he killed the 450 false prophets in one day? Or are the Minor Prophets' harsh pronouncements against ancient nations an example for Christian witness today?

Many studies have looked to Jonah for principles of mission.[10] Certainly this book does teach about God's gracious forbearing mercy and his desire to bless all nations. But the prophet Jonah is not a role model for missionaries! On the contrary, he is a better example of what

---

10 See Johannes Verkuyl, *Contemporary Missiology* (Grand Rapids, MI: Eerdmans, 1978), 96–100; and Daniel C. Timmer, *A Gracious and Compassionate God: Mission, Salvation and Spirituality in the Book of Jonah* (Downers Grove, IL: IVP Academic, 2016).

a missionary must not be since his heart was filled with ethnic superiority, selfish nationalism, and anger against God for being too gracious.

Yet while Jonah the person failed, the book of Jonah gives us a hint about the role of prophets and their message for mission.[11] It presents a lesson of God's mercy toward all nations despite the myopic selfishness of his disobedient prophet, the one who was called to be the official voice of God's showcase community. From the Prophets we learn another Old Testament method for Christian witness: in addition to living as God's showcase community, God's people also participated in God's mission as his advocates and witnesses within his international courtroom. Reflecting on the Prophets' role in God's mission gives us foundational insights for the church's witness among the nations today.

First, as already considered, God's plan from the beginning *included all the nations*. It is no surprise, therefore, that the Prophetic Literature consists of many oracles for the nations or that Jeremiah was called to be a "prophet to the nations" (Jer. 1:5).[12]

Second, the prophets speak into the *global scene of international rebellion* against God. The nations are raging against God; they refuse to recognize his sovereign authority (Ps. 2:1–3). These nations, enslaved by their own idolatries, must be rebuked by the prophets for their false beliefs and unethical practices. God's moral order still stands despite the fact it has been rejected internationally and replaced with many deviant religions and syncretistic traditions.

The prophets often speak into this scene of opposition, presenting it in starkly contrasting terms: the rebellious nations versus God's redeemed people, those deceived by Satan's lie versus those keeping God's covenant, and the gods of the nations versus the incomparability of the

---

11   See Kaiser, *Mission in the Old Testament*, 69–71; and Andreas J. Köstenberger and Peter T. O'Brien, *Salvation to the Ends of the Earth* (Downers Grove, IL: InterVarsity, 2001), 44–45.

12   We must keep in mind, however, that God's people were the primary audience of the oracles since the Gentile mission had not yet been inaugurated. The nations are not judged for general sin but specifically for their attacks on God's people (Ezek. 28:24–26). In this way, God also affirms the other part of the Abrahamic blessing: "Him who dishonors you I will curse" (Gen. 12:3).

Lord. The prophets announce God's impending judgment upon the sinful nations (Isa. 13–23) and also a coming salvation from judgment offered to all nations (Isa. 45:22–23).

Third, we see occasional glimpses in the Old Testament of the *cosmic contest between God and the so-called gods* (Job 1:6; Ps. 82; Zech. 3:1).[13] The rebellious nations worship their own gods in place of the only true God. In reality, these gods are not real deities; they are only projections of human idolatries that have been deified by sinners in their devious religiosity and rebellion against God (2 Kings 19:22; Isa. 37:19; 41:21–24, 29). These idols are empty and useless, leading only to confusion and shame (Isa. 44:6–20; Jer. 10:2–11; cf. Ps. 115:4–8). But these metaphysical realities must be confronted, since the devil stands behind them to give them a life of their own (Deut. 32:16–17; Ps. 106:37; Isa. 26:14; cf. 1 Cor. 10:20; Rev. 13:2).[14]

The prophets proclaim the exclusive truth of God's incomparability over against the so-called gods of the surrounding nations.[15] There is only one God, the sovereign Creator and Judge of the nations (Isa. 40:18–26). God has undisputed authority to summon the surrounding nations to his courtroom for a public trial (Isa. 41:21; Jer. 25:31). He will pronounce judgment upon them, regardless of whether or not these sinful nations heed his solemn warnings (Isa. 43:8–12; Joel 3:2;

---

13   See Richard R. DeRidder, "God and the Gods: Reviewing the Biblical Roots," *Missiology* 6 (1978): 11–28.

14   For example, the history of 2 Kings 17–19 highlights Hezekiah's exclusive trust in the Lord, the one true God (2 Kings 19:15–19), in contrast to the religious pluralism and syncretism of the surrounding nations. In response to Hezekiah's prayer, God reveals his supreme power over the gods of the other nations, including powerful Assyria that had overpowered all other nations (2 Kings 18:33–35). This story is not only about Hezekiah's faith when confronted by the boasts of a powerful foreign messenger. More importantly, the bigger story is about God's supreme power as proclaimed by his faithful messenger, the prophet Isaiah, and believed by his humble servant, King Hezekiah. Isaiah's message to Hezekiah about the demise of the Assyrian king (2 Kings 19:21–28)—and most of Isaiah's prophecy—must be understood within this context of international rebellion and a cosmic power encounter between God and the so-called gods.

15   See Casper J. Labuschagne, *The Incomparability of Yahweh in the Old Testament* (Leiden, NL: Brill, 1966).

cf. Ps. 2:4–6). God is making a name for himself: what God has already done over the gods of Egypt is a harbinger of his future total triumph (Ex. 9:16; 15:11; Num. 33:4; Zeph. 2:11).

Fourth, the task of the prophets included loving confrontation: *exposing and rebuking sin.* The prophets spoke on God's behalf in his international courtroom. They were not speaking on Israel's behalf against her enemies, as if the sovereign Lord were like one of the many gods who fought on behalf of the nation that worshiped them. Rather, the Lord's prophets exposed the sin of both Israel and the nations since both had disregarded his holy character of righteousness, justice, and compassion.

The prophets rebuked God's people for their covenant unfaithfulness. When God's people failed to live as a holy witness, God sent his prophets to expose their sin and call them back to true worship. The prophets especially confronted the immorality and injustice of the leaders. Through the prophets, God also pronounced judgment on his own people for their covenant unfaithfulness despite his gracious deliverance and forbearance.

God's prophets also implicitly rebuked the international community with various oracles against the nations (Isa. 17:13; 34:1–2, 8; 66:15–16). As God's advocates, they spoke on God's behalf, publicly declaring God's controversy with the nations and summoning the nations to stand trial in order to prove his preeminence. Through the prophets, God announced impending judgment upon all rebellious nations, especially for their opposition against his people and plan.

Fifth, God's Old Testament people are *his witnesses within this international scene.* The prophet Isaiah describes their place in God's international courtroom:

> Bring out the people who are blind, yet have eyes,
>   who are deaf, yet have ears!
> All the nations gather together,
>   and the peoples assemble.

Who among them can declare this,
  and show us the former things?
Let them bring their witnesses to prove them right,
  and let them hear and say, It is true. . . .
"I, I am the LORD,
  and besides me there is no savior.
I declared and saved and proclaimed,
  when there was no strange god among you;
and you are my witnesses," declares the LORD, "and I am God."
    (Isa. 43:8–12)

The supreme God has summoned all nations to his courtroom. In response to their idolatrous deception and global rebellion, he challenges them to dispute the fact that he is the exclusive and incomparable God. He then presents his own people as his witnesses who declare this truth. Though often blinded by unbelief, God's redeemed people still function as his witnesses within the context of the nations. They give evidence to the fact that he is the only God and Savior (Isa. 44:6–9; 45:20–23).

We know that God's people in the Old Testament often failed to live as faithful witnesses to this truth. But this is not the end of the story. Isaiah and the other Old Testament prophets announced the coming of the Messiah, God's chosen servant (Isa. 43:10). The Messiah would succeed where God's people had failed; he is the faithful witness (Isa. 55:4; Rev. 1:5) and he is the triumphant victor in the cosmic contest (Col. 2:15; Eph. 4:8; Heb. 2:14), as we will consider in the next chapter.

The Old Testament prophets, therefore, have an important place in a biblical theology of mission. They are God's spokesmen, teaching his people by repeating the history of God's deliverances, discipling them in the way of wisdom, and calling them back to true worship. They are God's advocates on the international scene, vindicating God's truth and righteousness, similar to the Holy Spirit's work of rebuking sin

(John 16:8) and New Testament witness as gospel defense. They also proclaim a message of judgment and mercy, sin and salvation: all people—including God's own people—will soon be punished, but mercy will be shown to all who repent and trust in God alone (Isa. 45:20–23).

Witness as Expectant Worship

In addition to their witness as a showcase community and by loving confrontation, God's Old Testament people also participated in his mission through the witness of their expectant worship. The Old Testament writings, especially the book of Psalms, give us important lessons for Christian witness.[16]

The Psalter has always been central in the praise of God's people, throughout all ages and across all lands. As inspired liturgy for God's people to use in worship, the Psalms are poetic expressions of Scripture's foundational themes. It is no surprise, therefore, that the themes of God's mission and our participation in it reverberate throughout the entire collection.

The Psalms proclaim *God's supreme being*. Monotheism is never questioned; it is always assumed and celebrated publicly. There is no contest between our God and other so-called gods: the Lord is incomparable, unsurpassed, and matchless (Pss. 89:7; 95:3; 135:5; 145:3). For example, Psalm 96 invites all "families of the peoples" to worship the Lord alone:

> Declare his glory among the nations,
>   his marvelous works among all the peoples!
> For great is the LORD, and greatly to be praised;
>   he is to be feared above all gods.

---

16 George W. Peters writes, "The Psalter is one of the greatest missionary books in the world." Peters, *A Biblical Theology of Missions* (Chicago: Moody Press, 1972), 116. John Piper has wonderfully expressed the same truth in *Let the Nations be Glad: The Supremacy of God in Missions* (Grand Rapids, MI: Baker, 1993). See also Geerhardus Vos, "The Eschatology of the Psalter," *Princeton Theological Review* 18/1 (January 1920): 1–43.

For all the gods of the peoples are worthless idols,
>>   but the LORD made the heavens. (Ps. 96:3–5; cf. 1 Chron.
>>   16:24–26; Isa. 66:19)

The Psalms celebrate *God's global purpose*. More than any other Old Testament book, the Psalms proclaim God's universal plan for all nations. Likewise, the apostle Paul turns to the Psalter to celebrate the global scope of the gospel as the outcome of Christ's mission (Rom. 15:9–11).

All the ends of the earth shall remember
>>   and turn to the LORD,
and all the families of the nations
>>   shall worship before you. (Ps. 22:27)

Let the peoples praise you, O God;
>>   let all the peoples praise you! (Ps. 67:3)

All the nations you have made shall come
>>   and worship before you, O Lord,
>>   and shall glorify your name. (Ps. 86:9)

The LORD has made known his salvation;
>>   he has revealed his righteousness in the sight of the nations.
>>   (Ps. 98:2)

Praise the LORD, all nations!
>>   Extol him, all peoples! (Ps. 117:1)

The Psalms recount *God's gracious dealings* with his particular people. They explain how God's people enjoy a privileged place among all the families of the earth (Pss. 33:12; 105:6; 106:5; 135:4; 144:15). For example, Psalm 105 narrates God's special blessings and wondrous works for his covenant people, while Psalm 106 recounts God's repeated deliverance despite his people's repeated disobedience, ending with a prayer that God will again show mercy to gather his dispersed people from among the nations.

The scope of worship in the Psalms is both exclusive and inclusive. God's Old Testament people were instructed by their liturgy to worship the only true God exclusively and to ascribe to him absolute allegiance. They were also trained by their liturgy to reject tendencies of myopic pride often caused by a misapplication of covenantal privileges. Thus their focus was continually redirected in worship to see God's global plan that intentionally included all nations, not merely their own tribe or people: "May God be gracious to us and bless us . . . that your way may be known on earth, your saving power among all nations" (Ps. 67:1–2; cf. 22:27–28; 47:9; 98:3; 105:1).

The religious pluralism within the sociocultural context of the surrounding nations, therefore, is countered by a refreshing balance in the Psalms that is both an exclusive confession of God's supremacy and also an inclusive message of hope for the nations. This balance is reaffirmed in the New Testament (Rom. 10:9–13; 1 Tim. 2:1–8; Titus 2:11).

Furthermore, the Psalms declare *God's international power* as the sovereign Judge. Psalm 2 introduces this theme, which is common throughout the Old Testament and also foundational for New Testament mission and eschatology (Acts 1:8; 4:24–26; 13:32–33; Heb. 1:5; Rev. 2:27; 12:5; 19:15). Despite international opposition, God holds unshakable global authority, and he will soon come to judge all nations (Pss. 9:8; 59:5, 8; 98:9; cf. Acts 17:31).

God has taken his place in the divine council;
    in the midst of the gods he holds judgment:
"How long will you judge unjustly
    and show partiality to the wicked?" . . .
Arise, O God, judge the earth;
    for you shall inherit all the nations! (Ps. 82:1–2, 8)

Say among the nations, "The LORD reigns!
    Yes, the world is established; it shall never be moved;
    he will judge the peoples with equity." . . .
Then shall all the trees of the forest sing for joy
    before the LORD, for he comes,
    for he comes to judge the earth.
He will judge the world in righteousness,
    and the peoples in his faithfulness. (Ps. 96:10–13)

Like the apostle Paul, many of the psalms are not ashamed of the righteousness of God that is revealed through his just judgments upon the wicked (Pss. 11:4–7; 58:1–11; 110:5–6; cf. Rom. 1:16–17).

Finally, the Psalms anticipate *God's future kingdom.* Many of these inspired songs are glimpses of a glorious time when God's mission will advance and be fully accomplished (Pss. 68:18; 85:9–13; 145:10–13). Psalm 72 is the classic expression of this anticipation:

Give the king your justice, O God,
    and your righteousness to the royal son! . . .
May he have dominion from sea to sea,
    and from the River to the ends of the earth!
May desert tribes bow down before him,
    and his enemies lick the dust!
May the kings of Tarshish and of the coastlands
    render him tribute;
may the kings of Sheba and Seba
    bring gifts!
May all kings fall down before him,
    all nations serve him! . . .
May his name endure forever,
    his fame continue as long as the sun!

May people be blessed in him,
    all nations call him blessed!
Blessed be the LORD, the God of Israel,
    who alone does wondrous things.
Blessed be his glorious name forever;
    may the whole earth be filled with his glory! (Ps. 72:1, 8–11,
        17–19)

The Psalter contains many similar celebrations of the royal Son's future kingdom (Pss. 2:8; 22:27–31; 47:1–9; 110:1–3). This future kingdom is also anticipated by the Old Testament prophets: for example, Isaiah and Micah describe visions of a centripetal ingathering of the nations that would take place in the latter days (Isa. 2:2–5; 24:14–16; 60:3–7; Mic. 4:1–5).[17] God's Old Testament people learned by faith to sing with expectation of what God would soon accomplish.

The book of Psalms, therefore, records these significant themes related to God's mission. It also teaches us how God's Old Testament people participated in his mission by means of their expectant worship. By faith, they publicly confessed their devotion to this one true God within the international context of religious pluralism. They celebrated the mighty acts of God and his wonderful deeds in the world, and at times declared the good news of God's global purpose for all nations. Even in exile, God's people witnessed to the world

---

17 Some have described mission in the Old Testament as a centripetal *coming in* force while mission in the New Testament was a centrifugal *going out* force. This distinction is an unhelpful bifurcation because it describes the Old Testament period by what the Old Testament itself says will characterize the New Testament period. That is, the Old Testament visions of centripetal ingathering (Ps. 72; Isa. 2:2–4) do not describe the occasional historical inclusion of foreigners in the covenant community; rather they describe future times of revival among the nations that will occur in the latter days of the New Testament. The centripetal/centrifugal bifurcation should be replaced with an understanding of God's unfolding vision for mission, still incomplete in the Old Testament that anticipates its fulfillment though Christ and the Gentile mission he inaugurates (Acts 3:25–26; Rom. 15:8–12; Gal. 3:8; 1 Pet. 1:10–12). The centripetal/centrifugal distinction comes from Bengt Sundkler, *The World of Mission* (Grand Rapids, MI: Eerdmans, 1965).

with a confession of faith and hope while singing the Lord's song in a foreign land (Ps. 137:4) In hope, God's church in the Old Testament anticipated the coming of the Messiah's future kingdom and the time when God would judge all nations with righteousness and rule a restored creation in equity.

Mission and Witness Before Christ

A short study can never capture all the interwoven themes and inter-related concepts of God's word. This chapter has highlighted the main themes of God's mission while also describing three central methods of witness in the Old Testament.

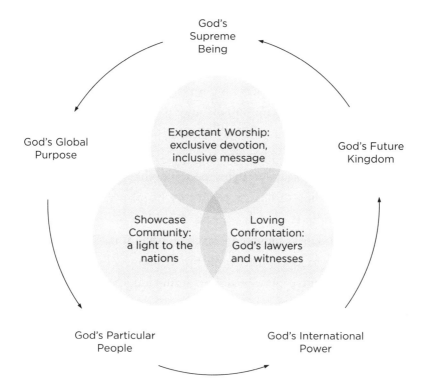

Figure 3. Mission and witness in the Old Testament.

We started this chapter with a dual focus on God's mission and the church's witness. We considered three methods by which God's people were his witnesses in the world, and we reflected on five themes that are central to the Old Testament metanarrative of God's mission (fig. 3). The Old Testament church's witness is, as it were, braided together within the bigger background reality of God the Father's plan for all nations.

The story of Old Testament mission must be told with these themes and methods in view. In conclusion, let's briefly note the seven major movements of God's mission in the Old Testament.

1. God begins his global mission, after the fall in Genesis 3, by coming to his world to evangelize the first sinners with the first message of hope.

2. God selects one family and nation, redeeming them and establishing them among the nations as his showcase community that was called to display his grace and glory.

3. God makes a name for himself among the gods of the nations by triumphing over the Pharaoh of Egypt and all metaphysical forces of evil, thus preparing to bless all nations.

4. God preaches the gospel to his special covenant people, progressively revealing through their history his plan of redemption for all nations (Gal. 3:8, 14; Eph. 3:3–11).

5. God pronounces judgments on the rebellious nations, calling all peoples to repentance, while proclaiming by his prophets a message of mercy in view of impending judgment.

6. God judges his own unfaithful people for their failure to remain holy and separate from the nations by dispersing them when disobedient and restoring them again after exile.

7. God foretells the mission of his servant, the Messiah, who would fulfill God's promises and perfectly perform what God's Old Testament people had failed to be.

The Old Testament is a textbook for mission. Yet it does not give us a full theology of mission or a comprehensive set of biblical methods for Christian witness. Rather, it carefully lays the foundation for what follows. It tells the story of what God the Father was already doing in preparation for the mission work that would soon be accomplished by Christ, and for the mission work that would then be inaugurated by Christ and empowered by his Spirit. The Old Testament also teaches us, with living examples, several essential principles for Christian witness that remain foundational today.

Discussion Questions

1. The Hebrew Bible can be divided into three sections: the Torah, the Prophets, and the Writings (including the Psalms and other Wisdom Literature). What do we learn about Christian witness from each of these sections of the Old Testament?

2. How did our Sovereign God providentially use the weaknesses and failures of his people's witness in the Old Testament to advance the cause of his mission during this period and to prepare for what was coming in the New Testament?

3. Discuss how three different church leaders in the New Testament each applied lessons from the Old Testament for Christian witness.

4. Reflect on Hezekiah's prayer in 2 Kings 19:15–19 in the context of 2 Kings 17:6–19:37 and Isaiah's prophecy. How did God's faithful people in Hezekiah's day try to obey the three central themes of Christian witness outlined in this chapter: showcase community, loving confrontation, and expectant worship? Where does this same historical narrative also clearly highlight the five themes of God's mission?

2

The Mission of Jesus Christ

JESUS CHRIST IS THE CENTER of God's mission. He is the focus and fulfillment of mission in the Old Testament. He is the inception and impetus of New Testament mission. Christ is also both the message and leader of the church's witness. God's mission and the church's witness are all about Jesus.[1]

The centrality of Jesus Christ in mission is undisputable. The magnitude of his person and work for mission, however, often makes it very difficult to describe accurately with all the proper perspectives. It can be like defining the concept of *light* in two sentences or describing *African culture* to people not living in Africa. The mission of Christ is a beautiful concept with many important perspectives that are diverse and interconnected.[2]

In this chapter, we will trace an outline of Christ's mission by viewing it through four lenses: the divine missionary, the suffering

---

1 Our missiology must be grounded on, shaped by, and saturated with biblical Christology. Or put differently, since Christology determines faithful missiology, anything other than biblical Christology will, at best, produce questionable missiology in both theory and practice. John R. W. Stott writes, "our understanding of the church's mission must be deduced from our understanding of the Son's." Stott, *Christian Mission in the Modern World* (Downers Grove, IL: InterVarsity, 1975), 23.

2 See Donald Senior and Carroll Stuhlmuller, *The Biblical Foundations for Mission* (Maryknoll, NY: Orbis, 1983); William J. Larkin Jr. and Joel F. Williams, eds., *Mission in the New Testament: An Evangelical Approach* (Maryknoll, NY: Orbis, 1998); and Peter Bolt and Mark Thompson, eds., *The Gospel to the Nations: Perspectives on Paul's Mission* (Downers Grove, IL: InterVarsity, 2000).

servant, the anointed leader, and the exalted sender (fig. 4). In essence, these four perspectives are one; we distinguish them only to aid our study, just as you can separate out the colors of the light spectrum in order to better understand light itself. We then conclude by looking through these lenses together as one, in order to see how the person, message, and mission of Christ are central for both God's mission and the church's witness.

Figure 4. Four lenses for viewing Christ's mission.

Christ the Divine Missionary

The author of Hebrews urges us to "consider Jesus, the apostle and high priest of our confession, who was faithful to him who appointed him" (Heb. 3:1). The title *apostle*, as is well-known, can be translated as "sent one" or "missionary." Though used only once in reference to Jesus, the concept of Christ's apostleship is found throughout Scripture, especially in John's Gospel (3:17, 34; 5:36; 6:29, 57; 7:29; 8:42; 10:36; 11:42; 17:3, 8, 18, 21, 23, 25; 20:21). All believers bear witness to the truth that "the Father has sent his Son to be the Savior of the world" (1 John 4:14; cf. 4:9–10; Matt. 10:40; Mark 9:37; Luke 4:18,

43; 9:48; 10:16; Acts 3:20, 26; Gal. 4:4–5). Our first lens for viewing the mission of Christ, therefore, is the biblical perspective of Jesus as God's apostle, the divine missionary.

Jesus was commissioned by God the Father. He did not come on his own accord or for his own purpose; rather, he was sent by the Father, and he spoke only the words given to him (John 8:42; 12:49; 14:10; 17:8). He is the last of a long line of prophets sent by God to his people (Luke 11:49–51; 13:34; 19:14; 20:10; Heb. 1:1–2). Unlike the Old Testament prophets, however, Jesus received authority directly from the Father and was glorified by him. For example, in response to the Jewish leaders who challenged his authority, he stated, "I came from God and I am here. I came not of my own accord, but he sent me" and, "It is my Father who glorifies me" (John 8:42, 54). Jesus was uniquely commissioned by God and reported back to God. In fact, Jesus's prayer to the Father in John 17 is a mission report to the one who sent him: "I glorified you on earth, having accomplished the work that you gave me to do" (John 17:4).[3]

Jesus was conscious of his unique identity and calling. The self-awareness of his calling is seen in the bold statements he makes about himself: "I am the light of the world" (John 8:12; cf. 1:9; 3:19; 9:5; 11:9; 12:46) and, "My food is to do the will of him who sent me and to accomplish his work" (John 4:34).

On various occasions, Jesus verbally declares specific objectives of his mission: to "suffer many things and be rejected" (Mark 8:31; cf. Matt. 16:21; Luke 9:22; 17:25; 24:7, 26, 46); "to give his life as a ransom for many" (Matt. 20:28; Mark 10:45; cf. Isa. 53:10; 1 Tim. 2:6); "to proclaim good news . . . liberty . . . the year of the Lord's favor" and "to preach the good news of the kingdom of God" (Luke 4:18–19, 43; cf. Matt. 4:23; Mark 1:38; Luke 8:1); to come "only to the lost sheep of the house of Israel" (Matt. 15:24; cf. 10:5–6; Acts 3:26; Rom. 15:8);

---

3 Richard R. DeRidder, *Discipling the Nations* (Grand Rapids, MI: Baker, 1975), 169.

"to seek and to save the lost" and "to call . . . sinners to repentance" (Luke 19:10; 5:32; cf. 15:4; John 3:17); and "to give eternal life" to the elect (John 10:28; 17:2).[4]

The apostles give further clarity about Christ's mission. For example, Paul states that Christ came to "show God's truthfulness" and to confirm Old Testament promises (Rom. 15:8). John later writes that Christ came "to take away sins" (1 John 3:5; cf. John 1:29; 1 Pet. 2:24) and "to destroy the works of the devil" (1 John 3:8; cf. John 12:31; Col. 2:15; Heb. 2:14).

Jesus came to declare God's glory by making him known in the world. There are numerous objectives associated with Jesus's earthly mission—the many passages referenced in the last two paragraphs make this clear. Related to each, however, is the central aspect that Jesus states at the start and end of his mission report to the Father: "I have manifested your name" and "I made known to them your name, and I will continue to make it known" (John 17:6, 26).

Christ's mission on earth was to declare God's glory by making his name known. God's mission from the beginning was to make a name for himself, in contrast to all attempts of human self-glory (Gen. 11:4 with 12:1–3; Ex. 9:16; Ps. 2). The Old Testament saints were witnesses of God's glory, but only in small part. Moses glimpsed this glory when God proclaimed his special name (Ex. 34:6–8). Isaiah was privileged to see a vision of it (Isa. 6:3; cf. Rev. 4:8), and the Old Testament church celebrated God's name and glory in hopeful song: "Blessed be his glorious name forever; may the whole earth be filled with his glory!" (Ps. 72:19). But Christ is God's final Word, the climax of the universal declaration of God's glorious name: he "who is at the Father's side, he has made him known" (John 1:18). Thus Jesus summarizes his mission by stating: "I made known to them your name" (John 17:26).

---

4   These lists of Jesus's mission objectives are only summaries. We will consider some of these with more detail in the sections that follow. For further discussion, see Eckhard J. Schnabel, *Early Christian Mission: Jesus and the Twelve* (Downers Grove, IL: InterVarsity: 2004), 207–19.

The earthly ministry of Jesus Christ, therefore, must be seen in light of his unique role as the divine missionary. His life-mission and miraculous works are better understood when viewed through this perspective. First, the life-mission of Jesus is best pictured by the "J-shaped" descending-ascending movement of the divine missionary. Jesus understood his own life-mission in this way; he was conscious that "he had come from God and was going back to God" (John 13:3; cf. 16:28). Paul later describes it with the same shape: his humiliation in coming down from God and his exaltation in going back up to God (Phil. 2:6–11; cf. Heb. 1:3–4). The Apostles' Creed also confesses this truth in nine well-known stages in Christ's life-mission: incarnation, suffering, crucifixion, agony, death, resurrection, ascension, session, and return.

Second, the miracles of Jesus are central to his unique witness as the divine missionary. His miracles are signs that prove his divine identity and role in God's mission. They authenticate his special commission and authority as the Son of God: "the [witness] that I have is greater than that of John [the Baptist]. For the works that the Father has given me to accomplish, the very works that I am doing, bear witness about me that the Father has sent me" (John 5:36). Jesus's miracles also supplemented his mission of making God known. The person and ministry of Jesus was characterized by his attitude of compassion (Matt. 9:36; 14:14; 15:32; 20:34; Mark 1:41; 6:34; 8:2; Luke 7:13; 10:33; 15:20). More than mere human affection for those in need, this divine display of "tender mercy" beautifully personified the gracious character of the Father who is "merciful and gracious . . . and abounding in steadfast love" (Ex. 34:6; cf. Luke 1:78–79). The miracles aided and amplified Jesus's display of compassion as he healed the blind, lame, lepers, deaf, and so on (Luke 7:22).[5]

---

5 Christ's ministry, however, never displayed one attribute of God to the exclusion of another. Bosch describes Jesus's mercy in the face of pending vengeance, and Flemming notes his mixture of compassion and confrontation. See David J. Bosch, *Witnesses to the World* (Atlanta: John Knox, 1980), 53–57; and Dean Flemming, *Recovering the Full Mission of God* (Downers Grove, IL: IVP Academic, 2013), 73–78. See also Vern S. Poythress, *The Miracles of Jesus* (Wheaton, IL: Crossway, 2016), 27.

Furthermore, Jesus's miracles serve as signs of the coming kingdom. His miraculous works on many occasions gave a foretaste of the messianic era anticipated by the prophets when shalom would be restored in the creation, causing the wolf and lamb to lie down and rest together (Isa. 11:6). In the person of Jesus, the King of Creation had come to this broken restless world; and though creation was still under the curse of sin until the final redemption, the results of the curse were temporarily reversed in the presence of Jesus the Creator-Redeemer.[6]

Additionally, Jesus's miracles are evidence of his mission to crush Satan's head and to destroy the works of the devil (Gen. 3:15; 1 John 3:8). The miracles, therefore, must also be understood in view of the cosmic power encounter by God's truth against the forces of darkness (Col. 2:15; Heb. 2:14). The first coming of Christ and his earthly mission was a direct assault on the devil's kingdom, resulting in Satan's downfall followed by a mission to the nations that continues to advance upon the gates of hell (John 12:31; Rev. 12). Christ the victorious King now rules from heaven with universal power, and he will soon return with his "rod of iron" to crush all opposition forever (Rev. 19:15; cf. Ps. 2:9; Rev. 12:5). The demons in Jesus's day were very aware of this truth; they often responded to him with fear, knowing that their time was short (Matt. 8:29; Mark 5:7; Luke 8:28).

Christ the Suffering Servant

The author of Hebrews describes Christ's ministry with two titles: *apostle* and *high priest*. Both roles are paramount in God's mission (Heb. 3:1). Having viewed the mission of Christ through the lens of his apostleship, we now look through the second lens: Christ's high priestly atoning work on earth as the suffering servant.

---

6   "The wonders of Jesus are closely connected with the kingship of God. As convincing 'signs' of the kingdom of heaven, they belong to the new world order, in which God will disclose his kingly power in this world. . . . Where Jesus comes, the demons flee, the storm is stilled, the fever subsides, and a new day dawns above this world cursed by sin and misery." J. H. Bavinck, *An Introduction to the Science of Missions* (Phillipsburg, NJ: P&R, 1960), 91.

The prophets anticipated this aspect of Christ's mission (Matt. 13:17; 1 Pet. 1:10–12). Isaiah gives the clearest description of God's suffering servant who would bring redemption to the world (Isa. 42:1–7; 49:1–7; 50:4–9; 52:13–53:12; 61:1–3). The prophets foresaw that this righteous servant would suffer for sin and bear iniquity, endure shame and injustice, make intercession for sinners, establish justice and equity, save people from all nations, and bring peace for all peoples.

The Gospels proclaim the ministry of God's suffering servant. Jesus is the perfect and final Passover Lamb of God (John 1:29; Luke 22:19–20). He is the rejected cornerstone (Luke 20:17; cf. Ps. 118:22; Acts 4:11; 1 Pet. 2:6–7). He is the Savior of the world (John 4:42; cf. 1 Tim. 4:10; 1 John 2:2; 4:14). The paramount high priest's once-for-all atoning sacrifice of himself as the perfect Lamb is the crowning moment of God's mission of redemption (Heb. 9:11–12).

The primary mission of Christ was to accomplish redemption by means of substitutionary atonement (Heb. 9:24–28; cf. John 17:2; Col. 1:14; 1 Pet. 2:24; 1 John 3:5).[7] Other aspects of his earthly mission are significant: displaying compassion in word and deed, proclaiming liberty to the oppressed, gathering God's lost sheep, and destroying the devil's works. Most significant and essential, however, is Christ's mission of suffering and death (Matt. 20:28; Mark 8:31).

Christ's own interpretation of his life-mission makes this truth central (Luke 24:26, 46). The Gospels often state how Jesus's suffering and death are direct fulfillments of God's plan of redemption anticipated long before by Scripture. It was necessary for Christ to suffer, not only to fulfill Scripture but also because his death was essential for his central work in God's mission.[8]

---

7   As Walter A. Elwell notes, "Jesus' fundamental mission on earth was redemptive and revelatory of God's saving will for the world." Elwell, "Jesus and Mission," in *Evangelical Dictionary of World Mission* (Grand Rapids, MI: Baker, 2000), 517–19.

8   For a helpful recent study, see Brian J. Tabb, *After Emmaus: How the Church Fulfills the Mission of Christ* (Wheaton, IL: Crossway, 2021), 39–59.

Christ's primary mission in the history of God's redemption was fully accomplished by his suffering and death. This central truth is the gospel message, the good news that must now be proclaimed to all nations. As the person of Christ is the chief agent in God's mission, so also the good news about Christ is the central message of Christian witness. Hence Jesus concludes his earthly mission with these words: "Thus it is written, that the Christ should suffer and on the third day rise from the dead, and that repentance for the forgiveness of sins should be proclaimed in his name to all nations, beginning from Jerusalem. You are witnesses of these things" (Luke 24:46–48).

Christ the Anointed Leader

The next lens for viewing Christ's mission focuses on Jesus as the Messiah, God's anointed leader. The Old Testament saints all died in faith, having seen from afar the fulfillment of God's promises (John 8:56; 12:41; Heb. 11:13). In faith, they had envisioned him with many prophetic titles: the anointed one (Dan. 9:25; cf. Pss. 2:2; 18:50; 45:7; Acts 4:26–27; Heb. 1:9); the leader and commander of the peoples (Isa. 55:3–4; cf. Jer. 23:5; 30:9; Hos. 3:5; Acts 5:31; 13:23–41); and the judge and ruler of Israel (Mic. 5:1–2; cf. Ezek. 34:23; 37:24; Zech. 13:7; Matt. 2:6; Luke 1:69). Indeed, the Old Testament church was taught with many types—both positive and negative—to anticipate the coming Messiah: the better prophet (Deut. 18:15; Mal. 3:1; cf. Acts 3:22); the perfect high priest (Ps. 110:4; cf. Heb. 7:3, 10:20); and the righteous king (Jer. 23:5; Zech. 9:9; Dan. 2:44; cf. Acts 7:52; 1 John 2:1).

Jesus Christ, God's Messiah, fulfills all these ancient longings as he begins his earthly ministry in Galilee. Each of the four Gospels emphasizes the significance of this event, the turning point in God's mission and history of redemption. Jesus enters the scene precisely at the fullness of time (Mark 1:15; Luke 4:21; cf. Dan. 9:25; Gal. 4:4; Eph. 1:10). He fulfills Scripture (Matt. 1:22; 2:5, 17; 3:15) and perfectly matches all aspects of the anticipated role, as Andrew exclaimed to Peter: "We have found the Messiah!" (John 1:41; cf. 1:45; 4:25).

The baptism of Jesus, recorded by all four Gospels, is also much more than just a story about the start of his ministry. In the Old Testament, God's anointed leaders were consecrated for holy service by the special oil that was poured over them as a symbol of God's Spirit anointing them for a special office or task. But now, in the fullness of time, Jesus was anointed without measure when the Spirit of God descended visibly to rest upon him and to remain with him (Matt. 3:16; Mark 1:10; Luke 3:22; John 1:32; cf. Isa. 11:2; Matt. 12:18; Acts 10:38; Heb. 1:9). The Father's audible voice from heaven also confirmed this unique anointing, which inaugurated the earthly ministry of the Messiah, the center-point of the mission of the triune God.

Therefore Jesus Christ is God's paramount and perfect anointed leader, the long-awaited Messiah, who came to confirm the promises given to the Old Testament church, and whose anointed ministry is the beginning of something even greater. Two areas of Jesus's ministry expressly highlight this truth.

Jesus is the *anointed evangelist*. He announces this divine role in his hometown synagogue:

> The Spirit of the Lord is upon me,
>> because he has anointed me
>> to proclaim good news to the poor.
> He has sent me to proclaim liberty to the captives
>> and recovering of sight to the blind,
>> to set at liberty those who are oppressed,
> to proclaim the year of the Lord's favor. (Luke 4:18–19; cf. Isa.
>> 61:1–2)

Mark records the same reality from a different perspective: "Jesus came into Galilee, proclaiming the gospel of God, and saying, 'The time is fulfilled, and the kingdom of God is at hand; repent and believe in the gospel'" (Mark 1:14–15).

Much has been written about the coming kingdom of God[9] and about the recipients of these blessings.[10] This kingdom announcement and its recipients, however, are best understood when defined by and seen as supportive to the Messiah's ministry within God's mission.

At the fullness of time, God's evangelist proclaims the good news of the kingdom.[11] The anointed prophet begins his ministry to declare God's truthfulness and to disciple God's people to live according to God's law in this present age. The anointed high priest proclaims the long-anticipated year of jubilee, the start of a new age—the Day of Salvation for all nations—in which all the families of the earth would become recipients of God's covenant blessings. The anointed king announces the beginning of a spiritual community, a growing foretaste on earth of the spiritual restoration and peace that would only be fully realized in the coming age.

Jesus is also the *messianic shepherd*. Many Old Testament prophets anticipated a future shepherd, a better leader of God's people, who would gather the remnant of Israel, God's sheep that had been scattered among all countries (Jer. 23:1–4; Ezek. 34:11–24). Jesus unequivocally states, "I am the good shepherd" (John 10:11), fulfilling the words of

9   See Herman N. Ridderbos, *The Coming of the Kingdom*, trans. H. de Jongste (Philadelphia, PA: P&R, 1962); and G. E. Ladd, *The Gospel of the Kingdom* (Milton Keynes, UK: Paternoster Press, 1964).

10   While rejecting the excesses of liberation theology, many evangelicals argue that Jesus's example and words in Luke 4:18–19 (as well as many other places) call for a holistic ministry that is more than only verbal gospel proclamation. See Harvie M. Conn, *Evangelism: Doing Justice and Preaching Grace* (Grand Rapids, MI: Zondervan, 1982); Bruce J. Nicholls, ed., *In Word and Deed: Evangelism and Social Responsibility* (Grand Rapids, MI: Eerdmans, 1986); and A. Duane Litfin, *Word versus Deed: Resetting the Scales to a Biblical Balance* (Wheaton, IL: Crossway, 2012).

11   We will give attention to eschatology later. For now, briefly, the good news is the gospel message that the suffering servant—as outlined above—has come to redeem all those who repent and believe in him alone. The kingdom is the new spiritual community of disciples who worship the King and receive eternal life, liberty, and spiritual peace through him. These spiritual blessings are not yet fully experienced since, in these last days, the disciples of the King—the New Testament church—still live in the present world even though they already experience a foretaste of the world to come. During these last days the good news of redemption in Christ must be proclaimed to all nations.

Ezekiel: "I myself will be the shepherd of my sheep," and "Behold, I, I myself will search for my sheep and will seek them out. . . . I will seek the lost" (Ezek. 34:11, 15–16; cf. Luke 19:10). The Gospels often use the imagery of gathering, echoing this common Old Testament theme (Matt. 9:36–38; 22:10; 23:37; 24:31; cf. Deut. 30:3–4; Ps. 106:47; Isa. 11:12; Mic. 2:12).[12] Likewise, Jesus states that he came for "the lost sheep of the house of Israel" (Matt. 15:24), and he depicts his people as a flock that is gathered together after being scattered (Luke 12:32; Matt. 26:31; cf. Isa. 40:11; Zech. 13:7). Furthermore, Jesus has "other sheep" of other folds that must also be gathered into "one flock" with "one shepherd" (John 10:16; cf. 17:20–21; Isa. 56:8), anticipating the ingathering of the nations after his resurrection.

We better understand Christ's mission, therefore, when we consider Jesus as God's anointed leader who proclaimed the good news of the coming kingdom to Israel and who began to gather his people from all nations. Several underlying tensions, however, should be unpacked before we conclude this section.

First, Jesus's earthly ministry was focused only on the people of Israel. Jesus made several statements that, on the surface, may seem shocking. Jesus explicitly instructed the twelve apostles to "go nowhere among the Gentiles" but only to "lost sheep of the house of Israel" (Matt. 10:5–6). Even more directly, Jesus told the Canaanite woman that he was sent "only" to Israel, even implying that his ministry was for Jews and not despised Gentiles (Matt. 15:24–26; John 4:22).

Certainly, Jesus's ministry did not ignore or avoid those outside of the Jewish nation. There are other notable examples: the Samaritan woman (John 4:7–42), the Roman centurion (Matt. 8:5–13; Luke 7:2–10), and some Greeks at the feast (John 12:20–26; cf. 7:32–36). But these were unsought exceptions; clearly, Jesus did not focus on the Gentiles. His earthly ministry was focused on Israel, the Old Testament covenant people.

---

12 Michael W. Goheen, *A Light to the Nations: The Missional Church and the Biblical Story* (Grand Rapids, MI: Baker Academic, 2011), 75–85.

Second, Christ's mission as anointed leader is best explained in two stages. God described the Messiah's two-part mission through the prophet Isaiah many years in advance:

> It is too light a thing that you should be my servant
>> to raise up the tribes of Jacob
>> and to bring back the preserved of Israel;
> I will make you as a light for the nations,
>> that my salvation may reach to the end of the earth. (Isa. 49:6)

The apostle Paul summarizes it theologically after the fact: "For I tell you that Christ became a servant to the circumcised to show God's truthfulness, in order to confirm the promises given to the patriarchs, and in order that the Gentiles might glorify God for his mercy" (Rom. 15:8–9).

As God's "servant to the circumcised," Jesus corrects and completes the mission of Old Testament Israel. But that's not all he does; God had decreed long before that Christ's mission would be much greater, including all nations and extending to the end of the earth (Pss. 2:7–8; 72:8, 11, 17, 19). Jesus's ongoing messianic ministry was also the inception and impetus of New Testament mission to the Gentiles, as considered below.[13] This is why Paul emphasized the same two-stage pattern at that unique time when the focus of God's mission was expanded, after Christ's resurrection, from only the lost sheep of Israel to also include all nations of the earth (Acts 13:46–47; cf. 18:6; 22:21; 28:28; Rom. 1:16; 2:9–10). In fact, the New Testament mission that Christ inaugurated is a continuation of the Old Testament mission, now revived and expanded.

Third, Jesus's ministry was for both the hardening and the restoration of Israel. Simeon saw this truth while holding baby Jesus in his

---

13   Joachim Jeremias notes "two successive events, first the call to Israel, and subsequently the redemptive incorporation of the Gentiles into the kingdom of God." Jeremias, *Jesus' Promise to the Nations* (London: SCM Press, 1948), 71; cf. Goheen, *Light to the Nations*, 81.

arms: not only was this child prepared to be both the glory of Israel and a light to the nations, he also was "appointed for the fall and rising of many in Israel" (Luke 2:31–32, 34). The "rising of many in Israel" was foreseen by Simeon as an outcome of Christ's mission. Jesus came for the restoration of God's covenant people; he came to gather the remnant of Israel, as seen above. Furthermore, the rebuilding and restoration of Israel by God's anointed leader was the very means that God would now use to gather the nations (Acts 15:16–17; cf. Amos 9:11–12).

Furthermore, Simeon foresaw the "fall . . . of many in Israel" as a second outcome of Christ's mission. This hardening of Israel, already described by the prophets (Isa. 6:9–10; Jer. 5:21; Ezek. 12:2), is seen in Jesus's ministry (Matt. 13:13–15; John 12:36–40) and more clearly in the ministry of the apostles who followed (Acts 7:51–54; 28:25–27; cf. Rom. 11:7–10). It results from God's judgment on Israel for rejecting their Messiah (Matt. 23:37–38; Luke 20:16–18; John 9:39). Though tragic and heartbreaking (Rom. 9:2–3), this "partial hardening" is also part of God's plan for the nations (Rom. 11:25; cf. 11:11–12).[14]

Christ the Exalted Sender

The prophets anticipated both the earthly mission of Jesus and the glories that would follow (1 Pet. 1:11), often seeing each stage as one future event. We can focus separately on each perspective, however, looking back on the various stages in his life-mission, as considered above. Now, for the final lens, we zoom out to view Christ's mission in the period following his resurrection. Jesus Christ, who is the divine missionary, suffering servant, and anointed leader, is also the exalted sender for the final period of God's mission.

---

14 Like the apostle Paul (Rom. 10:1), we should continue praying for the salvation of ethnic Jews today, since we have the same hope in God's gracious mercy (Rom. 11:23, 31–32), and since we can envision with Paul how their revival would be an amazing blessing for all nations (Rom. 11:15).

The New Testament church bore witness to the risen Christ, describing his person and ministry with many exalted titles. For example, he is worshiped as "the Holy and Righteous One . . . the Author of life" (Acts 3:14–15) and the "Lord of lords and King of kings" (Rev. 17:14; 19:16). Though not found together in Scripture, the compound title *exalted sender* combines two central aspects of his postresurrection mission.

Christ is the *exalted one*. The apostles bore witness to this truth: "God exalted him at his right hand as Leader and Savior" (Acts 5:31; cf. 2:33; Isa. 55:4). Upon completing his earthly ministry, Christ was further exalted by God the Father and seated in glory, waiting until all his enemies will be vanquished (Ps. 110:1; Phil. 2:9–11; Heb. 1:13). The greatly expanded mission during the New Testament period is a direct result of Christ's victory over evil (Luke 10:18; John 12:31; Eph. 1:21; 4:8; Col. 2:15; Rev. 12:9–10) and his coronation as the exalted King (Dan. 7:13–14; cf. Ps. 2:6–9; Matt. 28:18).[15]

Christ is also the *divine sender*. After his resurrection, the divine missionary becomes the divine sender: "As the Father has sent me, even so I am sending you" (John 20:21; cf. 13:20; 17:18). As the Father sent the Son, and as the Father and Son send the Spirit, in the same way Christ now sends his church into the world to bear witness (John 15:26–27). This truth is essential for the witness of the church in the New Testament period, as we will consider in later chapters.

Christ the exalted sender is now seated in glory, with supreme power and authority, executing his global mission according to God's perfect plan (Rev. 5). With this reality in view, we will now briefly focus on six biblical aspects about Christ's mission during this period.

15 Some have made the mistake of becoming triumphalist in view of Christ's victory and glory. But we who humbly follow in Christ's triumphal procession have learned to celebrate Christ's victory while also confessing that the spiritual battle still rages on earth and that we still have much indwelling sin—like a body of death—that keeps us humble and causes us to long for the final victory we will enjoy when Christ returns (Rom. 8:37; 1 Cor. 15:57).

Table 1. Parallel passages of the Great Commission

	Matt. 28:18–20	Mark 16:15–18	Luke 24:46–49	John 20:21–23	Acts 1:4–8
Authority	"All author- ity in heaven and on earth has been given to me" (18)		"Thus it is written" (46)	"as the Father has sent me" (21)	"the Father has fixed by his own authority" (7)
Activity	"Go . . . make dis- ciples" (19)	"Go . . . proclaim the gospel" (15)	"repentance . . . forgive- ness . . . proclaimed in his name" (47)	"even so I am sending you" (21)	"witnesses in Jerusalem and in all Judea and Samaria" (8)
Scope	"all nations" (19)	"all the world . . . to the whole creation" (15)	"to all na- tions, begin- ning from Jerusalem" (47)	"any" (23)	"to the end of the earth" (8)
Means	"baptizing them in the name . . . teaching them to observe" (20)	"Whoever believes . . . saved . . . not believe . . . con- demned" (16)	"You are witnesses of these things" (48)	"If you forgive . . . withhold forgiveness" (23)	"you will be my wit- nesses" (8)
Power	"all that I have com- manded you" (20)	"in my name" (17)	"stay . . . until you are clothed with power" (49)	"he breathed on them. . . . 'Receive the Holy Spirit' " (22)	"you will re- ceive power when the Holy Spirit has come" (8)
Promise	"I am with you always, to the end of the age" (20)	"these signs will accompany those who believe" (17)	"I am send- ing the pro- mise of my Father upon you" (49)	"Peace be with you" (21)	"you will be baptized with the Holy Spirit" (5)

First, and most famous, we see the event of the Great Commission. Five parallel passages describe this significant event, each highlighting different perspectives and nuances (table 1). The content of this commission is worthy of careful reflection. Not only does this commission build upon Old Testament mission and flow from Christ's own mission, but it also directly precedes the Holy Spirit's expanded mission and is foundational for the New Testament mission that followed (Acts 1:2; 10:42).[16]

Second, we observe the launch of the Gentile mission. From the broader perspective of Christ's mission, the Great Commission marked the inauguration of the long-awaited mission to all nations. The prophets had anticipated the special time when God's mission would be greatly enlarged and expanded in the world (Gen. 28:14; Isa. 54:2–3; Amos 9:11–12). Now, under the guidance of the exalted sender, this special time had begun as the final stage in God's mission. Now God's purposes from the beginning would be realized on the global scene as people from all families of the earth begin to receive his gracious covenant blessings. From this perspective, the Great Commission also shows how Christ is still the leader of God's mission on earth, now ruling from the place of ultimate power in heaven. He is the exalted sender who commissions his witnesses, empowering them with his Spirit and directing them in all related activities. Thus the witness of the church in this New Testament period is simply an extension of Christ's mission, the activity of Christ exercised by his Spirit and through his church.[17]

Third, we reflect on the scope of Christ's present mission. Though Jesus's earthly ministry was focused on Israel, he always had all nations

---

16 See DeRidder, *Discipling the Nations*, 170–96, and Tabb, *After Emmaus*, 17–33.

17 Köstenberger notes that John "conceived of the mission of the Christian community as ultimately the mission of the exalted Jesus carried out through his followers." Köstenberger, *The Missions of Jesus and the Disciples According to the Fourth Gospel* (Grand Rapids, MI: Eerdmans, 1998), 224–25. The Heidelberg Catechism (q. 54) confesses the same about the church: "The Son of God through his Spirit and Word, out of the entire human race, from the beginning of the world to its end, gathers, protects, and preserves for himself a community chosen for eternal life and united in true faith" (*CCC* 306).

in view (Matt. 8:11–12; Luke 13:28–30). For example, he knew that the temple should be a house of prayer for all nations (Matt. 21:13; Mark 11:17; Luke 19:46; cf. 2 Chron. 6:32–33; Isa. 56:7), and he desired that his "house may be filled" both with those first invited and with others also (Luke 14:23; cf. Matt. 21:43–45). God's purpose had always been for his covenant people to be light to the nations and, in Christ, this purpose is being realized as the church bears witness among all nations to Christ, the light of the world (Isa. 42:6; 49:6; Matt. 5:14–16; Luke 2:32; John 1:9; Acts 13:47; Rev. 21:23–24). The scope of God's mission had always been universal: all the families of the earth (Gen. 12:3; 18:18; 22:18; 26:4), among all peoples and all nations (Pss. 22:27; 67:3, 5; 72:11, 17; 96:3; 117:1; Rom. 1:5; 15:11), to the ends of the earth (Ps. 2:8; Isa. 49:6; 52:10; Acts 1:8).

Fourth, we perceive how God's ancient mystery is now revealed in Christ. This mystery is that people from all nations are "fellow heirs" with people of ethnic Israel, "members of the same body," and "partakers" of the same covenant promise in Christ (Eph. 3:6; cf. 3:1–13; Col. 1:26–27). God's divine purpose and plan, hidden for long ages before Christ's coming, is now revealed in Christ and proclaimed by Christ's witnesses to the world.[18] Paul describes the Gentile mission that Christ inaugurated as the public declaration among all nations of this divine secret (Rom. 16:25–26; Col. 4:3–4).

Fifth, we watch the glorious ingathering of the nations. Isaiah envisioned the latter days when "many peoples" from "all the nations" would come up for worship to "the mountain of the house of the LORD" (Isa. 2:2–5; cf. 27:13; 66:20; Mic. 4:1–5). Christ, the messianic-shepherd who gathers all his people (Isa. 56:7–8), foresaw the day when many peoples, from all corners of the earth, would come to sit down with Abraham in the kingdom (Matt. 8:11). Paul also foresaw the fulfillment

---

18 On this mystery, see P. T. O'Brien, "Mystery," in *Dictionary of Paul and His Letters* (Downers Grove, IL: InterVarsity, 1993), 621–23; and Lesslie Newbigin, *The Open Secret: An Introduction to the Theology of Mission* (Grand Rapids, MI: Eerdmans, 1995).

of Isaiah's vision: his missionary calling was a "priestly service" that included the "offering of the Gentiles" (Rom. 15:16).[19] This vision of an international ingathering is now being realized in this present age under the direction of the exalted sender. The remnant of God's people, like spiritual refugees from all nations (Isa. 45:20), are being gathered together in Zion, God's holy mountain. Not only those of ethnic Israel, but also all those who by faith have become the spiritual children of Abraham. We now see more than ever what Paul saw, as we observe—across two millennia of mission history—how many "from every nation, from all tribes and peoples and languages" are still being gathered into an innumerable, multiethnic multitude of worshipers of the exalted lamb-shepherd (Rev. 7:9, 17).

Finally, we discern Christ's ongoing mission in heaven and on earth. Christ the risen prophet-teacher sends forth his word by means of his Spirit and his church (Acts 23:11; 2 Tim. 4:17).[20] Christ the risen high priest continues his ministry of particular intercession, praying for his people and for their effective witness in the world (John 17:9, 20; Heb. 7:25). Christ the risen shepherd-king directs all events of world history for the good of his people and the glory of God's name; his mission will continue until the kingdoms of this world become the kingdom of our God (Rev. 11:15; cf. Ex. 15:18; Dan. 2:44; 7:14; Zech. 14:9; Luke 1:33).

Christ the exalted sender will come to earth again, at the conclusion of this present age. His second coming will crush all opposition in vengeance (2 Thess. 1:8; Heb. 10:30), as the final destruction of the devil's works and for the final judgment of all peoples. Christ's final return will mark the end of mission, since then God's mission plan will have been perfectly concluded and the kingdom fully consummated.

---

19 Compare Romans 15:16 with Isaiah 66:20, and compare Romans 15:18 with 1:5, 15:27, and 16:26. Concerning this international ingathering, see Bavinck, *Introduction*, 20–24.

20 As J. I. Packer argues, "There is only one agent of evangelism: namely, the Lord Jesus Christ. It is Christ Himself who through His Holy Spirit enables His servants to explain the gospel truly and apply it powerfully and effectively. . . ." Packer, *Evangelism and the Sovereignty of God* (Downers Grove, IL: InterVarsity, 1961), 85.

God's Apostle and Witness

Having viewed Christ's mission from the perspective of four distinct lenses, we now conclude by looking through all these lenses together as one. Stepping back in this way, we view the whole mission of Christ in summary and then briefly note several applications important for following chapters.

First, Christ's mission highlights his unique role as *God's apostle*. As already observed in part, the mission of Christ is singular in many ways: his special calling and commission by the Father as God's divine missionary; his once-for-all ministry of substitutionary atonement and redemption; his unlimited anointing by the Holy Spirit for messianic ministry; and his divine coronation and campaign as the exalted sovereign. Christ is preeminent in all things, including his role in God's mission (Col. 1:15–20).

Scripture also highlights this fact by drawing attention to Christ's unique position in the timeline of God's mission. His first coming was at the "fullness of time" according to God's plan (Mark 1:15; John 7:8; Gal. 4:4; Eph. 1:10), and the time between his first and second comings is the "intervening period" during which God's mission on earth is accomplished. The earthly ministry of Christ is both the final moment of God's mission in the Old Testament and the precursory moment to God's mission in the New Testament. Christ fulfilled Old Testament mission by correcting and completing the witness of Israel. He accomplished redemption and instituted his kingdom on earth. He inaugurated New Testament mission, sending out his Spirit and church as witnesses in the world. He now reigns from heaven until the end of mission with the coming of the completed kingdom (Matt. 24:14; Eph. 1:14). Christ's incarnation and earthly ministry is the climax of God's plan of redemption.

Second, Christ is called the *faithful witness*, having completed his earthly mission (Rev. 1:5; 3:14; 19:11; cf. Isa. 55:4). As such, Christ is the perfect exemplar for his church (John 13:15; 1 Cor. 11:1). His earthly mission sets patterns for his people to follow (1 Pet. 2:21; cf. 1 Tim. 6:13;

Heb. 3:1–6; Rev. 2:13). Christians are not commissioned to become "a little Christ" to the world; this is impossible for mere humans who are sinners still.[21] Rather, we are called to bear witness to Christ in this sinful world, a topic we will discuss more fully in later chapters.

Third, the church today follows Christ, the faithful witness, *by mentoring his disciples* within covenant communities. This truth is summarized in the well-known words of the Great Commission: "Go therefore and make disciples of all nations . . . teaching them to observe all that [Christ has] commanded" (Matt. 28:19–20). The place of discipleship in Christ's mission is not an afterthought, a few verses added to the end of Matthew's Gospel. During Jesus's earthly ministry he intentionally schooled carefully chosen disciples and sent them out by twos into the surrounding region. This method had Old Testament symbolism, perhaps patterned after the ministry of the early prophets (2 Kings 2:3).[22] After his resurrection, Christ commissioned the New Testament church leaders to make disciples of all nations in the same way.[23] Jesus's ministry set the pattern for us; he calls us to follow in his footsteps. Discipleship is the desired consequence and next step after evangelistic witness; it is also a method for the multiplication of witnesses. Making disciples includes many activities, such as spiritual formation, Bible education, and equipping for ministry (Acts 18:24–28; Eph. 4:12; 2 Tim. 2:2), which we will consider in later

---

21 On this point I disagree with C. S. Lewis who wrote: "Every Christian is to become a little Christ. The whole purpose of becoming a Christian is simply nothing else." Lewis, *Mere Christianity* (New York: Macmillan, 1952), 177. While it is true that—in a limited sense—we are sent by Christ as he was sent by the Father (John 20:21; 17:14–19), the uniqueness of Christ's mission must not be overlooked or minimized. No mere Christian—either personally as an individual or corporately as a church—can ever become "a little Christ" in the world to any extent close to Christ's incarnation and unique ministry; rather, Christians can only bear witness in the world to Christ, proclaiming the excellencies of every aspect of his unique person and mission. For correctives, see D. A. Carson, "Christology," in *Evangelical Dictionary of World Mission* (Grand Rapids, MI: Baker, 2000), 191; Southgate Statement, "Affirmations and Denials Concerning World Mission," *Themelios* 45, no. 1 (2020): 108–35.

22 See Schnabel, *Early Christian Mission*, 270–71 and 320–22.

23 For classic texts on discipleship following Christ, see A. B. Bruce, *The Training of the Twelve* (New York: Harper, 1930) and Robert E. Coleman, *The Master Plan of Evangelism* (Old Tappen, NJ: Revell, 1978).

chapters. The early church continued this task in obedience to Christ's commission (Acts 6:7; 11:26; 14:21; 18:23, 26; 19:9; 21:16; and so on).

Fourth, the church today also follows Christ, the faithful witness, *by showing his compassion* to all people in the world. As considered above, an attitude of compassion was the signature of Christ's mission; it is the distinct characteristic by which he displayed the Father's generous mercy. We are called to follow Christ—though in a limited and imperfect way—by displaying God's compassion to the world. We must display this compassion in both word and deed ministry. Christ our teacher invites us to follow his example; he commands us to love one another. In this way, the world will know we are his disciples, and the world will believe in God's divine missionary (John 13:14–15; 17:21). Reflecting on this new commandment, John later notes the direct relationship between spiritual love for God and tangible love for our neighbors (1 John 4:20–21). Likewise Paul participates in Christ's mission to the nations "by word and deed" (Rom. 15:18), and James rebukes those who say they have faith in Christ but do not follow his example of doing good deeds (James 2:14–17).

Christ's mission, therefore, when studied in each proper perspective, will result in both biblical worship and biblical witness. We learn better to behold God's divine missionary in all his beauty. We also learn better to follow Christ, the faithful witness, as we bear witness to the world of his grace and glory.

Discussion Questions

1. Explain how Jesus Christ is God's great missionary, and support your answer with Scripture.

2. Reflect on this statement: "As the person of Christ is the chief agent in God's mission, so also the good news about Christ is the central message of Christian witness." What does this mean for all mission ministries today?

3. Describe Christ's ministry as both the messianic shepherd and the anointed evangelist.

4. Explain at least five aspects of Christ's ministry as the exalted sender.

5. How does Christ's compassion both fulfill his calling as God's apostle while also setting an example for the church's witness, and how should our ministries today both proclaim and demonstrate God's generous mercy?

3

The Mission of the Holy Spirit

THE HOLY SPIRIT is the vital force of God's mission in the New Testament. He is the divine apologist who convinces the world of sin, righteousness, and coming judgment, and the divine evangelist who bears witness to Christ in this broken world. He is the divine pastor-teacher who reminds God's people about Christ and guides them into his truth. He is the divine church planter who gathers, grows, and guards the church until Christ's final return. All these and much more are the ongoing ministries of the Holy Spirit, crucial for the success of the mission of the triune God.

The mission of the Spirit proceeds directly from Christ's mission, as considered in chapter 2. His mission is the outcome of Christ's resurrection, ascension, and session; it is the overflow of Christ's blessings in this present age. Furthermore, God's redemptive plan and universal purpose for all nations, as considered in chapter 1, are being fulfilled globally through the mission of God's Spirit. The Spirit's mission, therefore, comes third in the biblical story of God's mission.

The Spirit within God's Mission

The Spirit's vital work in mission often does not get enough attention.[1] Scripture usually does not focus directly on the third triune person

---

1   My dissertation addresses this lack of attention: Brian A. DeVries, "Witnessing with the Holy Spirit: Pneumatology and Missiology in Evangelistic Theory" (PhD diss., Southern Baptist Theological

since he, as the divine author, desires to speak of Christ rather than draw attention to himself. His role in God's mission, however, is clearly evidenced across the pages of Scripture, from his life-giving presence first at creation (Gen. 1:2) to his gospel witness with the church until the end of mission (Rev. 22:17).

The vital role of the Holy Spirit has always been confessed by the church. Though still obscure in the Old Testament, the Spirit's work was more fully revealed in the New Testament, and faithfully summarized by the early church in AD 381: We believe "in the Holy Spirt, the Lord and Giver of life, who proceeds from the Father and the Son; who with the Father and the Son together is worshiped and glorified; who spoke by the prophets."[2] We echo this confession, and others, as we outline below seven main points in a concise biblical theology of the Spirit's mission.

First, we confess that the Spirit is the "Giver of life" in both creation and redemption. From the beginning, the Spirit is revealed as God's breath of life. Physical life is given and sustained by God's Spirit (Gen. 2:7; Job 34:14–15). The Spirit is also, within God's redemptive mission, the giver of eternal life to God's people, in addition to the physical life given to all (John 6:63; 2 Cor. 3:6). The Spirit works savingly, giving spiritual life to all those who are by faith in union with Christ and raising them into eternal life (Rom. 8:11). There is one Spirit of God with two distinct life-giving works:[3] giving physical life to Adam and all his children, and regenerating spiritual life in all the children of the last Adam (1 Cor. 15:45).

Seminary, 2007), especially 18–94. See also Roland Allen, *Pentecost and the World: The Revelation of the Holy Spirit in the "Acts of the Apostles"* (London: Oxford University Press, 1917); and Harry R. Boer, *Pentecost and Mission* (Grand Rapids, MI: Eerdmans, 1961).

2   Nicene Creed (381) (*CCC* 18). See the Belgic Confession of Faith, art. 11; Heidelberg Catechism, q. 53; and Westminster Larger Confession, q. 11. The classic Reformed confessions give less direct attention to the person of the Holy Spirit, instead giving considerable attention to the ministry of the Spirit, especially in the area of individual salvation.

3   We must highlight this distinction since otherwise the specialness of redemptive grace in the new and better covenant is obscured by too much continuity, and general and special revelation may then be confused in practice.

Second, the Spirit "spoke by the prophets" in the Old Testament. This phrase of the creed summarizes the Spirit's ministry before Christ's baptism. Since the same Spirit of God was at work in both Old and New Testaments, his ministry before Pentecost was not different in nature but only in degree, including his work of regenerating (Deut. 30:6), indwelling (Ex. 29:45–46; Hag. 2:5), restraining (Isa. 63:10–11; Mic. 3:8), and empowering specific people for specific tasks (Ex. 31:2–5). His Old Testament mission also gave hope to God's people by announcing beforehand the gospel of Christ (Gal. 3:8; 1 Pet. 1:10–12).

Third, the Spirit was active at every point in Jesus's life and ministry. Scripture gives abundant evidence of this special work: conception (Matt. 1:20), baptism (John 1:32–34), ministry (Luke 4:18; Acts 10:38; cf. Isa. 11:2), miracles (Matt. 12:28), atonement (Heb. 9:14), resurrection (Rom. 1:4; 8:11), and so forth.[4] Concisely stated, the Spirit enabled and empowered Christ to accomplish his mission of redemption, and then the Spirit was sent on mission by Christ to enable and empower the church to obey the Great Commission.

Fourth, Pentecost is the defining moment of the Spirit's mission. After Christ's ascension and session, the Holy Spirit takes a more prominent role in the story of God's mission, a role we examine thoroughly in the rest of this chapter. The New Testament gives much more attention to the Spirit who bears witness to Christ in all the world, empowers the launch of the Gentile mission, and applies Christ's redemption in all God's people.

Fifth, the Spirit was sent on mission by the Father and the Son to bear witness to Christ. Scripture clearly describes the Spirit's double commission by both the Father and the Son (John 14:26; 15:26; Acts 2:33).[5] Thus the Spirit's mission completes the triune mission.

4 John Owen explains eleven works of the Spirit in relation to Christ's human nature. See his *The Holy Spirit: His Gifts and Power* (Fearn, UK: Christian Focus, 2004), 115–131. See also Sinclair B. Ferguson, *The Holy Spirit* (Downers Grove, IL: InterVarsity, 1996), 35–56.
5 Note also the order of sending: the Father sends the Son (John 20:21), and then the Father *and the Son* send the Holy Spirit. Affirming the *filioque* clause ("and from the Son") is necessary for

Furthermore, the Spirit's mission is not somehow separate from God's mission in Christ,[6] since all three triune persons work together to accomplish and apply redemption.

Sixth, the Spirit's work in the New Testament is described both personally and corporately. In many places, Paul's letters explain how the Spirit works personal redemption in the hearts and lives of God's people. Conversely, Luke's second book, sometimes called "the Acts of the Spirit," tells the history of gospel witness by the corporate church community in the power of the Holy Spirit.

Seventh, the Spirit's work continues in the world today. In some ways, this states the obvious. Yet this observation is necessary to fence the discussion that follows. All Christians confess the uniqueness of the apostolic age, the period of church history directly following Pentecost. It was a wonderful time of special revelation when the apostles led the church, as Christ's eyewitnesses, and when the Spirit inspired the authors of New Testament books. But the apostles all died before the end of the first century, and the canon of Scripture is now complete (Rev. 22:18–19), which necessarily implies that some aspects of the Spirit's ministry have ceased.[7] Yet the Spirit's witness continues, despite

---

faithful mission. Those who deny this clause (e.g., the Eastern Orthodox Church) tend to limit the church's mission—at least in practice—to merely an attractive witness like the Old Testament showcase community.

6   So we affirm the unity of God's saving work in both Christ and the Spirit, while we maintain the nature/grace distinction of the "one Spirit with two works." Some inclusivists say that God's two hands (Christ and the Spirit) work, at times, in the world and in salvation independently from each other. For refutations, see Daniel Strange, *The Possibility of Salvation among the Unevangelized: An Analysis of Inclusivism in Recent Evangelical Theology* (Waynesboro, GA: Paternoster Press, 2001), 197, 263; and Stephen J. Wellum, "An Evaluation of the Son-Spirit Relation in Clark Pinnock's Inclusivism," *Southern Baptist Journal of Theology* 10 (Spring 2006): 4–23.

7   This is not the place for a cessation versus continuation discussion. For various voices on this issue, see Richard B. Gaffin, Jr., *Perspectives on Pentecost: New Testament Teaching on the Gifts of the Holy Spirit* (Grand Rapids, MI: Baker, 1979); D. A. Carson, *Showing the Spirit: A Theological Exposition of 1 Corinthians 12–14* (Grand Rapids, MI: Baker, 1987); Vern S. Poythress, "Modern Spiritual Gifts as Analogous to Apostolic Gifts: Affirming Extraordinary Works of the Spirit within Cessationist Theology," *Journal of the Evangelical Theological Society* 39, no. 1 (March 1996), 71–101; Iain H. Murray, *Pentecost—Today?: The Biblical Basis for Understanding Revival*

the cessation of the Scriptural inspiration and the unique eyewitness of the apostles. The Spirit of Christ still indwells the church and he continues to speak through the Scriptures, in and by the church, until the return of Christ (Matt. 28:20; Eph. 1:14; Rev. 22:17).

The Spirit's Coming at Pentecost

God's mission and the church's witness cannot be understood fully without first appreciating the pivotal significance of Pentecost. The Spirit's advent at Pentecost is the turning point in the history of God's mission; it is the crowning moment of Christ's ongoing ministry and the full revelation of the Spirit's mission. Pentecost is the point in redemptive history when the church and its witness were reminded of its Old Testament roots, reconstituted by Christ's gracious power and gospel commission, and refocused with a much wider angle on God's original purpose and redemptive plan. Pentecost marks the start of a new stage in redemptive history, the final part of God's story of mission in which the various themes are drawn together for a final conclusion. This is why Scripture carefully anticipates and explains Pentecost in advance, and why it gives the phenomena and timing of Pentecost Day substantial attention.[8]

First, Pentecost was anticipated by the prophets. The Old Testament predicts a future outpouring of God's Spirit that would result in universal blessings. The classic passage is Joel's prophecy: "And it shall come to pass afterward, that I will pour out my Spirit on all flesh . . ." (Joel 2:28). The Holy Spirit, through Peter's mouth, interprets Pentecost as the time when this prophecy began to be fulfilled (Acts 2:17–21, 33; 1 Pet. 1:12). Other prophets also look forward to the Spirit's coming in the last days,

---

(Carlisle, PA: Banner of Truth, 1998), 80–133; and Wayne Grudem, *The Gift of Prophecy in the New Testament and Today* (Wheaton, IL: Crossway, 2000).

8   While the Great Commission is important for mission in this present age, Scripture emphasizes the Spirit's advent at Pentecost as a more central New Testament theme. Though it has often been overlooked, Pentecost is of vital significance, not only for our study of the Spirit's mission, but especially for properly understanding the church's witness in the world.

describing his ministry with the imagery of abundance: floods on dry ground (Isa. 44:3), showers of blessing (Ezek. 34:26), and rivers in the desert that flow and make glad (Ps. 46:4; Isa. 32:15; cf. John 7:38; Rev. 22:1). For example, Ezekiel describes an amazing river, flowing from the temple and ever increasing into a great flood that brings life to many regions, resulting in fruitfulness and healing (Ezek. 47:1–12)—an anticipation of the Spirit's blessings in the world after Christ.

Second, Pentecost was also explained in advance by Christ. Before his ascension, Jesus gave careful instruction to his disciples that they must wait for the promise of the Father (Luke 24:49; Acts 1:4). We know from the rest of Scripture that the embodiment of this promise was none other than the indwelling person of the Spirit and his gracious empowerment (Rom. 8:9–11; Eph. 1:14; 1 John 2:27). Earlier, in the upper room before his death, Jesus had explained the role of this promised person: he was another Helper, like himself, who would be sent to them after he departed, in order to dwell with and in them, to bear witness with them, and to guide them into all truth (John 14:15–17, 26; 15:26; 16:8, 13). These words, spoken only fifty-three days prior and then poignantly repeated (Acts 1:4), must have been fresh in the minds of the waiting disciples on the day of Pentecost. They were expecting him soon, which is why they interpreted Pentecost as the direct fulfillment of the Father's promise (John 16:7; Acts 1:5; 2:33; 11:15–16).

Indeed, the primary focus of Christ's parting instructions, as well as much of Luke's account in Acts, is placed on the significance of the Spirit's coming and his empowerment of the church for mission. No mention is made in the rest of Scripture about the church's duty to obey the Great Commission. Yet many churches today focus most attention on obeying the Great Commission, while often overlooking the Spirit's sovereign mission in and through the church.[9]

---

9 Methodologies and strategies for obedience can quickly eclipse the church's dependence on the Spirit of Mission. Imbalances in practice result from this mistake: overattention to human agency

Third, Scripture documents the phenomena of Pentecost Day within the New Testament church. Prior to the Spirit's advent, we already see God's grace at work in the church community: waiting for the Father's promise in obedience, devotion to prayer and the application of Scripture, and unity of all believers in fellowship (Acts 1:14; 2:1). The exact moment of the Spirit's coming is evidenced by special signs and wonders: wind and fire, spiritual filling, and special tongues. These signs and wonders, though temporary phenomena on Pentecost Day, are very significant. For example, the wind and fire are both Old Testament symbols of the Spirit (Ex. 3:2–6; Ezek. 37:1–14). The speaking in other tongues and hearing in one's own language is clearly linked to the Babel account (Gen. 11:7–9). The Spirit's filling of believers and the church is also of crucial importance, as discussed below. Taken as one event, these temporary phenomena are used by God to highlight the great significance of what happened that day.

The enduring phenomena in the book of Acts, though often given less attention, are the greatest signs and wonders resulting from that unique day of Pentecost.[10] The long-anticipated day had finally arrived. God was now starting in a big way to fulfill his promise to Abraham (Gen. 12:1–3); now the curse of Babel would begin to be reversed so that all families of the earth could become children in God's covenant family. Now that the exalted-sender was seated at God's right hand

---

in gospel witness that excludes or minimizes the sovereign Spirit; a form of legalism that makes personal evangelism a required proof of authentic spirituality; or spiritual paralysis and inactivity resulting from a sense of guilt for the "great omission" rather than thankful grace-empowered obedience in a joyful commission. See Brian A. DeVries, "The Spirit Has Come!," *The Messenger* 66, no. 6 (June 2019): 14–15.

10 Much has been written about the temporary phenomena in Acts 2, and especially on the subject of tongues. More important for the church's witness, however, are the enduring phenomena of spiritual gifts. See C. R. Vaughan, *The Gifts of the Holy Spirit* (Carlisle, PA: Banner of Truth, 1975); Carson, *Showing the Spirit*, 77–88; Poythress, "Modern Spiritual Gifts," 71–101; and Brian A. DeVries, "Spiritual Gifts for Biblical Church Development: The Holy Spirit Working through Believers to Build Up the Body of Christ," *Puritan Reformed Journal* 13, no. 2 (2021): 183–205.

with all authority, the Spirit of God was being lavishly poured out into the church (Acts 2:33). Now the Spirit of Christ had finally come in fullness! Now Christ, by his Spirit, would continue his global mission unrestrained: to bring good news to the poor, to proclaim liberty to the captive nations, to give the church the oil of gladness and the garment of praise (Isa. 61:1–3). The book of Acts starts to record the long history of the enduring phenomena of Pentecost: genuine revival with great numbers and the launch of Christ's church-planting movement, directed by the Spirit himself, even to the ends of the earth. Peter and the other apostles were only beginning to understand the enduring significance of Pentecost.

Fourth, Scripture also delineates the timing of the day of Pentecost in God's redemptive history. Clearly, something new and unique occurred that day. This event was the long-awaited fulfillment of Old Testament longings for the last days when God's Spirit would indwell God's people (Ezek. 36:26–27; Jer. 31:31–34). Now after Pentecost, the Spirit's work is greatly intensified and expanded, and the rest of the New Testament teaches more about the Spirit's gracious role in both personal salvation and gospel witness. Furthermore, Pentecost is the official launch of the Gentile mission and the beginning of the church's spontaneous obedience to the Great Commission. The newness of Pentecost is twofold: it is the midpoint in God's mission story, after Christ's mission and before the end; and it also is the point at which the Spirit's mission is launched with much greater power and scope.

Yet the Spirit's ministry, both before and after Pentecost Day, was not new or different in essence. The same Spirit of God had already been working in the world since the beginning, both in nature and grace (Neh. 9:20; Ps. 51:11; Isa. 63:11).[11] The Holy Spirit also continues,

---

11 Boer speaks of "the work of the Spirit in the Old Testament as the retroactive work of the Spirit of Pentecost . . . as an arching backward, of the historical reality that did not exist until Pentecost. In thus effecting earlier operations of the Spirit of Pentecost, God preserved both the unity of the redemptive process, and the unity of the congregation of the Old Testament with the Church of the New Testament." Boer, *Pentecost and Mission*, 83–84.

after Pentecost, to be poured out into the church in specific places for special times of revival (Acts 4:31; 10:45; 19:6).[12] So while the Pentecost event in Acts 2 uniquely marked the beginning of something new and greater, the presence of the Spirit and his reviving work within and through God's people continues from the beginning to the end of mission.

The Spirit's Ministry in the World

We can at times be tempted to think that it would be wonderful if Jesus were physically present in the church today, as he was with the disciples in the days of his earthly ministry. But this thinking is incorrect since it contradicts what Christ clearly states: "I tell you the truth: it is to your advantage that I go away, for if I do not go away, the Helper will not come to you. But if I go, I will send him to you" (John 16:7).

The church today is greatly empowered and advantaged by the living presence of the Spirit of Christ and his ongoing ministry in the world. Now the church, after Pentecost, has worldwide gospel influence, doing "greater works" in this regard than Christ's earthly ministry (John 14:12; cf. Matt. 11:11; Acts 1:5). This truth we humbly confess as we joyfully bear witness to Christ! The key to this truth, however, is certainly not our work or our faith. Instead, it is the presence and empowerment of the sovereign Spirit of Christ and his ministry in and with us.

What is the Spirit's ministry in the world today, especially as it relates to mission? A systematic approach is most helpful for answering this question (fig. 5). Hence we consider the Holy Spirit's ministry from three theological perspectives: for our salvation (soteriology), with God's people, the church (ecclesiology), and in God's history (eschatology).

---

12 "From Pentecost onward, the work of the Spirit can be viewed in two aspects, the more normal and the extraordinary . . . [that] differ not in essence or kind, but only in degree. . . ." Thus genuine revivals are an extraordinary outpouring of the Spirit resulting in many conversions and much growth in grace. Murray, *Pentecost—Today?*, 17–25.

For Our Salvation
- The Divine Apologist
- The Divine Evangelist
- The Divine Teacher

With God's People
- The Divine Helper
- The Divine Life-Giver
- The Divine Anointing
- The Divine Guide

In God's History
- The witness of God
- In this present age
- To convict the world
- As gift and giver

Figure 5. The Spirit's ministry in the world.

The Spirit's Ministry for Our Salvation

Many excellent books explain the Holy Spirit's ministry in the salvation of God's people.[13] This doctrine, usually structured by the order in which we experience salvation, can also be framed as three divine works in the Spirit's mission: apologetics, evangelism, and discipleship.

The Spirit is *the divine apologist for Christ,* calling out sincerely to all sinners. As in Genesis 3, the Spirit of Christ comes to the place where sinners are hiding, drawing them out with searching questions and probing the precise point of their sinful departure from God's truth. As Jesus promised, the Spirit came to "convict the world concerning sin and righteousness and judgment" (John 16:8). He uncovers their guilt and shame, and he exposes their rebellion and unbelief, all in order to

---

13 The Reformers and Puritans gave us many classic texts in this area, for example: Owen, *Holy Spirit*; Thomas Goodwin, *The Work of the Holy Spirit in Our Salvation* (Carlisle, PA: Banner of Truth, 1979); George Smeaton, *The Doctrine of the Holy Spirit* (Carlisle, PA: Banner of Truth, 1988); and Abraham Kuyper, *The Work of the Holy Spirit* (New York: Funk & Wagnalls, 1900).

convince sinners to admit their sinfulness. He also exposes Satan's lie that stands behind all sinful idolatries, unbiblical ideologies, and false religions, while his divine power destroys these strongholds of spiritual darkness (2 Cor. 10:4; Eph. 5:11).

The Spirit's uncovering and exposing ministry of conviction is always a compassionate work, though it is usually not received as such. As J. H. Bavinck writes, the Spirit "awakens in man that deeply hidden awareness of guilt. He convinces man of sin, even where previously no consciousness of sin was apparently present. The Holy Spirit uses the word of the preacher and touches the heart of the hearer, making it accessible to the word."[14] All people by nature resist his work and rebel against it, continuing rather to run further away from God down into the vortex of vice (Rom. 1:18–32). Sinners respond by exchanging God's truth for a lie, reshaping what once was good into objects of idolatry and further rebellion. Yet due to God's sovereign grace, some sinners are convinced of their sinfulness and drawn back by the Spirit in repentance and faith.

The Spirit's ministry of conviction works in tandem with his ministry of illumination. He calls out to all people in the world with the voice of reason and the undeniable light of God's truth (Prov. 8:1–4; John 1:9). His law is written upon everyone's heart, and he shows them enough about God to know they are without excuse (Rom. 1:19–20; 2:15). The Spirit also opens the minds of some people to begin understanding the gospel (Gal. 3:2; Heb. 2:4; 6:4), and he fully enlightens the hearts of true believers (Acts 16:14; 2 Cor. 4:6; Eph. 1:18; Heb. 10:32).

The Spirit's ministries of conviction and illumination are preparatory for his ministry of evangelism. As with conviction, this ministry of illumination begins before spiritual regeneration and continues through

14 J. H. Bavinck, *An Introduction to the Science of Missions* (Phillipsburg, NJ: Presbyterian & Reformed, 1960), 229, cf. 221–46. Bavinck sees this conviction as central and essential for all gospel apologetics with non-Christians. The Spirit's work, he writes, "unmasks to heathendom all false religions as sin against God, and it calls heathendom to a knowledge of the only true God" (222).

sanctification. However, the work of the divine apologist does not result in salvation unless it is made effectual by the work of the divine evangelist.[15]

The Spirit is *the divine evangelist for Christ*, communicating the gospel to unbelievers. He continues the work of Jesus the anointed evangelist, as considered previously. He now extends the announcement of Christ's kingdom to the ends of the earth. He bears witness to Christ (John 15:26), publicly declaring by his word the good news of salvation for all people. He works effectually with the word of Christ's gospel,[16] resulting in regeneration, the new spiritual life for sinners formerly separated from God (Eph. 2:5). He indwells believers (John 14:17; Rom. 8:11; 2 Tim. 1:14) and sovereignly works in them a living faith with all its fruits. We will give further attention to our cowitness with the Spirit's apologetic and evangelistic ministries in chapters 8 and 9.

The Spirit is also *the divine teacher for Christ*, guiding God's people to follow Jesus. As Christ discipled his followers during his earthly ministry, so now the Spirit disciples all Christians today. He administers the gracious blessings of Christ to God's people, by both the public and private means of grace. He also opens our minds to understand the Scriptures and teaches us to obey all that Christ has commanded (Matt. 28:20; Luke 24:45).

Indeed, the Holy Spirit is the only person who perfectly performs what the Great Commission prescribes—he is still working unceasingly

---

15 The "light of nature" (Canons of Dort, heads 3/4, art. 4) is enough to leave sinners without excuse (Rom. 1:20) but not enough to save sinners. John Calvin compared the Spirit's illumination in unregenerate persons apart from the evangelistic word of God to "a traveler passing through a field at night who in a momentary lightening flash sees far and wide, but the sight vanishes so swiftly that he is plunged again into the darkness of the night before he can take even a step—let alone be directed on his way by its help." Calvin, *Institutes of the Christian Religion*, ed. John T. McNeill, trans. Ford L. Battles (Philadelphia: Westminster Press, 1960), 2.2.18.

16 As J. I. Packer explains, the Spirit works both *mediately* with the word on the mind and *immediately* with the word in the heart, and thus his work is both moral by persuasion and physical by power. "Grace is *irresistible*, not because it drags sinners to Christ against their will, but because it changes men's hearts so that they 'come most freely, being made willing by his grace.'" Packer, "Puritan Evangelism," in *A Quest for Godliness* (Wheaton, IL: Crossway, 1990), 294–95. See also Canons of Dort, heads 3/4, art. 11; and Westminster Confession of Faith 10.1.

to make disciples from all nations. The missionary Spirit works savingly in God's elect: he irresistibly convinces, enlightens, regenerates, converts, and disciples them, all to the praise of God's glorious grace.

The Spirit's Ministry with God's People

The Spirit's mission together with God's people is especially important for Christian witness. Unfortunately, this subject has often been eclipsed by extensive attention to issues of church growth or government, and distracted by divisive discussions about spiritual gifts or the more sensational signs and wonders. It is of crucial importance, therefore, to consider the Spirit's ministry with the church as the divine Helper, life-giver, anointing, and guide.

The Spirit is *the divine Helper like Christ.* The Spirit is the counselor, Comforter, and keeper of God's people; he is the Spirit of truth who embraces us with gracious love, gives us assured faith, and fills us with renewed hope. As Christ is our advocate, who is now with the Father, so the Spirit is another advocate, who is with us forever (John 14:16–17; 1 John 2:1). The Spirit is the divine agent that empowers all church ministry.[17] He works together with all believers, the human agents who also bear witness to Christ (John 15:26–27). He empowers each believer with differing spiritual gifts in order to serve for the common good to build up Christ's body (1 Cor. 12:4–11). Yet as the divine Helper, the Spirit's ministry is sovereign and independent since he works whenever and wherever and however he desires (John 3:5; 1 Cor. 12:11; Heb. 2:4). Thus the church as Christ's human agents must always maintain a posture of humble dependence upon the Spirit of Christ.[18]

---

17 Jonathan Edwards wrote, "If it be that 'tis the work of the Holy Ghost thus to convince men of sin, of righteousness, and of judgment, then we learn where ministers should have their dependence in their endeavors, even upon the Holy Ghost." Edwards, "The Threefold Work of the Holy Ghost" quoted in Stephen J. Nichols, *An Absolute Sort of Certainty: The Holy Spirit and the Apologetics of Jonathan Edwards* (Phillipsburg, NJ: P&R Publishing, 2003), 155.

18 The Spirit has been called the "supernatural factor" (or even the "forgotten factor") in all church ministry and mission. While correct, this distinction can be confused by a natural/supernatural

The Spirit is *the divine life-giver in Christ.* He is the giver of life in both creation and re-creation, and his life-giving work is seen in both the regeneration of individual sinners as well as the planting and revitalization of local churches. Genuine revivals are not produced by the will of man, but by the Spirit who sovereignly chooses to work with great power, at certain times and places, in a way that purifies the church of decay, renews its love for Christ, and often yields rapid church growth. Likewise, local churches are not revitalized by the methodologies of man but, ultimately, by the Spirit who works with human agents to produce the results he desires.

The Spirit is *the divine anointing of Christ.* Jesus specifically instructed the apostolic church leaders to wait until they received power when clothed by the Holy Spirit (Luke 24:49; Acts 1:4; 8). This promised spiritual power, which at times fills and covers all believers, is the Spirit's empowering presence for gospel witness, often called his anointing or unction (Acts 10:38; 2 Cor. 1:21–22; 1 John 2:20, 27).[19] In the Old Testament we see this anointing at special times upon specific people. But after Pentecost, the Spirit has been poured out lavishly, so that even the lowliest servants bear witness to Christ with boldness and clarity (Num. 11:29; Acts 2:17–20).

The Spirit's filling of the church, as the divine anointing, animates all faithful witness. Believers who were once ashamed of the gospel, like Peter, are transformed into courageous gospel witnesses. The Spirit makes us competent ministers of the new covenant and motivates us to follow Christ in the way of suffering (2 Cor. 3:4–6; 1 Pet. 4:13–14).

---

dichotomy. It is better to conceive of the relationship of the divine Helper and the church as his co-agents of Christ. See J. I. Packer, *Evangelism & the Sovereignty of God* (Downers Grove, IL: InterVarsity, 1961), 85–86.

19 John Owen writes: "It is not the Spirit who anoints us; but he is the unction wherewith we are anointed by the Holy One [i.e., Christ]." He then describes two effects of this unction: (1) as a "teaching, with a saving, permanent knowledge of the truth thereby produced in our minds"; and (2) as the official function of all believers, "being made kings and priests (Rev 1:5)." Owen, *The Holy Spirit*, 370–71. See also Vaughan, *Gifts of the Holy Spirit*, 276–90; and Smeaton, *Doctrine of the Holy Spirit*, 122–45.

He mobilizes churches for mission and spontaneous obedience to the Great Commission. The Spirit's mission as the divine anointing has amazing spiritual effects. We see courageous witness and enormous church growth in the book of Acts. We also know times of great revival in church history, and many faithful believers have described their experience of this anointing in their preaching, evangelism, or other forms of gospel witness.[20]

The Spirit is *the divine guide for Christ*. Jesus assured the apostolic church leaders that they would be guided in Christ's word by the Spirit of truth (John 16:13). The Spirit of Christ continues to guide the church on earth, primarily by means of his word of truth, in concert with his presence among them. In addition to his personal guidance of individuals (Rom. 8:14; Gal. 5:18), the Spirit's mission as divine guide is to lead the church in gospel witness. He specifically directs mission work (Acts 8:29; 15:28; 16:6–10). He especially unites all believers around the truth of Christ, also to promote gospel witness (John 17:21; Eph. 4:3). He powerfully defends the church, encouraging it to war against spiritual disobedience and ensuring the defeat of all demonic opposition (2 Cor. 10:3–4; Gal. 5:17; 1 Pet. 2:11). The spiritual success of the church on earth is central to the Spirit's mission, and his ministry work will not fail.

The Spirit's Ministry in God's History

We must also view the Spirit's ministry from a wide-angle perspective, considering it within the whole story of the mission of the triune God.

First, the Spirit is himself the divine witness of the triune God. Not only does he bear witness to the truth, but also he is, in his own person, the witness of God in the world. Known in the Old Testament as the "Spirit of Prophecy," he is further revealed in the New Testament

---

20 For example, see D. Martyn Lloyd-Jones, "Demonstration of the Spirit and of the Power" in *Preaching and Preachers* (Grand Rapids, MI: Zondervan, 1971), 304–25; and Andrew Fuller, "The Promise of the Spirit, the Grand Encouragement in Promoting the Gospel" in *Southern Baptist Journal of Theology*, 17, no. 1 (2013): 359–63.

as the "testimony [*witness*] of God" (1 John 5:6–12) and "testimony [*witness*] of Jesus" (Rev. 19:10). Thus it is clear that the Spirit's person and presence in the world, especially after Pentecost, is essential to the big-picture story of God's mission.

Second, the present stage in God's story is the age of the Spirit's global witness, in and with the church, during this time between Pentecost and Christ's return.[21] Peter, by the Spirit, interprets Pentecost as the beginning of the "last days" that were anticipated by the prophets (Joel 2:28; Acts 2:17; cf. Isa. 32:15; 44:3; Zech. 12:10). Pentecost was the turning point of God's mission, as mentioned above, beginning the long-awaited "last days" that continue now until the end, when the gospel of Christ will have been proclaimed to all nations (Matt. 24:14; 28:20).

We must not think of the present age, however, as something separate or disconnected from the previous age, as if the old was removed and exchanged with something different.[22] Rather, this age of the Spirit's global witness is a continuation and fulfillment of God's mission from the beginning. We can picture it as a sparkling waterfall that cascades down with increasing beauty, or as an ever-increasing spring of water that flows into a stream and overflows into a mighty river (Ezek. 47:1–12).

Third, the Spirit bears witness in the world for divine judgment. He comes to "convict the world concerning sin and righteousness and judgment" (John 16:8). This conviction is part of the Spirit's apologetic work, as noted above. It is also necessary for God's sincere gospel offer and the righteous judgment of all people who have rebelled against him: "So that every mouth may be stopped" (Rom. 3:19) and every knee bow before Christ (Isa. 45:22–23; Phil. 2:10–11).

---

21 "At Pentecost the new aeon became a reality in the life of the Church. It was then that the *still here* of the old age became conjoined with the *already here* of the new age to bring into being the New Testament *now*, the 'time between the times.'" Boer, *Pentecost and Missions*, 149.

22 This disjointed eschatology is found in several classic books about the Spirit's ministry; for example, see Adoniram J. Gordon, *The Holy Spirit in Missions* (New York: Revell, 1893), 12–13. John B. Lawrence corrects this thinking but is still influenced by it in *The Holy Spirit in Missions* (Atlanta: Home Mission Board, SBC, 1947), 3–4.

The Spirit's cosmic conviction has various purposes in God's mission.[23] He thereby restrains the wicked, displaying God's forbearance and unwillingness that any should perish (Ezek. 33:11; 2 Pet. 3:9). He vindicates God's righteousness, proving that willful disobedience is without excuse (Rom. 1:20). His "ministry of condemnation" makes way for his more glorious new covenant "ministry of righteousness" (2 Cor. 3:9). He also furthers God's plan, as suggested in the Old Testament by the zeal of the Lord for his people and the consuming fire of God's jealousy for his glory (Isa. 26:11; 2 Thess. 1:5–8). Though everyone might attempt to reject God's truth, the Holy Spirit convicts all people in the world of their sinfulness according to God's law, God's righteous justice, and the certainty of future judgment.

Fourth, the Spirit is God's gift and the channel of all spiritual gifts. After Christ's exaltation, God gave the Spirit to the church, as he had promised; and all believers receive this gift of the Spirit by faith in Christ (Acts 2:33, 38). This gift of the Spirit, then, in turn is the divine channel of spiritual gifts and blessings for each member of Christ's spiritual body (1 Cor. 12:4–11; Eph. 4:7–12). But these gifts and blessings must not be selfishly hoarded or idolized. Rather, just as Abraham's family was chosen to be a blessing to all families, so the church today is blessed by the Spirit and empowered to proclaim these blessings in Christ to all nations.

The reverse of Babel's curse at Pentecost was only the beginning of the Spirit's more glorious new covenant ministry in the church (2 Cor. 3:7–9), as evidenced by great gospel advances in the book of Acts and

---

23 Though the Spirit is at work in the unregenerate world, he does not work savingly apart from Christ. See Vaughan, *Gifts of the Holy Spirit*, 17–40; and Michael S. Horton, *Rediscovering the Holy Spirit* (Grand Rapids, MI: Zondervan, 2017), 105–21. J. H. Bavinck wrestles with this truth in relation to mission but should have been more guarded. Yet it remains an important insight, as well as an ancillary aid for apologetics, that the Spirit is often already at work within unbelievers long before any human encounter for gospel witness. See Bavinck, *The Church between the Temple and Mosque: A Study of the Relationship between the Christian Faith and Other Religions* (Grand Rapids, MI: Eerdmans, 1966), 125.

the spiritual success of Christian witness in the centuries that followed. Together with the Spirit and his gifting, Christian witnesses are now made competent ministers of the new covenant, empowered to do greater things for Christ (John 14:12). Therefore, "we do not lose heart," despite fears within and foes without, since we have been given the "Spirit as a guarantee" of future spiritual success (2 Cor. 4:1, 18; 5:5; cf. Rom. 8:23; 15:13).

The Spirit of the Church's Witness

Having studied the mission of the triune God (fig. 6), we turn to the church's witness in the next chapter. In preparation for that study, however, we conclude this chapter on the Spirit's mission by reflecting upon the vital force of God's divine witness, who animates, directs, and unites the New Testament church for witness.

Figure 6. The mission of the triune God.

First, we are coworkers with the Spirit of God (2 Cor. 6:1). This truth undergirds the entire witness of the church. It is essential to everything that follows in our study of Christian witness. The Spirit is the apologist, evangelist, and teacher who prepares us for this work. The Spirit is the Helper, life-giver, anointing, and guide who goes before us, works with us, and perfects what was attempted by our feeble efforts. In every way, we are cowitnesses when we cooperate, by grace and in faith, with Christ's Spirit.

Though an unequal relationship, this divine-human cooperation is God's preferred method for effectual gospel communication. Since the Spirit is sovereign, we remain dependent upon him, both for personal grace as well as for the results of our cowitnessing. Yet his saving work is always effectual, so we should always be expectant as we partner with him to bear witness to his truth. The Spirit works in ways far beyond our knowledge and ability. Though we can only bring the word of Christ to the ears and minds of fellow sinners, the Spirit can use our words to pierce the heart of the hardest sinner. We simply echo his word as we cooperate with him, going into all the world to bear witness to Christ: both "the Spirit and the Bride say, 'Come'" (Rev. 22:17).

Second, genuine spirituality in Christ is prerequisite for the church's witness. The church has often given too much attention to methods and strategy, without first grounding its witness within personal and corporate spirituality. Yet Jesus clearly indicates a priority: wait until you receive power (Luke 24:49; Acts 1:4). Natural abilities, academic knowledge, methodologies and strategies informed by the social sciences, and communication skills—all these can be helpful. But genuine spirituality is absolutely essential. This is true for all genuine revival; it is also true for all experiential witness. How can we be a powerful witness for Christ if we are living in ways that grieve his Spirit? Why should we expect to be filled with the Spirit if we are not keeping in step with the Spirit? A faithful Christian witness is a person who knows Christ experientially and who is nourished daily in spiritual relationship with him. Thousands of faithful witnesses since Pentecost have discovered this secret of spiritual success.[24]

---

24 Hudson Taylor knew this secret: "To him, the secret of overcoming lay in daily, hourly fellowship with God; and this, he found, could only be maintained by secret prayer and feeding upon the Word through which He reveals Himself to the waiting soul. . . . The hardest part of a missionary

The Holy Spirit prepares each believer and the whole church for witness, making us ready to be empowered and guided as his tool, used in ways we often cannot fully comprehend. He graces us with the required attitude: the love of Christ (2 Cor. 5:14). He shapes our character and behavior (Gal. 5:16–25). He gifts us with spiritual abilities, making us competent for his ministry (2 Cor. 3:4–12). In short, he makes us holy, to live in the world but not be of the world (John 17:14–19). As with the Old Testament showcase community, the holiness of the church is of central importance for its effective witness in the world. The church must be consecrated for holy worship; it must live separate from the world in order to be a powerful witness to the world. The Spirit's primary work in the church is sanctification in order to prepare the bride of Christ to invite sinners more effectively to come out of the world.

Third, the church's witness must remain dependent on the Spirit and controlled by his word. Those most influenced by Western philosophy often struggle with tensions between divine sovereignty and human responsibility, such as the place of human strategy and technique, or the relation of prayer to planning. The solution for many of these problems is a biblical understanding of the Spirit's mission, which delivers us from much evil in this area.[25] The foundation and framework of Scripture give us the starting point for mission methodology, evangelistic communication theory, apologetic strategy, and related techniques for Christian witness.

We must also carefully examine our methods and strategies to ensure they do not in any way contradict the Sprit's way of working or create

---

career, Mr. Taylor found, is to maintain regular, prayerful Bible study. 'Satan will always find you something to do,' he would say, 'when you ought to be occupied about that. . . .'" Howard Taylor, *Hudson Taylor's Spiritual Secret* (Chicago: Moody Press, 2009), 239.

25 "Honor the Spirit by confessing that in evangelism everything depends on him, and by committing ourselves to labor in evangelism as if everything depends on us. Honor the Spirit by giving ourselves afresh to Jesus Christ, whom the Spirit honors, to be his means of evangelism wherever he leads." J. I. Packer, "The Power and Work of the Holy Spirit I," in *Proclaim Christ Until He Comes* (Minneapolis: World Wide Publications, 1990), 104.

distractions to the gospel message of Christ. Attempting to witness using methods inconsistent with the Spirit's ministry will lead inevitably to questionable practices, often out of step with the Spirit. Many modern evangelistic methods and strategies are unhelpful distractions and can even be obstacles to the Spirit's evangelistic ministry. Since we confess the Spirit's sovereignty, we must be careful not to contradict our confession with inconsistent methods and techniques.[26]

Finally, the church's witness is authenticated and strengthened by its spiritual unity. The Spirit's ministry produces and protects this unity. He unites the church, not around organizational polity or human traditions, but by reshaping each believer into the image of Christ and by drawing each spiritual church member closer to Christ and his truth. He also guards and defends the purity of the church. Hence much of the New Testament is devoted to exposing and refuting false teaching, since the Spirit must work apologetically to fiercely protect Christ's bride from capitulation to Satan's lie. Spiritual unity, therefore, is an authentic proof of the Spirit's presence in the church—the true church on earth is the people who worship Christ in spirit and truth (John 4:23–24).

Gospel witness is a central purpose of this spiritual unity: "That the world may believe" in Christ (John 17:21). Thus the church must keep in step with the Spirit, "eager to maintain the unity of the Spirit" (Eph. 4:3), which binds us together in Christ (Gal. 5:25; Col. 2:19; 3:14). The church must also, as part of this unity, keep in step with the Spirit by promoting holiness and by disassociating from all those who deny Christ

---

26 Examples of such distractions include a reliance on signs and wonders or on sensational power encounters. The Spirit is not a golden key we use to unlock spiritual blessings; nor is he a powerful spiritual technique we follow to guarantee successful results. Jonathan Edwards speaks of spiritual dependence upon the sovereign Spirit: "I think I have found that no discourses have been more remarkably blessed, than those in which the doctrines of God's absolute sovereignty, with regard to the salvation of sinners, and his just liberty, with regard to answering prayer, and succeeding the plans, of natural men, continuing such, have been insisted on." Edwards, *The Works of Jonathan Edwards* (New Haven, CT: Yale University, 1977), 2.849–50.

and his truth (2 Cor. 6:14–7:1; Phil. 3:2–3; 1 Tim. 4:1; Heb. 10:29; 1 John 4:1–6). This spiritual unity, with Christ's sovereign blessing, often results in powerful gospel witness and genuine church growth (Acts 2:44–47; 4:32–33; 5:13–14), which is the goal of the Spirit's mission.

Discussion Questions

1. What changed in the Spirit's ministry at Pentecost? In what ways is his post-Pentecost ministry different and in what ways is it the same?

2. Describe the Spirit's ministry in your own salvation as the divine apologist, evangelist, and teacher, and with your church as the divine Helper, life-giver, anointing, and guide.

3. How should our prayers, strategies, and methods for witness all be shaped by a biblical understanding of God's sovereignty and human responsibility?

4. Review the methods used by your church in its various areas of Christian witness. Do these methods cooperate with the sovereign Spirit? Do they flow from humble trust in him, or do they tend to be influenced more by other factors?

5. Why is our relationship with the Spirit of Christ of vital importance to the success of our witness? Reflect on the tension of waiting for the Spirit's empowerment while also being faithful in using the means he has provided.

4

Witness in the New Testament

PENTECOST IS THE MIDPOINT in the history of God's mission. It is the watershed, a decisive dividing line in Scripture. Pentecost marks the end point of Old Testament mission and the starting point of New Testament mission. It also begins the penultimate scene, since the only major event to follow in God's story of mission is the final coming of Christ at the end of this age. As we considered in the last chapter, the outpouring of the Holy Spirit at Pentecost is of central significance for and the launching pad of the church's witness in the New Testament.

A new age began at Pentecost. This new age, anticipated long before by the prophets (Gen. 12:3; Joel 2:28–29), is when the nations would glorify God for his mercy (Rom. 15:9–12). Now the church will arise and shine among the nations (Isa. 60:1–3). The Spirit of Christ now empowers God's people to be witnesses of Christ to the whole world. Now begins the final stage in God's story of mission.

Jesus's parting words in Acts 1:1–11 introduce this new age. We already considered this passage in the introduction, especially verse 8: "But you will receive power when the Holy Spirit has come upon you, and you will be my witnesses in Jerusalem and in all Judea and Samaria, and to the end of the earth" (cf. Luke 24:48). These words are Christ's commission to the New Testament church, a prescription which they must fulfill until he comes again at the end of this age (Matt. 24:14).

The groundwork for New Testament mission was laid in the Old Testament (see chap. 1). Then Christ's earthly mission commissioned the church's witness in the present age (see chap. 2), and the Holy Spirit's mission empowered the church for this purpose (see chap. 3). So now, in this chapter, we consider the witness of the New Testament church, first by looking in more detail at the biblical concept of *witness* and then by unpacking five key aspects of witness clustered around this concept.

You Will Be My Witnesses

What is a witness? A witness is a person who gives evidence, often within a judicial context. The word is also used to describe someone who speaks with personal knowledge of an event or truth. This word is central in Christ's commission to the New Testament church, so it is essential in our understanding of New Testament mission.

As noted in the introduction, *witness* is a key biblical concept, especially in the book of Acts and the books of the apostle John (John 15:26–27; 16:16; Rev. 1:5).[1] Yet it is much more than merely an important theological concept; it is the personal identity of every true believer in Christ, and it is the faithful impassioned public expression of this identity.

A practical example will help us understand this concept of witness. Suppose you were awakened from sleep shortly after midnight by a loud bang coming from your neighbor's house. You jump out of bed, go to the window, push the curtains aside, and peer out into the darkness. You hear shouting voices, perhaps your neighbor's and others'. You watch as two men run out of the house and jump into a car. The engine revs, the wheels squeal, the car bolts off in a hurry, and you see your neighbor run out of the house shouting while his teenage boy follows

---

1 See James M. Boice, *Witness and Revelation in the Gospel of John* (Grand Rapids, MI: Zondervan, 1970); and Allison A. Trites, *The New Testament Concept of Witness* (Cambridge: Cambridge University Press, 1977).

him into the yard. A few minutes later the police arrive on the scene and the neighbor's whole family comes out to meet them.

In this example, you are a witness. You have personal knowledge of what happened next door shortly after midnight. You are able to give evidence of the events, to report the facts in order. You can speak with the police, making a clear public statement about the truth of what you saw and heard that night. You may also be willing to testify in court about this truth, describing the situation and perhaps even details about the two men and the escape car. You are an eyewitness of the crime scene and, if needed, you could be a key witness in court. Even if you were to close the curtains quietly after viewing the commotion next door and go back to bed without saying anything in the morning to your neighbor—even then, you are still a witness.

Who is a witness of Christ? Every true believer. All Christians have experienced forgiveness of sin and new life in Christ. We all give evidence of this salvation by displaying the fruits of Christ's Spirit, by publicly confessing this salvation in our communities, and by testifying publicly that Jesus Christ is the Son of God and that the Bible is God's authoritative word. As the apostle John writes many years after Christ's resurrection, "We have seen [experienced] and testify [witness] that the Father has sent his Son to be the Savior of the world" (1 John 4:14; cf. 1:2). We all as true believers, like Jesus, "speak of what we know, and bear witness to what we have seen" even though people "do not receive our testimony" (John 3:11). Bearing witness to Christ, therefore, begins with an experiential knowledge of Christ and his salvation. How can we tell others about Christ if we do not know him personally ourselves?

Bearing witness to Christ is the central activity of the church's mission. As a noun, the word *witness* denotes the identity of God's people who by their character and conduct give public evidence to the truth about Christ; they themselves are living proof of what they personally know and have experienced. The apostle Peter is consciously aware of his appointment as Christ's witness. In his preaching he repeatedly draws attention to this identity and commission: "We all are witnesses" (Acts 2:32, 40; 3:15; 4:33; 5:32; 8:25; 10:39, 40, 42). Likewise, the apostle Paul understood his calling as a witness of Christ (Acts 13:31; 22:15; 26:16).

As a verb, *witness* denotes the activity of God's people who are commissioned to communicate the truth about Christ (John 15:26–27). Witnessing, as an activity, encapsulates all forms of New Testament gospel ministry, including speaking the gospel of Christ (John 1:34; Acts 23:11), testifying to the truth of Christ despite opposition (Acts 28:23; Rev. 11:3), and suffering persecution or even death for Christ's sake (Rev. 2:13; 17:6).

For the purpose of our study in this chapter, we summarize the concept of witness under five dominant New Testament themes: gospel living, gospel speaking, gospel defense, gospel increase, and gospel suffering (table 2). These themes help us organize our study of witness as a biblical concept, with each theme highlighting a significant aspect of mission in the New Testament.

Table 2. Bearing witness to Christ

Gospel Living	To display the truth as disciples of Christ	Acts 4:32–33 1 Peter 2:12
Gospel Speaking	To declare the truth as ambassadors of Christ	Acts 26:16 2 Cor. 5:18–6:1
Gospel Defense	To defend the truth as apologists for Christ	Acts 17:2–3, 17 1 Peter 3:15
Gospel Increase	To disperse the truth as coworkers for Christ	Acts 8:4–5 2 Cor. 3:5–9
Gospel Suffering	To die for the truth as martyrs with Christ	Acts 5:41 Rev. 2:13

Witness as Gospel Living

God's people in the New Testament church were, first and foremost, called to be followers of Christ. Their task was to display the truth of Christ. The personal character and gospel living of these believers powerfully witnessed the undeniable reality about salvation in Christ. Saved sinners were being united in gospel community and, like the blind man healed by Peter and John in Acts 3, this spiritual miracle could not be hidden or refuted. We will further consider many of these themes in later chapters, but for now we note briefly four elements of witness as gospel living that are seen in the New Testament church.

Gospel living occurs *within social communities.* All who love God's church are inspired by the beautiful witness of united fellowship following Pentecost (Acts 2:42–47; 4:32–35; 5:12–13; 11:15–18; 13:1–2; 15:30–35; 20:18–38). Indeed, as Jesus had prayed, the world believes the gospel when the church lives in unity (John 17:21). Likewise, the unity of Christ's new humanity is a powerful witness, as former socio-religious barriers between outsiders and insiders are broken down by the gospel (Eph. 2:11–22). The very presence of this new community was a powerful testimony in society to the truth of the gospel, and it was also the base from which ministries of mercy and hospitality could be performed most effectively.

Gospel living forms a *new social identity.* It was the multiethnic church plant at Antioch where "the disciples were first called Christians" (Acts 11:26). This observation by Luke is not an afterthought or insignificant detail. It highlights something new, something exciting that had taken place. In the church, the barrier between Jew and Gentile had been broken down, which created a new social category as other social barriers were also removed.

What should the world call this new social configuration? They were not only Jews, for now Gentiles were members, even within the leadership (Acts 13:1–2). They were not an ethnic gathering, nor a political or ideological group. It was something unique, so it needed a new name in society. At first it may have been intended as a negative term: those Christ-followers, those Christians. But this new identity was fitting since it describes the essence of who we are: disciples of

Christ. As Peter later wrote, echoing God's own description in Exodus 19:4–6, the church is "a chosen race, a royal priesthood, a holy nation" so that it "may proclaim" God's wonderful deeds in the world (1 Pet. 2:9–10). Further attention will be given to these truths in chapter 7.

Gospel living expands the *ministry of making disciples*. Judaism in Jesus's day was known for its zeal to make proselytes from all nations, and it was successful in gathering converts from many places.[2] Though often with the wrong motives (Matt. 23:15), this missionary zeal was rooted in the Old Testament and it is possible that Jesus deliberately continued this pattern with corrected motives (Matt. 10:5). Now after Pentecost, the church's ministry of making disciples is renewed. Christ's followers are given the expanded instruction to make disciples from all nations, not only from among Jewish communities. Thus disciple-making continued as a central activity in the church's ministry.

Gospel living continues the *church's public testimony*. Jesus had instructed his followers to "let your light shine," which Peter repeats as a command for public witness: "Keep your conduct among the [nations] honorable" (Matt. 5:16; 1 Pet. 2:12). Similarly, God's Old Testament people were called to be a "light for the nations," a truth which featured prominently in Paul's thinking as he began his missionary ministry to all nations (Isa. 42:6; 49:6; 51:4; Acts 13:47; 26:23). The visible display of spiritual peace and joy within a loving church community is living proof in society of God's kingdom that has already come in part (Rom. 14:17). Indeed, the shining presence of a holy church with honorable conduct is a powerful witness in the New Testament of the gospel message (Eph. 5:8–15; Phil. 2:15).

Witness as Gospel Speaking

God's people in the New Testament church were called to be ambassadors of Christ. Their task was to declare the truth of their Lord and

2   The international crowd in Acts 2 was likely composed of many Jews from the dispersion as well as many proselytes. See Richard R. DeRidder, *Discipling the Nations* (Grand Rapids, MI: Baker, 1971), 93–94.

Savior. Here we distinguish the *identity* of a witness (noun) from the *activity* of a witness (verb). While in practice both identity and activity are united holistically in one person, it is helpful to distinguish between them for the sake of clarity. Gospel speaking, as such, includes the following five common activities of witnessing.

The first activity is "gossiping" the gospel, which is done by all Christians. We will consider below the more formal and official activities of gospel speaking in the New Testament church. We must not overlook, however, the significance of informal conversations between ordinary people.[3] For example, believers from the Jewish diaspora (Phoenicia and Cyprus) evangelized other people in Antioch, both Jews and Hellenists, after being scattered due to persecution in Jerusalem (Acts 11:19). Evangelism, from the Greek *euaggelizo*, is sharing the good news about Christ, which has both formal and informal elements.[4] Yet while the activity of evangelism is very common in the New Testament, the formal function of an evangelist is seldom mentioned.[5] Witness by informal gospel conversations has always had a chief role in spreading the gospel since Pentecost.

Another activity is the preaching of the gospel by church leaders. Preaching, from the Greek *kerysso* and a cluster of related words, is the official proclamation and application of God's word. The authoritative witness of God's word together with the internal witness of the Holy Spirit are the means by which God has chosen to save sinners: "How

---

3   Michael Green quotes missionary historian Adolf von Harnack: "The great mission of Christianity was in reality accomplished by means of informal missionaries." Harnack, *The Mission and Expansion of Christianity in the First Three Centuries*, 368, quoted in Green, *Evangelism in the Early Church* (Grand Rapids, MI: Eerdmans, 1970), 172–78.

4   J. I. Packer defines evangelism as presenting "Christ Jesus in the power of the Holy Spirit, that men may come to put their trust in God through Him, to accept Him as their Saviour, and serve Him as their King in the fellowship of the church." Packer, *Evangelism and the Sovereignty of God* (Downers Grove, IL: InterVarsity, 1961), 37–38, 41.

5   The title *evangelist* is used only three times in Scripture (Acts 21:8; Eph. 4:11; 2 Tim. 4:5). Perhaps coined by Christians, it is a term used for all those who were active in gospel proclamation. See Eckhard J. Schnabel, *Early Christian Mission*, 2 vols. (Downers Grove, IL: InterVarsity, 2004), 657, 1462–65.

beautiful are the feet of those who preach the good news!" (Rom. 10:14–18; cf. Isa. 52:7; Nah. 1:15).

Third is the activity of bearing witness about the kingdom of God (Acts 8:12; 19:8; 28:23, 31). Jesus had begun to establish his kingdom on earth, and he promised to come again for its completion (1 Cor. 15:24–28). Thus now in this interim period, the New Testament church continues to announce the coming of Christ's kingdom. Proclaiming the good news of this kingdom includes many facets: the confident declaration that Jesus is Lord, reigning over the universe with sovereign power (Acts 2:32–36; cf. Matt. 28:18); the tangible proof of his reign on earth that is visibly displayed by the church, the spiritual community in which he is worshiped as King (Rom. 14:17; 2 Thess. 1:5); the hopeful anticipation of the future inheritance that God's people will receive when Christ returns in glory (1 Cor. 6:9–10; Heb. 12:28; James 2:5); and the public announcement that Christ, the King of all creation, will soon return to judge all nations with righteousness and rule a restored creation in equity (Acts 17:31). As a continuation of Old Testament expectant worship, the New Testament church witnesses to all peoples about the coming kingdom of God.

The teaching of Christ's gospel in the church is a fourth activity of gospel speaking. Teaching ministries in the New Testament are a continuation of the Old Testament ministry within covenant communities. The task of Old Testament priests and prophets was often to teach the Torah and to call God's people back to covenant living. Likewise, a primary function of New Testament church leadership involves the same: Barnabas and Paul instituted a discipleship program in the Antioch church plant, and Apollos was educated by Priscilla and Aquila (Acts 11:25–26; 18:24–28). Pastor-teachers are called to educate the church and lead discipleship programs, thus equipping the saints for the work of the ministry (Eph. 4:11–12).

Finally, there is the activity of Christ's ambassadors who go out to the nations. Paul describes this gospel witness in 2 Corinthians 5:20:

"Therefore, we are ambassadors for Christ, God making his appeal through us. We implore you on behalf of Christ, be reconciled to God." This ministry of reconciliation is also, in some ways, a continuation of the role of Old Testament prophets who spoke on God's behalf to rebuke national and international sin. Now in the New Testament, Christ's ambassadors are empowered as cowitnesses with the Spirit to plead with sinners to be reconciled with God.

Christ's witnesses represent God in his global lawsuit against the nations, not only announcing the good news of reconciliation in Christ but also pronouncing God's judgment on those who reject the gospel message (Rev. 11:3–7). This ministry is greatly expanded in the New Testament, also since God's righteousness has now been fully revealed in the person and earthly mission of Christ (Rom. 1:16–17). So the New Testament appeal of the gospel is intensified and expanded: we sternly warn that the rod of Christ's sovereign power will soon crush all opposition, and we lovingly urge sinners to repent and believe the good news of God's mercy in the face of his pending judgment.

There are many other modes of witness as gospel speaking. Letter writing features prominently in the New Testament mission (Col. 4:16; 2 Pet. 3:1, 16), as do the counseling ministries of exhortation and consolation (1 Thess. 2:12). Dialogue can also be used as a mode of gospel speaking, as long as it is not a truth-seeking quest but rather a truth-speaking mode of communication. In fact, there is an impressive range of communication modes for gospel witness in the New Testament.[6] We will give further attention to witness by gospel communication in chapter 8.

Witness as Gospel Defense

God's people in the New Testament church were called to be advocates for Christ. Their task was to defend the truth of Christ in response to

---

6   For these and other terms, listed according to their Greek occurrences as descriptive of the evangelistic activities of Paul, see "Appendix," in Robert L. Reymond, *Paul: Missionary Theologian: A Survey of his Missionary Labours and Theology* (Fearn, UK: Christian Focus, 2000), 589–95.

opposition. In the same way, our task as witnesses of Christ is to testify about him and to defend this truth publicly.

Today, we often define a witness simply as someone who has had a personal experience of the truth. This is a valid use of the word, but biblical words for witness, in both Hebrew and Greek, include strong legal connotations: a witness is a person who testifies in a judicial case or who is willing to make a public defense of the truth. Bearing false witness is a crime punishable by death; it is equivalent to presenting untrue evidence in a courtroom when testifying under oath (Deut. 19:15–21; 1 Cor. 15:15). This judicial sense of the word is helpful for understanding witness as gospel defense.

Gospel defense by God's witnesses takes place within God's global court-room. As we considered in chapter 1, the Old Testament reveals God's cosmic controversy with all rebellious nations (Ps. 2:4–6; Isa. 43:8–12; Jer. 25:31). The nations—and even God's own people at times—have rejected God's truth; they have believed Satan's lie and created false gods. So God's prophets are his advocates who publicly proclaim his truth, and God's people are his witnesses who testify that only the true God is faithful to his promises. In this context God publicly declares his sovereign incomparability, and he demands an answer from all the world's inhabitants (Isa. 45:20–23). This judicial backdrop in the Old Testament foreshadows the final judgment when all people will be required to give an answer to God.

The New Testament story continues against the backdrop of this global courtroom.[7] Like the Old Testament prophets, Christ's New Testament witnesses are God's advocates among the nations. Sinful people in the world, however, try to reverse the roles: they try to put God in the dock, acting as if they are the judge and God with his truth is on trial. The world demands an answer, putting the church on trial and forcing Christians to publicly testify to the truth of Christ (Acts 4:5–7; 5:17–33; 9:15). But the message of the gospel is that Christ, the

---

7   The forensic concept of witness is especially clear in John's Gospel. See Andrew T. Lincoln, *Truth on Trial: The Lawsuit Motif in the Fourth Gospel* (Peabody, MA: Hendrickson, 2000), 454–84.

exclusive Savior, will soon return as the sovereign Judge of all people from every nation (Acts 4:12; 10:42; 17:31).

Christ's witnesses serve on God's behalf for the defense of God's truth against Satan's lie. Thus the New Testament church is called to be advocates for Christ, to publicly defend God's truth in the world. Furthermore, they themselves—in their very identity and conduct—are the evidence of the truth of God's redemption. Like Christ, they are called to make a good confession of God's truth even when on trial, assaulted by false witnesses, and in suffering (Matt. 26:59–68; John 18:37–38; 1 Tim. 6:12–13). This gospel witness is often called *apologetics*, from the Greek word *apologia*, meaning to speak in defense.

Gospel defense in the New Testament, within this legal context, includes many interconnected activities. Christ's witnesses speak in defense (*apologia*) of the gospel (Acts 22:1; 2 Cor. 12:19; Phil. 1:7, 16). They reason (*dialegomai*) with unbelievers (Acts 17:2, 17; 18:4, 19). They correct false teaching and persuade (*peitho*) objectors (Acts 19:8–9; 28:23–24). They expose and rebuke (*elenkho*) false teachers (Eph. 5:11; 1 Tim. 5:20; Titus 2:15). They contend for the faith (Jude 1:3) even in order to tear down gospel opposition (2 Cor. 10:4–6), all the while acting with wisdom and grace (Col. 4:5–6; 1 Pet. 3:13–17). We will give more attention to many of these activities in later chapters.

A final aspect of gospel defense remains to be considered briefly: the *manner* of gospel defense. Though Christ's witnesses are empowered by his Spirit and speak with his authority, they at all times are called to display Christ's character of compassion and meekness. They act with gentle boldness, not with flattery or greed, "being affectionately desirous" to share the gospel (1 Thess. 2:1–12).[8] They act with wisdom in the midst of opposition (Matt. 10:16; Col. 4:5) while living winsomely (1 Cor. 9:19–23). They do not promote themselves but rather, for the

---

8   In 1 Thessalonians 2:1–12, the apostle Paul gives us an excellent example of the manner in which we must witness. He lists more than ten ways in which he engaged in gospel defense, even calling upon God to witness that he acted in the proper manner and with pure motives.

sake of the gospel, they boast in their weaknesses and glory in the cross of Christ (2 Cor. 10–13). They do not rejoice in the power of their own witness (Luke 10:20) but rather, with humility and gentleness as witnesses of Christ, learn to follow him in suffering.

Witness as Gospel Increase

God's people in the New Testament church were called to be coworkers for Christ. Their task was to disperse the truth of Christ. The book of Acts tells the story of how Christ's witnesses were empowered by his Spirit to begin establishing his church across the world. As a result of their witness, the Lord graciously added to their number, often daily, and thus the church grew and increased greatly.

Gospel increase is a term that best describes the visible outcome of New Testament mission.[9] The church's increase is a central theme in the book of Acts (Acts 2:41, 47; 5:14; 6:1, 7; 9:31; 11:24; 12:24; 13:49; 19:20), clustered around three Greek words: to add (*prostithemi*), to grow (*auxano*), and to multiply (*plethuno*). It is conceptually related to the church's upbuilding (*oikodomeo*), which is a central theme in Paul's letters (Rom. 14:19; 1 Cor. 14:26; 2 Cor. 10:8; Eph. 4:12; 1 Thess. 5:11). Under this heading of gospel increase, therefore, we consider the propagation and planting of New Testament churches by coworkers of Christ and fellow workers in gospel ministry.

We all are inspired by the story of the New Testament church's spontaneous propagation, from Jerusalem, then in Judea and Samaria, to Antioch and Asia Minor, and then onward to the ends of the earth.[10]

---

9 We could use the term *gospel growth*, but the biblical idea of growth, from the Greek *auxano* (to grow), has been overused and even abused in the past century within the Church Growth Movement and other movements that followed. Alternatively, we could use the term *gospel multiplication*, which also is a Bible term, from the Greek words *prostithemi* (to add) and *plethuno* (to multiply), but this English word carries the connotation of success measured in numbers or other tangible results, which also can confuse the concept of New Testament witness.

10 Propagation is the act of spreading or multiplying into new regions. Roland Allen used the word *spontaneous* in 1927 to describe church growth. See *The Spontaneous Expansion of the Church: And the Causes That Hinder It* (Grand Rapids, MI: Eerdmans, 1962).

Yet it was suffering and persecution that God graciously used for the growth of his church. Like a wise sower scattering seed, God sent out his witnesses to disperse the truth of Christ into communities far and near. So the gospel message was lavishly scattered like precious seed, dispersed among the nations to take root in new regions. As a result, the church was established across the entire Roman Empire in a relatively short period of time, even in the face of growing opposition on many fronts.

How did the New Testament church grow? In addition to spontaneous propagation, church planting was an intentional method of witness. This is the process of establishing a spiritually mature church in a new area. While *church planting* has become the accepted term, there are other terms that also describe this method of New Testament witness.[11] Paul's mission included many activities related to establishing local churches: *church formation*, the gospel ministry of starting a new church (Acts 14:23; 1 Cor. 3:6–8); *church upbuilding*, the gospel ministry of building up an established church (1 Cor. 3:10–15; Col. 2:7); and *church revitalization*, the gospel ministry of leading an unhealthy church back toward a state of spiritual maturity (2 Cor. 10–13).

The growth of the New Testament church, however, must not be credited to human methodology. Ultimately, gospel increase is spiritual, the result of God's blessing (1 Cor. 3:7). It is true that human witnesses disperse gospel truth and edify the church, but it is Christ who builds his church by his word and Spirit (Matt. 16:18; Acts 2:47). This fact explains the agency of New Testament mission: gospel increase is produced by Christ's ongoing work in the world through his Spirit and human witnesses.

Christian witnesses are coworkers with the Holy Spirit, as considered in chapter 3. The book of Acts is a story about the witness of the apostles and those who followed them. The book's focus, however, often gives more attention to the acts of Christ's Spirit who empowered

---

11 Planting (*phuteuo*), an agricultural term, is used in only one passage (1 Cor. 3:6–8), while church upbuilding (*oikodomeo*, often translated *edification*), an architectural term, is used more commonly in Scripture (Acts 9:31; 1 Cor. 14:4; 1 Pet. 2:5).

these apostles, rather than their own acts. In fact, its main theme is the ongoing work of the risen Christ, acting jointly through his Spirit and his witnesses.[12] Christ's witnesses, working together with the Holy Spirit (2 Cor. 6:1), are his agents for church growth. They are the means Christ uses to produce the results he has already planned.[13]

Furthermore, as Christ's witnesses, we are fellow workers with other believers. For example, consider Paul's gospel cooperation with a great number and diversity of coworkers (Rom. 16; 2 Cor. 8:23; Phil. 4:3). This cooperation is also seen in cross-cultural partnerships for gospel ministry (Acts 14:26–28; Phil. 1:5). The Spirit of Christ gathered together a diverse group of gospel workers, he empowered them to serve together in gospel ministry, and he then sovereignly blessed this ministry by producing mature churches, Christ's new multiethnic humanity (Eph. 2:15).

Gospel increase in the New Testament, therefore, is sovereignly produced by Christ, by means of his witnesses who are coworkers with his Spirit. As a result, new church communities are formed, built up, and continue to multiply in many areas. In fact, even the social phenomena of gospel increase in each society is itself a testimony to the gospel's transforming power (Acts 4:21). Consider the powerful witness of a mature multiethnic church in a society divided by discrimination and injustice! Or consider the undeniable witness of a loving church community in a place of strife and open conflict!

Witness as Gospel Suffering

God's people in the New Testament church were called to be martyrs with Christ. At the time, they were called even to die for the truth of

---

12   J. H. Bavinck writes, "The work of missions in the book of Acts is portrayed as the work of the glorified Christ. . . . it should be called the Acts of Christ through his Apostles. . . ." Bavinck, *An Introduction to the Science of Missions* (Phillipsburg, NJ: Presbyterian & Reformed, 1960), 36; see also Heidelberg Catechism, q. 54.

13   So we as Christ's witnesses are significant; we are cowitnesses with the Spirit and God's chosen means to distribute gospel truth. Yet we cannot produce gospel increase ourselves; God is sovereign and we remain dependent upon him. See also Packer, *Evangelism and Sovereignty*, 85–86.

Christ. Gospel suffering is inherent to the identity of every faithful witness.[14] This truth may seem shocking at first to many of us who are accustomed to comfortable lifestyles in the Western world. The English word *martyr*, however, is a direct transliteration of the Greek noun for witness (*martus*). Christ's witnesses, throughout the New Testament, were called to follow him in suffering. Consider several related truths.

First, gospel suffering displays God's power in our weakness. Paul knew this secret of spiritual success (1 Cor. 2:1–5; 2 Cor. 4:7–11). Consider the gospel defense of Paul, a prisoner, standing before Felix, a cruel governor (Acts 24:24–25). In human society, Felix was in the position of power over Paul, a prisoner accused by his own people and bound in chains. But despite his external circumstances, Paul was conscious by faith of the more transcendent spiritual reality. So Paul, empowered by Christ's Spirit and with the authority of Christ's word, dialogued with Felix. Paul the prisoner testified on behalf of Christ the Judge, and Felix the governor trembled when rebuked by Christ's word and Spirit. This spiritual reality is often confirmed in Scripture and by countless missionary biographies: when we as Christ's witnesses are in ourselves weak, then in Christ we are strong (2 Cor. 12:10).

Second, gospel suffering should be expected as normal. Have you ever wondered why more than one-fourth of the book of Acts is devoted to the story of Paul in prison (Acts 21:27–28:31)? Why, if this book is about mission, does the Spirit give so much attention to Paul's bondage? The answer is the close connection between gospel witness and gospel suffering. Christ's witnesses are often persecuted and imprisoned, and they are often bound by sociopolitical or even physical chains. Yet "the word of God is not bound!" (2 Tim. 2:9). Christ's truth continues to triumph, even as his church must bear witness to the power of this truth

14 I use the term *gospel suffering* to distinguish this kind of suffering from other forms of suffering. The same distinction is made in 1 Peter 2:20. John Piper gives six reasons why God uses suffering to advance the witness of the church. See *Let the Nations be Glad* (Grand Rapids, MI: Baker, 1993), 71–112.

through much weakness and suffering (Acts 14:22). Gospel witness is at the spiritual frontlines, so the church expects spiritual opposition and prays for gospel advance in the midst of suffering (Eph. 6:19–20).

Third, gospel suffering completes the sufferings of Christ (Col. 1:24). The spiritual union between Christ and his people is so intimate that the sufferings of his people are considered—by Christ himself—to be his own suffering (Acts 9:4).[15] In the higher plan of God's mission, it is at times necessary for Christ's witnesses to suffer in the world, just as it was necessary for Christ himself to suffer (Luke 24:26). Christ commanded Peter to carry the cross of self-denial, and Peter later reminded his readers of their calling to follow Christ in suffering (Matt. 16:24; 1 Pet. 2:21).

Fourth, gospel suffering advances the cause of the gospel. It may seem as if the progress and triumph of the gospel is hindered by suffering and persecution, just as we may be tempted to think that Paul's ministry would have been more effective had he not been imprisoned for so many years. But God has a higher plan, and the purpose of his mission will not be hindered by suffering! In fact, it is the opposite: he skillfully uses suffering to further perfect his plan (Gen. 50:20; Acts 4:28; Rom. 8:35).[16]

By faith, Paul learned to look for God's higher purpose in his suffering (Phil. 1:12–18). In his all-wise providence, God allows suffering, not only to strengthen his people's faith, but also to amplify their gospel witness (2 Tim. 4:17). He often uses the persecution of his church to advance the cause of his mission in the world (Acts 8:1–4). Truly, the

---

15 Though Christ's sufferings in his work of atonement have been finished, having made perfect penal satisfaction to the demands of God's law on behalf of his people (John 19:30; 1 Pet. 3:18), it remains true that his sufferings in union with his people are still being completed by the gospel suffering of his witnesses in mission. The sufferings of Christian witnesses, of course, are nonexpiatory, yet they serve an important role in the economy of the church's witness under God's sovereignty.

16 Eric Liddell (1902–1945) writes, "Circumstances may appear to wreck our lives and God's plans, but *God is not helpless among the ruins.* Our broken lives are not lost or useless. God's love is still working. He comes in and takes the calamity and uses it victoriously, working out his wonderful plan of love." *The Disciplines of the Christian Life* (Nashville, TN: Abingdon Press, 1985), 125.

blood of Christ's witnesses is the seed of the church![17] Even if the specific value in gospel suffering remains a mystery, God's people are called to live by faith in his higher purpose and mission.

Gospel suffering is a joy and privilege for Christ's witnesses. This truth is countercultural; it is impossible to understand it without faith. Yet Christ's witnesses rejoice to be counted worthy to suffer for the sake of his name (Acts 5:41; Rom. 5:3; 2 Tim. 2:3; 1 Pet. 4:13). It is a joy to suffer for Christ, since by this means the gospel is advanced and God's mission accomplished, and since in this way Christ's witnesses publicly testify to the world about the power of the gospel and their intimate spiritual union with Christ. Indeed, many who have gone before us have joyfully sealed this testimony with their own blood.

Bearing Witness to Christ

Mission in the New Testament is best described as bearing witness to Christ. The five aspects of mission, highlighted in this chapter, all further describe the New Testament concept of Christian witness.

One question remains as we conclude this chapter: Are you a faithful witness of Jesus Christ? This is the calling of every true believer. Most people in the world, however, are deceived by false witnesses— those who twist God's truth to promote Satan's lie. Even worse, many Christians, at times, even act like false witnesses due to contradictions between what they profess and what they practice. Many Christians are also fickle witnesses; they are inconsistent and unfaithful, often vacillating between confessing and denying Christ.

We are called to be faithful witnesses, like Christ, even to the point of suffering and death. The apostle Peter was, at first, a fickle witness: at one time he gave a clear testimony (Matt. 16:16) but later he denied Christ with an oath (Matt. 26:72). Yet by the power of Christ's grace, Peter

---

17 Church Father Tertullian (AD 160–220) first made this observation in the second century: "The blood of the martyrs is the seed of the Church." Tertullian, *Apology* (Cambridge, MA: Harvard University Press, 1953), 50.

was forgiven and restored. Then he was commissioned and empowered by the Spirit to bear witness to Christ, faithfully, even unto death. We also are by grace restored and empowered. We don't trust in our own ability; we remain dependent on the sovereign Spirit of Christ. And we remain hopeful as we are sent forth to witness of Christ, faithfully, even if it means that we must seal our testimony with our own blood.

Discussion Questions

1. Define the term *witness* as used in the New Testament and explain from Scripture at least four different activities of a faithful witness.

2. What should you do to improve the witness of your own church community? Explain five methods for gospel witness that your church has found to be effective in your community.

3. What are the similarities and differences between gospel living (deeds) and gospel speaking (words)? How do they together strengthen the credibility of our witness?

4. Who are ambassadors for Christ (2 Cor. 5:18–6:1)? What is the message of reconciliation?

5. Read Romans 1:16–17 and describe how gospel witness serves to declare God's righteousness in the world.

6. Suppose your friend thinks that God does not want Christians to suffer. Prove from the Bible that this teaching is incorrect and explain how gospel suffering is an important form of witness.

7. How did God use Ananias in Paul's conversion (Acts 9:10–19)? What caused Ananias to be afraid? What keeps us from being faithful witnesses?

PART 2

CONCISE HISTORY OF CHRISTIAN WITNESS

5

The Church's Witness after Pentecost

CHRISTIAN WITNESS CONTINUES in the world today, unrelenting and unstoppable. This fact is the overwhelming testimony of the first anthology of missionary biography, the infallible history book authored by God himself—the book of Acts. Through Luke, the Holy Spirit tells us the beginning of an expansive and beautiful story about the ongoing success of God's mission to the end of the earth. We are not given all the details; we have only a few excerpts and snapshots, a few selected stories of men and women who, by grace, were counted worthy to suffer for the sake of Jesus's name. The details that we do know, however, give abundant evidence to illustrate the wonderful ways in which faithful Christian witnesses have continued to shine light on God's marvelous works in this sin-darkened world.

We laid the foundation for our definition of Christian witness in the first section of this book. Now we turn to illustrate this definition with a concise historical review of the church's participation in the bigger story of God's mission. But first we define more precisely the church's role in God's mission in order to give clarity for the historical review that follows.

What Is the Mission of the Church?

This crucial question is central to our present study: How do God's people after Pentecost participate in God's mission? A sharp contrast is often made between the concepts of *church* and *mission*, defining mission as something external and even far away, or at least somewhat disconnected from the local church in the sense of a subordinate or parachurch ministry. Furthermore, various aspects of the church's witness—evangelism, apologetics, hospitality, global partnerships, church planting, and so on—are often treated as separate activities, sometimes overlapping or at other times competing for space within a church or parachurch. More recently, however, there has been a greater focus on the missionary nature of the church, which in many ways has been a helpful corrective.[1]

How should *church* and *mission* be related? Much recent literature now addresses this question with helpful insights.[2] This book is my contribution to the discussion: church and mission are properly related by a biblical understanding and consistent practice of Christian witness. *Bearing witness to Christ is the mission of the church in the world today. Christian witness*, as described by this whole book, *is the participation of God's people serving within God's mission.*

This answer is not the final word, but hopefully it will give clarity to this ongoing discussion. In my opinion, the best answer must be grounded within the biblical theology of God's mission, and it must be shaped by a theological confession that is faithful to Scripture. The answer must also recognize the complexity of both terms: *mission* and *church.*

---

1   Some of the earlier voices in modern history are Roland Allen, *The Spontaneous Expansion of the Church and the Causes Which Hinder It* (London: World Dominion Press, 1927); Lesslie Newbigin, *The Household of God: Lectures on the Nature of the Church* (1953; repr., Carlisle, UK: Paternoster Press, 1998), 181–206; Johannes Blauw, *The Missionary Nature of the Church* (New York: McGraw-Hill, 1962); and Darrell L. Guder, ed., *Missional Church: A Vision for the Sending of the Church in North America* (Grand Rapids, MI: Eerdmans, 1998).

2   For example, see the views of Jonathan Leeman, Chris Wright, John Franke, and Peter Leithart in Craig Ott, *The Mission of the Church: Five Views in Conversation* (Grand Rapids, MI: Baker, 2016), or a broader comparison of views in Jason Sexton, *Four Views on the Church's Mission* (Grand Rapids, MI: Zondervan, 2017). See also Christopher J. H. Wright, *The Mission of God's People: A Biblical Theology of the Church's Mission* (Grand Rapids, MI: Zondervan, 2010); Kevin DeYoung and Greg Gilbert, *What Is the Mission of the Church?* (Wheaton, IL: Crossway, 2011); and Timothy Keller, *Center Church* (Grand Rapids, MI: Zondervan, 2012), 251–96.

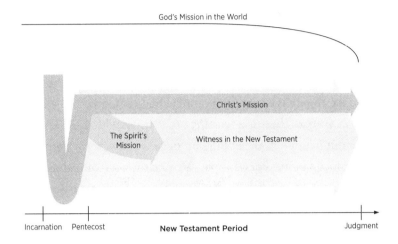

Figure 7. Mission and witness in the New Testament.

We have already defined various aspects of the term *mission*: God's mission in the Old Testament, the mission of Christ, and the Spirit's mission (fig. 7). Now we are defining the church's witness and illustrating it historically. Our study in the last four chapters often hinted at the church's mission within the bigger story of God's mission, and the third section of this book will further develop many of these points. Before going further, however, we will consider seven distinctions about the concept of *church* in order to give more precision to this discussion.

First, we recognize that the church is both the object of mission and an agent in mission. As stated previously, the church as an object of mission is God's trophy of grace, cosmically displayed in his holy showcase community, whose presence is a public proof of God's grace and truth. Yet God also uses the church as an agent in mission, his people who are commissioned to publicly witness of Christ in order to advance his mission in the world. Both aspects are important in God's mission, though the church's agency is primarily in view as we consider methods of witness.

Second, we differentiate between God's mission and the church's witness. As indicated previously, the church's mission is subordinate and contextual; it is always limited to a specific time and place in the much broader mission of God's redemption. It is helpful, for the sake of clarity, to speak of the *witness* of the church instead of the *mission* of the church: the church's witness serves within God's mission.

Third, the church is both the communal body of Christ and individual believers in Christ. There is a tendency to focus on either the individual or the communal, often depending on one's worldview presuppositions or cultural inclinations. For example, Western society is often highly individualistic, tending to overlook the importance of corporate witness and giving almost exclusive attention to individual expressions of witness, such as personal evangelism, personal obedience to the Great Commission, and even personal guilt when these activities are not emphasized. Yet Scripture highlights both the personal and corporate aspects of redemption: each individual believer saved through faith in Christ as well as the whole covenant community of faith that is united in Christ (Rom. 12:4–6; 1 Cor. 12:11–14). The church's witness is much more than the sum of all the parts of each individual believer's witness; we must also affirm and strengthen the collective witness of the church community within each society.[3]

Four more common distinctions are helpful to mention for further clarity. We distinguish between the church on earth in suffering, sometimes called the church militant, and the church triumphant in heaven that is beginning to enjoy perfected worship. The church's witness is limited to the church militant on earth, since perfected worship in heaven is the goal of mission.[4] We distinguish between the universal church, which is God's people in all times and places, and the many different church

---

3   Renewed attention in the past century to the church's missionary nature has been valuable in this regard, since much more attention is being given to the collective witness of the church as a local community of faith. For example, see Michael W. Goheen, *A Light to the Nations* (Grand Rapids, MI: Baker Academic, 2011), 191–99; Keller, *Center Church*, 251–96; and Stefan Paas, *Pilgrims and Priests: Christian Mission in a Post-Christian Society* (London: SCM Press, 2019), 187–204.

4   John Piper makes this point famously: "Missions is not the ultimate goal of the church. Worship is. Missions exists because worship doesn't." Piper, *Let the Nations Be Glad* (Grand Rapids, MI: Baker, 1993), 11.

communities in local expression. The membership of the church is both comprehensive and contextual, comprising a great multitude that is individually numbered and gathered from specific historic periods, particular local areas, and diverse ethnic groupings throughout the whole world (Rev. 7:9). We also distinguish between the church as an organization serving under Christ's authority and the church as a spiritual fellowship united in Christ (Eph. 4:11–16), as well as the church gathered for worship at specific times and the church scattered for witness in all of life (cf. Acts. 4:31; 5:42; 8:4; 11:19; 14:27; 20:7). Each of these seven distinctions help us recognize the complexity of the term *church*.

Therefore, in view of the complexity of both terms, I suggest the following definition: *The role of the church in the world after Pentecost is to bear witness to Christ by participating in God's mission through evangelism, apologetics, global gospel partnerships, church planting, compassion ministries, biblical counseling, cultural engagement, gospel worship, gospel suffering, and the many other related aspects of Christian witness.*

As previously defined, God's mission is his plan of redemption, decreed before creation and now made known through biblical history. God's people is his church on earth, of all ages (past, present, and future) and places (both local and global), both personal and communal, especially as a spiritual fellowship in Christ, that is gathered for worship and is living as witnesses in this un-Christian world. Christian witness is the activity of God's people serving within God's mission. Thus the church's task is to bear witness of Christ in the world today. We will illustrate this definition in the next chapter by tracing the major themes of witness in church history since Pentecost. For the rest of this chapter, we will consider methods of witness in the apostolic church and the vision of this mission history from God's perspective.

Methods of Witness in the Apostolic Age

A historical review of methods for Christian witness must start by giving attention to the methods for witness used by the apostolic church. We can be concise since there are many excellent studies of these meth-ods.[5] Unlike many books today, the New Testament does not focus on the methodology of Christian witness, such as techniques, strategies, procedures, or even a set of principles. Rather, it simply tells stories about the apostolic church faithfully bearing witness to Christ. Several observations can be made about the method of Christian witness in this formative age.

Witness in the New Testament is *usually preceded by prayer.* Though the spiritual dimension of methodology is often difficult to docu-ment, the book of Acts makes an association between prayer and witness. There is a general pattern: believers wait upon God in de-pendency, then believers are empowered by the Spirit, which leads to believers witnessing with clarity and boldness (Acts 1–2; 4:31; 11:5; 13:1–3; 16:25; 22:17–21; cf. Eph. 6:18–20; Col. 4:3). For example, the believers in Acts 4 were beginning to experience persecution. So they brought this fact to God in prayer, describing the problem to him. God then answered their prayer by filling them afresh with the Holy Spirit, causing them to respond with continued witness (Acts 4:23–31).

Witness in the apostolic church is *often explicitly Spirit-directed.* The history of Acts 16:6–10 illustrates this fact. Paul and his team were "forbidden by the Holy Spirit" to go to Asia and instead were guided to preach the gospel in Europe. From our perspective, two thousand years later, this divine direction had enormous consequences: consider the possible historical outcomes if Paul's team had stopped traveling west into Europe and instead turned east into Asia! Likewise, the Spirit directed the church to break down ethnic barriers with gospel witness: the "hand of the Lord" guided believers in Antioch to witness

---

5   For example, see Adolf Harnack, *The Mission and Expansion of Christianity in the First Three Cen-turies,* trans. James Moffatt (New York: Harper, 1962); Michael Green, *Evangelism in the Early Church* (Grand Rapids, MI: Eerdmans, 1970), 194–235; and Eckhard J. Schnabel, *Early Christian Mission: Paul and the Early Church* (Downers Grove, IL: InterVarsity, 2004).

cross-culturally, and then endorsed this witness with divine blessing (Acts 11:19–21). This new development was approved by the church leaders because the Holy Spirit had already prepared them for it (Acts 10:1–11:18) and guided them to ratify it (Acts 15:7–9, 28; cf. Eph. 2:18; 1 Cor. 12:13; Gal. 3:28).

The apostolic church's outward expansion of the gospel movement, both geographic and ethnic, is sovereignly directed by God, not by human strategy or methods. This does not mean our strategies and methods are not important. Rather it sets for us the foundation and framework within which we employ these subordinate means for the sake of gospel witness.

Witness in the apostolic church is *generally spontaneous*. Given the propensity of many Western worldviews for precise polity, procedures, and strategic planning, we may be surprised by what seems to be a glaring absence in the New Testament of specific methods for witness. Even the Great Commission, the clearest command for the church's mission, is not repeated and seldom suggested (the only exceptions being Acts 10:42 and Rom. 1:5; 16:26). Clearly, the story of witness is not about methods and strategy; rather, it is about believers who live faithfully and speak freely about Christ to everyone.[6] Again, this does not mean polity and procedures should be avoided; rather, it implies they must be designed to serve Christian witness and not hinder it.

Spontaneous witness in the New Testament church is the natural byproduct and necessary outcome of faithful Christian belief. This history focuses on the lifestyles and activities of ordinary believers in spiritual communities, giving very little attention to an office of evangelist or to

---

6   In response to the weaknesses of many mission methodologies in his day, Allen argued for spontaneous expansion that "follows the unexhorted and unorganized activity of individual members of the Church explaining to others the Gospel which they have found for themselves; I mean the expansion which follows the irresistible attraction of the Christian Church for men who see its ordered life, and are drawn to it by desire to discover the secret of a life which they instinctively desire to share." Allen, *Spontaneous Expansion*, 7; see also John L. Nevius, *The Planting and Development of Missionary Churches*, 3rd ed. (New York: Foreign Missionary Library, 1886).

the more formal witness of leadership functions in the church.[7] There is little strategic planning, if any, with Paul's personal desires in Romans 15:22–29 being the rare exception. This pattern of witness is set early in the history: God's people living in holy fellowship is itself a public witness that God uses to increase his church (Acts 2:42–47; 4:32–37; 5:12–14).

The New Testament depicts *the church community itself as the dominant form* of witness. Though the Great Commission is not repeated as a personal command to individual believers, the New Testament does give many commands to motivate church communities to live in ways that promote witness to the gospel of Christ. For example, Peter commands the church to abstain from sin and live honorably so that others will see the light (1 Pet. 2:11–12; cf. Matt. 5:16), and Paul instructs the church to walk as children of light in order to shine as lights in a sin-darkened world (Eph. 5:8; Phil. 2:15). Likewise, Paul thanks God for the gospel witness of the Thessalonian church throughout their whole region, and he encourages them to improve their public witness more and more by faithful Christian living (1 Thess. 1:7–8; 4:1–12). Witness in the apostolic age, therefore, is best described as contagious Christian living within an attracting church community.

Gospel communication is central in all apostolic witness. Peter's sermon in the home of Cornelius is the most concise example of what could be called the apostolic method: that God sent the good news of Jesus Christ to his people; that God anointed Jesus to display this good news; and that God commands his people to proclaim this good news and to

---

7   The *Epistle to Diognetus* (ca. 200) is the classic example of how these ordinary Christians witnessed simply by displaying their faith: "For Christians are not distinguished from the rest of mankind either in locality or in speech or in customs. For they dwell not somewhere in cities of their own, neither do they use some different language, nor practice an extraordinary kind of life. . . . They find themselves in the flesh, and yet they live not after the flesh. Their existence is on earth, but their citizenship is in heaven. . . . They are dishonored, and yet they are glorified in their dishonor. They are evil spoken of, and yet they are vindicated. They are reviled, and they bless; they are insulted, and they respect. Doing good they are punished as evil-doers; being punished they rejoice, as if they were thereby quickened by life. . . ." Joseph Barber Lightfoot, *The Apostolic Fathers* (Grand Rapids, MI: Christian Classics Ethereal Library, 1956), 193–94.

testify that Christ is coming again (Acts 10:34–43; cf. Luke 24:46–48). The church is a public testimony of this apostolic message. The witness of this message is communicated both verbally and nonverbally, and it is sometimes accompanied with other phenomena, such as extraordinary gospel encounters (Acts 8) or signs and wonders (Mark 16:17, 20; Rom. 15:19; 2 Cor. 12:12). However, the primary focus in the New Testament is on the communication of the gospel message that is authenticated by the faithful living of the witnessing community.[8]

The New Testament gives us *instructive personal examples of methods* for witness. We learn much from Paul's example of untiring cross-cultural mission, a co-laboring with the Holy Spirit with a huge multiethnic network of faithful witnesses.[9] We are stirred up by Stephen the apologist, whose place was soon filled with many others like Apollos and Jude. We learn about faithful evangelism from Philip and about church planting from Timothy, Titus, and others in their team. Peter teaches us to embrace suffering as a form of witness, and John warns us about false witnesses and the tarnished witness of worldliness. Indeed, time fails us to tell of the Spirit-filled Barnabas known for encouragement and mentorship; of Pricilla and Aquila who ministered through Bible education (Heb. 11:32; Acts 18:26); of the unknown author of the book of Hebrews who is famous for preaching Christ; of the nameless itinerant witnesses who gave their lives for the sake of the name (3 John 7); and of the methods used by so great a cloud of New Testament witnesses who lived and died in faith.

Methods of witness in the New Testament are *built on the foundation of Old Testament prophets and New Testament apostles*, with Jesus Christ

8   Central to the book of Acts is a vast array of *communication* words: speaking, teaching, proclaiming, exhorting, reasoning, appealing, urging, convicting, testifying, and so forth. David B. Barrett and Todd M. Johnson, *World Christian Trends* (Pasadena, CA: William Carey, 2001), 218–23.

9   Much has been written about Paul's methods. See Roland Allen, *Missionary Methods: St. Paul's or Ours?* (Grand Rapids, MI: Eerdmans, 1962); J. Herbert Kane, *Christian Missions in Biblical Perspective* (Grand Rapids, MI: Baker, 1976), 72–93; Roger S. Greenway, *Go and Make Disciples: An Introduction to Christian Missions* (Phillipsburg, NJ: P&R, 1999), 61–68; Eckhard J. Schnabel, *Early Christian Mission: Paul and the Early Church* (Downers Grove, IL: InterVarsity, 2004).

as the cornerstone. The witness of God's people in the Old Testament is continued in the New Testament, shaped by the same purpose and principles but now amplified by the Spirit and expanded by the completed revelation of the gospel promise. For example, Peter builds on the foundation of witness as showcase community, defining his doctrine of the church by directly quoting God's design for Israel. He affirms this method, builds on it in view of Christ our cornerstone, and expands it with New Testament truth (Ex. 19:4–6; 1 Pet. 2:9), which we will also do in chapter 7. Paul does the same with his concise statement of Christological missiology (Rom. 15:8–13), continuing the Old Testament method of witness as expectant worship that was affirmed by Christ's mission and is being amplified by the church's witness of Christ among all nations.

Mission methods in the apostolic age are best described as bearing witness to Christ. The five aspects of New Testament witness, as studied in chapter 4, are built upon the five aspects of witness as studied in chapters 1 and 2. All ten aspects of witness help us ground our theology of Christian witness in Scripture (table 3). They all describe essential elements and features of a comprehensive biblical theology of witness, including both God's mission and the church's participation in it.

Table 3. Ten aspects of witness in Scripture

Witness as showcase community	God's covenant nation
Witness as loving confrontation	God's devoted prophets
Witness as expectant worship	God's praise singers
Witness as discipleship training	God's loving mentor
Witness as showing compassion	God's merciful healer
Witness as gospel living	God's holy community
Witness as gospel speaking	God's bold evangelists
Witness as gospel defense	God's gentle apologists
Witness as gospel increase	God's new humanity
Witness as gospel suffering	God's faithful martyrs

Mission History from God's Perspective

How should we study the history of the church's witness? There are many excellent resources, both comprehensive and specific, including histories of mission, evangelism, apologetics, and of many other related forms of Christian witness.[10] There are also many different ways to structure this history. For example, some divide it into periods or paradigms while others tell the big story with a collection of biographies.[11] For this brief overview, we will start with a synopsis from God's perspective followed in the next chapter by a review of the major themes in Christian witness.

The book of Revelation gives us a glimpse of the church in history from God's perspective.[12] It is not a complete history; like Acts, it is intentionally selective to promote a message. Unlike Acts, it was written as a vision of future history, with much symbolism and mystery, showing us "the things that must soon take place" (Rev. 1:1). But the message is clear: the risen Christ is directing world history for the good of his church and toward his ultimate glory. Thus, the church on earth must endure suffering a little longer until Christ, who is already victorious over evil, returns to forever unite all his people in perfected multiethnic

---

10 For several comprehensive reviews, see Kenneth Scott Latourette, *A History of the Expansion of Christianity*, 7 vols. (New York: Harper, 1937–1948); Stephen Neill, *A History of Christian Missions* (New York: Penguin, 1964); J. Herbert Kane, *A Global View of Christian Missions* (Grand Rapids, MI: Baker, 1975); and John Mark Terry and Robert L. Gallagher, *Encountering the History of Mission* (Grand Rapids, MI: Baker Academic, 2017). For recent histories of evangelism, see Robert G. Tuttle Jr., *The Story of Evangelism* (Nashville: Abingdon Press, 2006); and David M. Gustafson, *Gospel Witness through the Ages* (Grand Rapids, MI: Eerdmans, 2022). On the history of apologetics, see Benjamin K. Forrest, Josh Chatraw, and Alister E. McGrath, eds., *The History of Apologetics* (Grand Rapids, MI: Zondervan, 2020); see also J. K. S. Reid, *Christian Apologetics* (Grand Rapids, MI: Eerdmans, 1969) and Avery Cardinal Dulles, *A History of Apologetics* (New York: Corpus Books, 1971).

11 David Bosch structured mission history as a series of social paradigm shifts in *Transforming Mission: Paradigm Shifts in Theology of Mission* (Maryknoll, NY: Orbis, 1991), especially 181–510. For mission biography, see Ruth A. Tucker, *From Jerusalem to Irian Jaya: A Biographical History of Christian Missions* (Grand Rapids, MI: Zondervan, 1983).

12 See J. H. Bavinck, *And On and On the Ages Roll* (Eugene, OR: Cascade Books, 2019); cf. J. H. Bavinck, *Between the Beginning and the End* (Grand Rapids, MI: Eerdmans, 2014), 1–4.

worship of God. In this light, we see the history of Christian witness from the perspective of the triune God and his mission.

First, we see *God's mighty acts and gracious dealings* with his church. We may be tempted to think that mission is advanced when the church is strong and that mission is failing when the church is weak. But this is not always true, just as it was not always the case in the Old Testament. God was glorified even by the disobedience and selfishness of Jonah, and he used the failures of Israel to prepare for the coming of Christ. Likewise, we may see times of great persecution as detours or delays in the church's mission. But God views history from a different perspective. His plan is always advancing on schedule, despite opposition from without and failure from within.

Biblical history often highlights this fact. God's mighty acts are most clearly manifested in times of great impossibility, since God often uses occasions of evil and opposition to make known his almighty power in ways that his "name might be proclaimed in all the earth" (Rom. 9:17). God's gracious dealings are most clearly displayed by the gentle ways in which he mentors his wayward people, making them useful agents in his mission when guided by his loving hand (Acts 9:15–16; Philem. 11).

Church history is a story with God as the main actor. He is performing mighty acts to advance his cause, as he guides his people to serve in his mission. God sovereignly controls all world events, even while he repeatedly calls his church back into holy community, reforming them and sending them out again for faithful witness. J. H. Bavinck illustrates this beautifully:

The book of Acts dramatically describes how God wrestled with his church. He permitted Cornelius to call the reluctant Peter, and afterward he used Peter to convince the reluctant congregation of Jerusalem. He caused the murmuring of Greek speaking church members to lead to the election of seven men, and he moved one of these seven men, Stephen, to preach the gospel everywhere among the Jews who had settled within Jerusalem from other parts of the world. He let this preaching end in a bloody persecution of the congregation, and then used the flight of many church members from Jerusalem to make the gospel known in a wider area. He called Saul on the way to Damascus and made him particularly competent to do a great and glorious work. He let the command of the Holy Spirit re-echo in the church of Antioch, within a small group of teachers and prophets. In short, God breaks through each barrier. He breaks down all obstacles and removes all hindrances. The deepest motive of the book of Acts therefore, is not the deeds of the apostles, but the mighty works of the risen Jesus Christ. For in spite of the church's reluctance and opposition, Christ takes the church with him on his triumphal march through the world. And this main thought of Acts is at the same time the theological perspective under which we must regard the further development of the history of missions. Acts provides the key to the mystery of the history of missions and makes it possible to view it as God intended. It is the history of God's mighty acts.[13]

Second, throughout church history we see the onward march of *Christ's triumphal procession.*[14] Paul gives us this mental picture: by his death and resurrection, Christ has crushed Satan's head and shamed all opposition (Col. 2:15; cf. Heb. 2:15). He now leads his redeemed people, as trophies of grace, in a triumphal procession, as the church spreads the message of his victory everywhere across all lands (2 Cor. 2:14; Eph. 4:8). Church history is a long line of men and women who have humbly followed in this spiritual victory march. It is the spiritual

---

13 J. H. Bavinck, *An Introduction to the Science of Missions* (Phillipsburg, NJ: Presbyterian & Reformed, 1960), 276–77.

14 This theme is common in the prayers of the European Reformers and Puritans. "A frequent theme in Calvin's writings and sermons is that of the victorious advance of Christ's kingdom in the world." Michael A. G. Haykin and C. Jeffery Robinson Sr., *To the Ends of the Earth: Calvin's Missional Vision and Legacy* (Wheaton, IL: Crossway, 2012), 53.

advance of the church militant, following Christ through suffering, who learn by faith to endure in view of future joy (Heb. 12:1–3).

For some, this gospel message of Christ's victory is like the stench of death; but to those being saved it is the fragrance of life (2 Cor. 2:15–16). For example, *Foxe's Book of Martyrs* is for the world a sorry tale of unfortunate fools who died terrible deaths. But for us—and for Christ—this history is a glorious account of a great cloud of witnesses who remained faithful unto death.[15] The biographies of Christian witnesses, from every period and place, remind us how God continues to use sinful people like ourselves in his service, and they motivate us to more faithful witnesses for Christ. We are not alone; there is a long procession of faithful witnesses ahead of us, and many more are still coming after. Christ is still distributing grace, with royal generosity, causing us all to follow him humbly in his triumphal procession, as witnesses in the world to his overcoming grace.

Third, we observe *the ministry of the Spirit* as he assembles the church for worship. Picture in your mind a famous conductor working with his orchestra in preparation for a grand international symphony. There is an extended period of practice sessions during which difficult pieces are rehearsed, often out of order and in different parts. Even immediately before the big event, there appears to be disorder as the various instruments are assembled, tuned, and adjusted in various places across the stage. The conductor is at the center of it all, correcting here and there, practicing again, and rearranging things as needed. This scene of rehearsal is a picture of the church on earth, presently being assembled and guided by the Spirit, the most famous conductor, in preparation for the coming celebration in heaven.

We can stand back to view all of church history as the ministry of the Holy Spirit who directs the spiritual body of Christ. The ministry

15 John Foxe, *Actes and Monuments of These Latter and Perillous Dayes* (London: John Day, 1563). From many other examples, see Paul Hattaway, *China's Christian Martyrs* (Grand Rapids, MI: Monarch Books, 2007) and Bryan M. Litfin, *Early Christian Martyr Stories* (Grand Rapids, MI: Baker Academic, 2014).

of the Spirit is both a personal work of grace in each individual believer, and a communal work that calls, sanctifies, and empowers God's covenant community. The Holy Spirit is busy maturing God's people for service and building them up into a temple of praise (1 Cor. 12:11; Eph. 2:22; 1 Pet. 2:5). Church history is a story of how the Spirit has worked in many times and places, often behind the scenes, to gather God's people from all nations and to mature the elect church for glory.

So we can picture the church in history as different sections of instruments that are being assembled for the grand international symphony of perfected worship in glory. Now is a time of practice, with each member of the body—the churches in Africa, in Asia, in Europe, and so on—being prepared to play their part, all to the praise of God's glorious grace. Some churches need to be corrected; others are matured through much testing. Each local church, with its unique abilities and contextual opportunities, is being prepared to play its part. Here and there we see the instruments being assembled, sometimes with much effort or against opposition. But the famous conductor is working tirelessly, often behind the scenes, to bring it all together at the appointed time, into a unified performance of perfected worship.

Therefore, we are filled with hope as we behold this ministry of the Spirit, now unveiled since Pentecost, as he transforms God's people, one degree at a time, in preparation for glory (2 Cor. 3:7–18). With much anticipation we look forward to the next page in God's big story of mission, each new page telling another little story about how we all are being prepared to participate together in this international symphony.

My Church in God's History of Mission

Long ago, Isaiah gave us a beautiful vision that is now becoming reality: many peoples from all nations flowing together unto Zion so that God's place of worship would become a house of prayer for all ethnic groups (Isa. 2:2–5; 56:6–8; cf. Mic. 4:1–5). When he cleansed the temple, Jesus knew this vision would soon begin to be realized (Matt. 8:11;

Mark 11:17), but its time had not yet come. Now after his ascension, Christ the messianic-shepherd is gathering his covenant people from all lands, by means of his Spirit and his church, bringing them into the New Jerusalem (Mal. 1:11; Rev. 21:24–26). Isaiah's vision, therefore, is being fulfilled in church history through mission.

Paul tries to comprehend the breadth, length, height, and depth of this glorious vision. It was a mystery, but now it is a secret revealed publicly: through the gospel, all nations are becoming members of Christ's body in covenant fellowship (Eph. 3:6). Paul understands his ministry as a priestly service of ingathering, bringing in the obedience of the nations as thank offerings to God's glory (Rom. 15:16; 16:25–26; cf. Isa. 66:18–20). In the Spirit, John also saw glimpses of this vision being fulfilled—he heard a preview of the new song of perfected worship: worthy is the Lamb who "ransomed people for God from every tribe and language and people and nation" (Rev. 5:9).

Therefore, together with all the saints, we pray for ability to comprehend this mystery (Eph. 3:18). Isaiah saw it in part; Jesus gave his life for it; Paul tried to comprehend it in every dimension; and John gave us a glimpse of its glory. Now, in view of mission history across two millennia, we know even more about how God, with mighty acts in history, is still fulfilling Isaiah's vision. So we as believers and churches follow in Christ's triumphal procession, along with a great cloud of witnesses, all of us flowing together toward the New Jerusalem in preparation for perfected worship. Consider this truth with amazement: your church is also included in this glorious history!

How is your own local church a part of God's universal mission? This is the question we started with at the beginning of this book. Together we are praying that our own churches—along with God's people in every region of the world today—will become more faithful in their witness of Christ. We want to learn more about God's mission and how our churches should serve in it more effectively. We especially desire that our church communities will mature in faithful gospel witness.

We who are indwelt by the Spirit of mission continue to pray that all of God's people will more clearly see God's vision for mission, and that we all will become more faithful in bearing witness to Christ.

Discussion Questions

1. How do you describe the role of the church in God's mission, especially in view of the different ways in which the words *church* and *mission* are often used?

2. Briefly explain each of the ten aspects of Christian witness.

3. Witness in the apostolic age is best described as contagious Christian living in an attracting church community. What does this truth mean for your church's witness?

4. Explain how the history of Christian witness can be viewed as God's mighty acts in the world, as Christ's triumphal procession, and as the Holy Spirit's ministry for worship.

5. Consider Isaiah 2:1–5 and 66:18–21, in association with Revelation 5:9; 7:9; 21:24–26 and Romans 1:5; 15:8–16; 16:26. How is God using your church to fulfill this prophecy?

6

Historical Themes in Christian Witness

HOW DOES CHRIST VIEW the past two millennia of mission history? We are merely participants in this history. Christ is above it all, directing each detail. Yet, with faith in Christ and by faithful historical review, we are raised higher to gaze upon the whole panorama of church history, glimpsing it from the perspective of Christ, the exalted sender, who guides all of history to its completion in future glory. From this perspective, we can recognize the contours of several major motifs and reoccurring themes in the history of Christian witness.

This history is diverse, complex, and variegated. But it is one story, the witness of God's people guided by one Spirit as they try to obey God's unchanging word faithfully and bear witness to the only Savior. It is not a constantly mutating story, with chaotic stages and novel paradigm shifts, stumbling haphazardly forward into an unknown future.[1] The story often surprises us, from our limited perspective, but it does not surprise God who planned it before the beginning. It is God's story, which Christ is directing from the throne (Rev. 6:1)—the history

---

1 David Bosch's paradigmatic approach diverges from the unity of mission history, with others taking it much further. See Bosch, *Transforming Mission: Paradigm Shifts in Theology of Mission* (Maryknoll, NY: Orbis, 1991), 181–89; and Stephen B. Bevans and Roger P. Schroeder, *Constants in Context* (Maryknoll: Orbis, 2004), 1–4.

of the church's witness in God's mission, with reoccurring themes and patterns across two millennia.

Our view of this history is like that of a child looking through a kaleidoscope. Each turn of the tube displays ever-changing combinations of the same colorful shapes. In this chapter, we describe some of these colorful shapes that have often been seen, in various combinations and from different angles, throughout each turn in the timeline of God's history. There are at least seven common themes in the history of Christian witness.

Expansion: The Advance of Witness

The history of Christian witness has most often been described using the theme of expansion.[2] Consider, for example, William Carey's famous sermon on "enlarge the place of your tent" at the beginning of what has been called the "great century of missionary expansion."[3] Or consider the various millennial expectations with geographic applications of God's glory physically filling the earth "as the waters cover the sea" (Hab. 2:14).[4] The history of Acts is also structured by the ethnic and geographic expansion of the gospel (Acts 1:8).

This theme of expansion closely aligns with the New Testament theme of witness as gospel increase. Mission history records many times

---

2   Much historical literature is organized around geographic expansion, new territories, and gospel progress. The titles of several influential modern histories of mission illustrate the essence of this theme: Adolf Harnack, *The Mission and Expansion of Christianity in the First Three Centuries*, trans. and ed. James Moffatt (New York: Harper, 1962); and Kenneth Scott Latourette, *A History of the Expansion of Christianity*, 7 vols. (New York: Harper, 1937–1948).

3   Carey's sermon was taken from Isaiah 54:2–3 (cf. 9:1–7; 26:15; 49:19). It was preached on May 30, 1792 at the Friar Lane Baptist Chapel in Nottingham, with two main points: "Expect great things from God, and attempt great things for God." Most historians mark this date as the start of the Great Century of mission expansion. See Justo L. González, *The Story of Christianity: The Reformation to the Present Day*, vol. 2 (Grand Rapids, MI: Zondervan, 2010), 419.

4   Compare Numbers 14:21, Psalm 72:19, Isaiah 11:9, and Zechariah 14:9. See Johannes Van Den Berg, *Constrained by Jesus' Love: An Inquiry into the Motives of the Missionary Awakening in Great Britain* (Kampen, NL: J. H. Kok, 1956); and Charles L. Chaney, *The Birth of Missions in America* (Pasadena, CA: William Carey, 1976).

of spiritual increase—gospel witness in new territories, to new ethnic groups and new languages, resulting in many new members for Christ's spiritual kingdom. The high points of the church's global witness help us organize and analyze the many amazing advances in mission, the story of God's growing fame among all nations. These undeniable facts of gospel expansion often motivate us with missionary zeal to conquer new territories for Christ, to win multitudes for the Lord, to start new church planting movements, or the like.

The expansion theme, however, has often been confused with political or personal ambitions. Think of the many church and state entanglements within Christendom, such as the Crusades of the Roman Catholic Church and European colonial expansion under the Christian banner. Similar mistakes are seen when zeal for Christian witness is combined with Western ideas of progress or pragmatism that attempt to measure spiritual success by physical numbers or social influence alone.

The expansion theme describes the spiritual advance of Christ's kingdom, not the physical conquest of the church. Christ's kingdom continues to come, but the influence of the church on earth ebbs and flows, in different times and areas. For example, very little remains physically of the seven churches that were given special notice in John's Revelation; yet Christ's rich promises remain for all those who conquer spiritually by faith (Rev. 2:7, 11, 17, 26; 3:5, 12, 21). Likewise, both John the Baptist, the greatest Old Testament prophet, and the apostle Paul, the great New Testament missionary, died alone in prison, deserted by all (Matt. 11:11; 2 Tim. 4:16–18). Yet through the faithful witness of them and many others, the rider of the white horse rides on, "conquering, and to conquer" (Rev. 6:2; cf. Rom. 8:35–37).

The certainty of eschatological hope should not be confused with geographic expansion or political ambitions, or even by the social success of the church on earth. Gospel expansion is not measured by the success of my denomination or my organization, and certainly not by the success of my culture, tribe, or nation. Gospel success is spiritual;

we sacrifice our own personal ambitions with absolute surrender as we spiritually follow Christ our King in his triumphal procession across all lands.

The expansion theme is helpful when held in humble balance with a holistic perspective. The history of Christian witness is a story of great gospel successes, due to God's grace and despite the many mistakes and misapplied ambitions of human witnesses. We rejoice to meditate on God's wondrous works throughout the world as we continue singing psalms and missionary hymns that celebrate his coming kingdom (Pss. 105:1–2; 145:4–6)! Yet the expansion motif is one of several; there have often been times and places where the church is a weak minority, where the dominant motif is witness in exile and suffering (considered below), or where Christ's kingdom comes in ways hidden from human reasoning (1 Kings 19:12; Zech. 4:6; Rom. 11:1–5). So while we celebrate the expanding triumph of Christ's spiritual kingdom, we do so without a triumphalist attitude, because we also recognize other historical themes of witness.

Translation: Witness to Every Nation

The history of Christian witness is also a story of cross-cultural gospel communication into many languages, nations, and worldviews. Our second historical theme is the reoccurring motif of gospel translation for the purpose of witness to every nation.

Gospel translation started at Pentecost when the message about Christ was heard for the first time in a multitude of different languages (Acts 2:8–10). This miracle of tongues was symbolically a reversal of the confusion that God caused at Babel to thwart the rebellious plans of humanistic globalism (Gen. 11:6–9). God's plan for gospel globalism—the covenant community in Christ's kingdom—began to be realized at Pentecost (Gen. 12:2–3; Ps. 2:8; Dan. 2:44). Cross-cultural communication of the gospel message is essential to this plan. The gospel of Christ's kingdom must be heard in every language and every land (Matt. 24:14; Mark 13:10). John's Revelation symbolically describes this translation theme as the gospel message that is now traversing the globe: "Then I saw another angel flying directly overhead, with an eternal gospel to proclaim to those who dwell on earth, to every nation and tribe and language and people" (Rev. 14:6).

The history of Bible translation tells how God has preserved, transmitted, and translated his word, using thousands of men and women in the process, so that the gospel can be proclaimed to all nations. Starting with Hebrew and Greek in the apostolic age, there are presently 736 languages with full Bible translations, 1,658 more languages with full New Testaments, and another 1,264 languages with Bible portions.[5] Early translation work included Origen's Hexapla in the third century, Jerome's Latin Vulgate around AD 400, a Gothic translation for mission in the fourth century, and then Armenian, Syriac, Coptic, Old Nubian, Ethiopic, and Georgian translations in the fifth century.[6] Translation was not without opposition, with much tension at each of the major turning points: from Greek into Latin, from Latin into vernacular European languages, and now from the West into non-Western contexts.[7]

Space does not permit us to review the whole history here. Notable stories on the European scene include John Wycliffe's translation into Middle English (1383), the Hungarian Hussite Bible (1416), and the German Luther Bible (1522). Outside of Europe, John Eliot's Algonquin Bible (1661) was the first translation into an indigenous American language, as well as the first Bible published in North America. Bible translation, though slow at first, gained momentum during the European Reformation, eventually becoming a mighty movement in the

---

5   Totals as of November 2023 according to the Wycliffe Global Alliance at https://www.wycliffe .net/resources/statistics/.

6   David B. Barrett and Todd M. Johnson, *World Christian Trends* (Pasadena, CA: William Carey, 2001), 114–16.

7   For example, Cyril and Methodius of Moravia translated the Bible into Old Church Slavonic, but opponents argued the Bible's official languages should be limited to Hebrew, Greek, and Latin, based on the trilingual inscription on the cross (John 19:19–20). See John Mark Terry and Robert L. Gallagher, *Encountering the History of Missions* (Grand Rapids, MI: Baker Academic, 2017), 69.

past century. In view of this history, we mention several tenets related to the translation theme.

First, we note the translatability of Christianity. From the beginning, the church was shaped by a Jewish heritage within a Greek culture, which soon led to cross-cultural gospel communication. The church council in Acts 15 affirmed the church's multicultural identity, concluding that Christianity is not inherently Jewish, but a faith confessed by all cultures and in all nations (Acts 15:1, 19; cf. Gal. 3:27). Christianity from the beginning, therefore, was inherently translatable.[8] The eternal gospel must be translated into every language so that the whole world can hear "the mighty works of God" (Acts 2:11; cf. 1 Pet. 1:25; Rev. 14:6).

Second, we consider the accessibility of God's word. Reading the Bible in the vernacular has always been important in Christian witness. Augustine's instruction to "take up and read" Scripture eventually became Tyndale's passion to give Scripture to every "boy that driveth the plough." Therefore, God's word must be made available in all languages; it must also be faithful to the divine author's original intent and understandable by people in all levels of society.[9]

Third, we acknowledge the indigeneity of gospel witness. Not only the Bible, but all forms of the church's witness—its identity, confessions, and ministry—must be translated into local contexts. As repeatedly affirmed by church history, each generation and community must hear God's eternal gospel in their own language and learn to apply it within their own context. Thus, indigenization is closely related to the translation theme.[10]

---

8   Lamin Sanneh notes: "The notion that the Qu'ran contains the very thoughts of Allah since they were directly dictated to the Prophet in Arabic, limits Islam's capacity to contextualize." Sanneh, *Translating the Message: The Missionary Impact on Culture* (Maryknoll, NY: Orbis, 2002), quoted in David J. Bosch, *Transforming Mission*, 20th ann. ed. (Maryknoll, NY: Orbis, 2011), 533.

9   Westminster Confession of Faith, 1.8: "Therefore [the Scriptures] are to be translated into the vulgar language of every nation unto which they come. . . ." (*CCC* 187).

10 *Indigenization*, like the newer term *contextualization*, includes gospel translation, cross-cultural communication, and intercultural ministry. These terms need further clarity to be used effectively; see Brian A. DeVries, "Contextualisation within Context: A Pedagogical Spectrum of Six Methodologies" in *In die Skriflig* 55, no. 1 (Oct. 2021): 1–8.

In fact, mission history can be viewed as a long story of repeated attempts to avoid both foreignness and accommodation in gospel witness. Consider, for example, the Jesuits' syncretism in the Chinese Rites controversy or John Eliot's attempts to civilize North American Indians according to a combination of Old Testament patterns and European social order.[11] The history of gospel translation is important since we must learn from both the successes and failures of those going before us.[12]

Reformation: The Renewal of Witness

A third theme in the history of Christian witness is reformation. The reformation theme complements the expansion theme: mission history records times of both reformation and expansion, with the reformation of the church often preceding and preparing for the expansion of witness.

This theme is described with many terms, including Spirit-worked revival, spiritual renewal, and church revitalization. Old Testament examples include the spiritual renewals of God's people during the judges, restorations during the reigns of Asa, Hezekiah, and Josiah, reforms of Jehu and Jehoiada, revival anticipated by the prophets (Ezek. 37:11–14; Amos 9:11–12), and even longings for revitalization: "Restore us again, O God" (Ps. 85:4; cf. Ps. 80). Calls in the New Testament for reformation are found in Paul's letters to Corinth and in the seven letters of Revelation. Several biblical metaphors of the church are also related to the reformation theme: a city on a hill, salt and light in society, and yeast hidden in a lump of dough. Other metaphors related to reformation include trimming the lamp (Matt. 25:7; Luke 12:35), fanning spiritual

---

11 See Sidney H. Rooy, *The Theology of Missions in the Puritan Tradition* (Grand Rapids, MI: Eerdmans, 1965), 201–8, 322. The weakness of these attempts is much easier to see four hundred years later. Despite their weaknesses, however, Eliot's pioneering efforts were hugely influential in shaping methods of many Western missionaries in the nineteenth century.

12 For further measured reflection, see Timothy Keller, *Center Church* (Grand Rapids, MI: Zondervan, 2012), 194–232. In addition to continued Bible translation for unreached peoples, the church in each region and generation must also learn to communicate the gospel to its own society, especially if its own culture has misunderstood or forgotten the gospel.

gifts into flame (2 Tim. 1:6), and purifying the temple (Mal. 3:3–4; cf. Matt. 21:12–14; John 2:14–17; 2 Cor. 6:14–7:1).

The story of Christian witness records many times of renewal, with the classic example being the Protestant Reformation in sixteenth-century Europe. The church's witness during this period was mostly focused on reforming the church by personal rebirth, the refinement of doctrine, church revitalization, the renewal of Christian practice, and radical biblical reforms in society.[13] This period has often been criticized as lacking in mission, since some still judge the sixteenth-century church with a definition of mission from the nineteenth century's time of expansion.[14] When viewed through the theme of reformation, however, the sixteenth-century Protestant church is another wonderful story of God's mighty reviving work to restore again his people for Christian witness.

Other historical examples of the reformation theme are also valuable for further reflection: the Waldensian movement in Southern Europe during the thirteenth century; the spiritual witness of David Brainerd, not only for revival among the North American Indians during the eighteenth century, but also for the influence of his personal experiences

13 Examples of the church's witness shaped by other historical themes can also be collected to prove this period was not without mission. The sending of a few men from Geneva to Brazil is often used in this regard. But such reasoning is not necessary since the dominant theme of mission at this time was reformation, not expansion. On Geneva's mission to Brazil, see R. Pierce Beaver, "The Genevan Mission to Brazil," in J. H. Bratt, ed., *The Heritage of John Calvin* (Grand Rapids, MI: Eerdmans, 1973), 55–73; and William Stanford Reid, "Calvin's Geneva: A Missionary Centre" in *Reformed Theological Review* 42, no. 3 (1983): 65–74.

14 The Protestant church was first criticized for its lack of mission by Roman Catholic opponent Robert Bellarmine. Judging them by their lack of international mission, he overlooked the Protestant church's strong reformation witness. German historian Gustav Warneck continued this unfair assessment, stating: "There was no missionary action by [the Protestant church] in the age of the Reformation." Warneck, *Outline of a History of Protestant Missions from the Reformation to the Present Time*, trans. George Robson (New York: Fleming Revell, 1901), 8. Warneck's mistake, like Bellarmine's, was to assess a period of reformation witness by comparing it with a period of expansion witness. Surprisingly, Warneck also overlooked the mission activity of the Dutch in the East Indies and the Puritan efforts at home in England and to North American Indians (actions which fit his definition of mission). More surprisingly, Warneck's mistake is still repeated today, despite the growing abundance of evidence to the contrary, though renewed attention on the missionary nature of the church and its local witness is also helping to correct it.

on many missionaries following; and the South African revival in 1860 with Andrew Murray and others, which resulted in the sending of many missionaries across Southern Africa.[15] Another example is the Pyongyang Revival of 1907, in what today is North Korea, where the preaching of Kil Sun-joo and other leaders was used by God for the establishment of Korean Christianity.[16] Historical patterns of the reformation theme are varied and difficult to describe precisely, partly since the Spirit cannot be predicted or controlled (John 3:8). But a few observations can be made from the historical record.

First, periods of reformation often follow times of prayer for God to intervene. Jonathan Edwards highlighted the importance of prayer for "the revival of religion and the advancement of Christ's Kingdom on earth" in his *An Humble Attempt*.[17] The believers in Acts 4 also experienced the same: they confessed God's sovereignty and prayed for boldness, and God answered them with renewed spiritual power for continued witness.

Second, periods of reformation are produced by special times of spiritual renewal. While each case and context differs greatly, reformation is ultimately the outworking of the mission of the Holy Spirit, who produces revival by working regeneration in the hearts of many people, and who revitalizes church communities to motivate them for witness. As a result, the church is renewed for purified worship as well as for bold witness.

---

15 Andrew Murray was involved in establishing missions in Malawi (1888), Zimbabwe (1891), Zambia (1899), Mozambique (1908) and Nigeria (1908), and indirectly involved in Angola, Swaziland, and Kenya. See Martin Pauw, "The Role and Influence of Andrew Murray Jr in Missions within the Dutch Reformed Church and in Wider Context" in *Stellenbosch Theological Journal*, 8, no. 3 (2022): 75–101. For more on the revival itself, see Olea Nel, *South Africa's Forgotten Revival: The Story of the Cape's Great Awakening in 1860* (Maitland, FL: Xulon Press, 2008).

16 William N. Blair and Bruce F. Hunt, *The Korean Pentecost and the Sufferings Which Followed* (Edinburgh: Banner of Truth, 1977).

17 Jonathan Edwards, "An Humble Attempt to Promote Explicit Agreement and Visible Union of God's People in Extraordinary Prayer for the Revival of Religion and the Advancement of Christ's Kingdom on Earth, Pursuant to Scripture-Promises and Prophecies concerning the Last Time" in *The Works of Jonathan Edwards* (New Haven: Yale University, 1977), 5:308–437. See also Iain H. Murray, *Pentecost—Today?: The Biblical Basis for Understanding Revival* (Carlisle, PA: Banner of Truth, 1998), 64–69.

Third, periods of reformation usually lead to great advances for Christ's kingdom, often evidenced by refined indigenous expressions of faith, restored public witness, revived mission expansion, and renewed social transformation. For example, the eighteenth-century Great Awakenings led to church renewal, political abolishment of slavery, and great missionary expansion. Likewise, we see similar effects—and we anticipate more—from the reformation of churches around the world.[18]

Organization: The Polity for Witness

A fourth theme is the history of organization for Christian witness. Organizational polity for witness includes institutional structures, commissioning and governance, personnel relations, mobilized resources, and much more. It is often viewed as tangential or of subordinate importance, sometimes an afterthought or even treated as unnecessary. Yet organization for witness has always been required since the time of the apostles.

Directly after Pentecost, the activity of witness was unanimous and spontaneous, the overflow of gospel joy resulting from a spiritual filling by the Spirit of mission. But organization and other formalities soon developed in the New Testament church. The Jewish leaders' challenge in Acts 4—"By what power?"—made clear the need for authority in witness that was delegated from Christ, guided by his Spirit, through the apostolic leadership (Acts 4:7, 10, 19–20; 5:29, 39). The challenge of financial hypocrisy in Acts 5 made clear the need for accountability in witness that was overseen by the appointed leaders according to God's Spirit and word, the governance of which became clearer at later stages (Acts 5:3–4; 15:28). The challenge of financial equality in Acts 6 made clear the need for strategy in witness to guide God's church and people in faithful ministry (Acts 6:1–7).

---

18 The revivals in South Africa (1860) and North Korea (1907) both led to healthy missionary movements in the decades following. The present renewal of the Protestant church in Brazil will hopefully produce many more similar spiritual advances in Christ's kingdom.

Later in the apostolic age, the offices of elder and deacon were formalized within established churches (1 Tim. 3:1–13). Polity for missionary and evangelist positions, however, is not specified in detail by the New Testament (Acts 13:1–3; Eph. 4:11). Financial support in witness, a challenging issue from the beginning, is frequently addressed by the New Testament, though also never with prescribed structures (Acts 11:29–30; 1 Cor. 16:1–2; 2 Cor. 8–9). It is clear, however, that organization for witness has always had to deal with issues of authority, accountability, strategy, and support.

We can learn from the many historical examples of organization in Christian witness. For example, some of the monastic orders during the Middle Ages were influential for the preservation, expansion, and renewal of church communities across Europe. Later the Moravian movement, founded in Herrnhut by refugees, formed small renewal societies within existing churches, and sent out hundreds of missionaries to plant churches around the world.

Organizational polity for mission has often been the space where issues of church and state overlap, leading to various forms of cooperation, competition, or conflict. The classic example is the checkered history of colonialism's influence on mission polity and the complex relationship of Christianity and commerce.[19] Another example is the church's mission structures that were entangled with and limited by the Dutch East India Company in the seventeenth and eighteenth centuries.[20]

Organization in the modern period has diverged in different directions: the formation and vast influence of Bible societies, mission agencies, and

---

19 As David Livingstone stated: "Those two pioneers of civilization—Christianity and commerce—should ever be inseparable." Livingstone quote in Norman E. Thomas, *Classic Texts in Mission and World Christianity* (Maryknoll, NY: Orbis, 1995), 68.

20 The company appointed a governor-general to supervise every preacher and schoolmaster in order to serve both the European community and the non-Christians "so that the name of Christ may be proclaimed and the service of the Company properly advanced." Unfortunately, however, the "service of the Company" often took precedence over "the name of Christ." Peter Y. De Jong, "Early Reformed Missions in the East Indies" in *Mid-America Journal of Theology* 6, no.1 (1990): 43.

other ministry structures, sometimes filling a void left by the church's weakness and other times working synergistically with the church; the faith missions movements of Hudson Taylor and many others to follow; and a host of polity issues like the three-self formula, comity agreements, and exit strategies. Today there are a great variety of organizational structures with varying degrees of success, such as denominational committees in competition for resources with parachurch ministries, or evolving structures in gospel partnerships between sending churches and younger churches.

Many other aspects of organization are seen in various combinations across church history. We recognize both the spiritual nature of the church's witness as organism, as well as the need to guide and guard the authenticity of this witness with organizational polity. It is also helpful to distinguish between institutions and movements for witness.[21] Closely related is the need for training and leadership development, considered in the next section, as a response to ministry challenges such as internal tensions (Acts 5–6), doctrinal disputes (Acts 15), or confusion and opposition (Acts 19).

Personnel relations include coworkers and team dynamics (Rom. 16:3–16; 3 John 1:5–12), gospel partnerships (Phil. 1:5; 4:15), mission societies and agencies, and the various groupings of religious networks, associations, and alliances. Also important are the structural relations of a witness ministry with the church as an organization, with the political state and social institutions, and with the church as a diverse spiritual community of local and global believers.[22] Nor can contextual relations be overlooked, including the culture of polity, organizational lifecycles, and issues within the social milieu.[23]

---

21 See Timothy Tennent, *Invitation to World Missions* (Grand Rapids, MI: Kregel, 2010), 432–57; and Keller, *Center Church*, 337–42.

22 Some of these complexities include discussions about church versus parachurch, denominational versus nondenominational, national versus international, unidirectional versus multidirectional, and so on.

23 For example, what is the church's status within the local social milieu: dominant or marginal, privileged or persecuted? There is much rethinking of polity for witness today as societies transi-

Education: Witness by Discipleship

The fifth historical theme of education flows directly from Christ's commission in Matthew: "Make disciples of all nations . . . teaching them to observe all that I have commanded you" (Matt. 28:19–20). Making disciples includes many activities, such as catechism instruction with spiritual formation, Bible education at different levels in various forms, and mentorship for ministry within and outside the church. Discipleship of believers is an essential ministry of the church; it is also a method for the multiplication of witnesses. Educational ministries are common throughout the history of Christian witness.

Jesus Christ's own earthly ministry is the strongest biblical precedent for the church's educational ministry, as considered at the end of chapter 2. His pattern of discipleship with the twelve and the seventy, rooted in the Old Testament, was continued by the church after Pentecost (2 Kings 2:3–5; Acts 5:42; 6:7; 14:21; 18:23; 19:9; 21:16). Barnabas's mentorship of Paul and others in the Antioch church plant and the training of Apollos by Pricilla and Aquila are examples of the church's emerging Bible education ministry (Acts 11:25–26; 18:24–28; 2 Tim. 2:2).

Historical examples of gospel education are many. What started as simple catechetical instruction for new church members in the early church soon grew into the famous theological schools in Alexandria, Antioch, Jerusalem, and elsewhere.[24] During the Middle Ages, formal education was offered in monastic and cathedral schools, primarily to train men for the ministry and with less attention to evangelistic education, though serving as a reforming force in society to counteract

---

tion away from Christendom and the West to situations of religious pluralism. Church history should guide how we organize Christian witness in the future.

24 Additionally, the ministry of Christian publication and literature distribution was started, albeit slowly at first, when leaders in the early church wrote books specifically for training spiritual leaders, as did many more of the European Reformers with the aid of Gutenberg's printing press: Ambrose's *On the Duties of the Clergy*, Gregory's *Pastoral Rule*, and Cassiodorus's *Institutions* followed later with publications during the Protestant Reformation such as Melanchthon's *Loci Theologici* and Calvin's *Institutes*. See Justo L. González, *The History of Theological Education* (Nashville: Abingdon Press, 2015), 119, cf. 1–14.

worldliness.[25] During the European Reformation, the school in Geneva was a powerful reforming witness, equipping and sending out hundreds of men who gave their lives for the spiritual conquest of the gospel in Europe.[26]

We find many more examples from around the world. The Log Colleges in New England (1750–1825) trained hundreds of men who planted churches across the American colonies and expanding frontier.[27] In Scotland alone, during the nineteenth century, theological education trained thousands of missionaries as well as hundreds of mission workers for urban ministry.[28] The ministry of Alexander Duff (1806–1878) in India laid foundations for the expansion of gospel education globally. Duff established the method of training students in all subjects with a Christian worldview so that they in turn would influence society as a whole, a method still followed in most mission education today.[29] More recently, many forms of Bible education were influential, from the informal schools on colonial mission stations for children and evangelists, to the established educational institutions across the globe in the last century, as well as newer forms of gospel education today such as Theological Education by Extension (TEE) and online learning.[30]

25 There was a revival of education during the time of Charlemagne in cathedral, monastic, and parish schools. See Frank P. Graves, *A Student's History of Education* (New York: MacMillan, 1915), 53–64; and Robert W. Pazmiño, *Foundational Issues in Christian Education* (Grand Rapids, MI: Baker Academic, 2008), 144–48.

26 Reid, "Calvin's Geneva," 65–74; and Erik A. de Boer, *The Genevan School of the Prophets: The Congregations of the Company of Pastors and their Influence in 16th Century Europe* (Geneva: Librairie Droz, 2012).

27 David W. Kling, "New Divinity Schools of the Prophets, 1750–1825: A Case Study in Ministerial Education" in *History of Education Quarterly*, 37, no. 2 (1997), 185–206.

28 Ian J. Shaw, "Thomas Chalmers, David Nasmith, and the Origins of the City Mission Movement" in *Evangelical Quarterly*, 76, no. 1 (2004): 31–46.

29 George Smith, *The Life of Alexander Duff* (London: Hodder and Stoughton, 1879); William Paton, *Alexander Duff: Pioneer Missionary of Education* (New York: George H. Doran, 1923).

30 For further examples, see Harvie M. Conn and Samuel F. Rowen, *Missions and Theological Education in World Perspective* (Farmington, MI: Associates of Urbanus, 1984); J. Dudley Woodbury, Charles VanEngen, and Edgar J. Elliston, *Missiological Education for the 21st Century: The Book, the Circle, and the Sandals* (Maryknoll, NY: Orbis, 1996); Bernhard Ott, *Beyond Fragmentation: Integrating Mission and Theological Education* (Oxford, UK: Regnum Books International, 2001);

Discipleship in many forms has been a powerful tool in the church's witness, both for catechizing church members and for witnessing to those outside the church. This duality of purpose is seen in the history of Sunday school ministries that provided training for the children of the church as well as for children from unchurched or un-Christian families. The same was true for the parish ministries of Richard Baxter, Thomas Chalmers, David Nasmith, and the many urban ministries that followed around the world, which were often equally effective in the evangelism of the unchurched as in the discipleship of the churched.

History also records how education ministries frequently lose their gospel focus over time, even though discipleship is the essential element of the Great Commission. Since Paul's day, many have been corrupted by false teachers or distracted by "silly myths" (1 Tim. 4:7; Titus 1:14). Christian higher education has often been compromised by the academic pursuit of a form of knowledge that is disconnected from rudimentary wisdom and piety, or that is divorced from witness in both word and deed. Even the vitally important ministry of Christian education for children of the church can lose its evangelistic vision by myopically focusing only on internal growth.[31] Understanding gospel education as a part of the church's witness helps guard against distortion and compromise.[32]

Compassion: Witness by Kind Acts

The history of gospel compassion, our sixth historical theme, is the holistic embodiment of gospel witness. Like education by discipleship,

---

and Linda Cannell, "Opportunities for 21st Century Theological Education" in *Theological Education as Mission*, ed. Peter F. Penner (Schwarzenfeld, Germany: Neufeld Verlag, 2005), 153–70.

31 The Heidelberg Catechism, itself designed to be an evangelistic teaching tool, gives special attention to Christian education in its answer about the fourth commandment (q. 103): "First, that the gospel ministry and schools for it be maintained" (*CCC* 323). This answer, while supporting education of the church's own children, is about promoting gospel ministry, which should include the evangelistic education of all children in the local community and beyond.

32 See Keith Ferdinando, "Jesus, the Theological Educator" in *Themelios* 38, no. 3 (2013): 360–74; and Brian A. DeVries, "Theological Education in the Service of Mission" in *Reformed Mission in Southern Africa: The Way Forward*, ed. Rob van der Kooy (Pretoria, South Africa: GKSA, 2022), 162–79.

this common theme in Christian witness directly follows the pattern of Christ, who "went about doing good" (Acts 10:38; cf. Matt. 9:36). Christians are called to display gospel benevolence, imitating their Father in heaven who is merciful, just, and generous (Matt. 5:44–48; Eph. 5:1), while living in society with honorable conduct so that the world will glorify God when they see these good deeds (Matt. 5:16; 1 Pet. 2:12).

The church has always had a powerful witness in society by means of compassion. Charity in the early church was holistic and tangible: support for widows and orphans, teachers and officials, and the sick and disabled, as well as care of prisoners, mine workers, slaves, those visited by great calamities, churches in poverty or peril, and many more.[33] Compassion continued in more institutional forms after persecution decreased in the fourth century. For example, Basil of Caesarea founded the first Christian hospital in Cappadocia, and a similar institution was founded in Syria by Rabbula of Edessa.[34] Likewise, the Knights Hospitaller, later famous as a Roman Catholic military order, was initially founded in the twelfth century to promote compassion and charity.

More recently, the medical ministries of most Christian witness since the nineteenth century are countless tributes to the story of gospel com-

---

33 Gospel compassion is applauded in a letter from the church in Rome to the church in Corinth (ca. AD 96): "Day and night you agonized for all the brotherhood, that by means of compassion and care the number of God's elect might be saved." Adolf Harnack, *The Mission and Expansion of Christianity in the First Three Centuries*, trans. and ed. James Moffatt (New York: Harper, 1962), 211, cf. 207–23. In this chapter, "The Gospel of Love and Charity," Harnack gives historical evidence for this long list of ways in which the early church displayed compassion.

34 Julian the Apostate recognized the importance of Christian compassion when writing to a pagan priest: "When it came about that the poor were neglected and overlooked by the [pagan] priests, then I think the impious Galilaeans [i.e., Christians] observed this fact and devoted themselves to philanthropy. . . . [They] support not only their poor, but ours as well, all men see that our people lack aid from us. . . . It is their benevolence to strangers . . . their . . . pretended holiness of their lives that have done most to increase atheism [i.e., Christian rejection of idolatry]." See *The Works of the Emperor Julian*, vol. 3, trans. Wilmer Cave Wright (New York: Putnam's Sons, 1923), 69.

passion in action. Likewise, modern missionaries have often strongly supported indigenous causes that preserve local culture, promote political and economic stability, and stand against institutional injustice in society. The church's witness by compassion continues today in many tangible ways: humanitarian assistance for disaster relief, ministries among a growing number of refugees, public action against human trafficking, or other forms of ministry to the marginalized.

Keeping the witness of the gospel primary and foremost has always been a challenge for the church, especially when overwhelmed by the urgency of human need for compassion. A common mistake is to separate the witness of compassionate deeds from the witness of spoken words, trying to promote the one in isolation of the other.[35] While the verbal proclamation of the gospel is central (Rom. 10:14), it is also impossible for a living faith to witness without corresponding deeds (James 2:26). This tension lives within us, and within the church community; even the word *witness*, which is both a noun and a verb, represents both gospel presence and gospel proclamation.[36]

Christian compassion throughout church history has been a powerful form of gospel witness, especially when the church was marginalized and powerless in society. As proven by the early church, charity in Christ's name, especially when least deserved, often speaks the loudest in gospel witness (1 Cor. 13:1–3). Gospel compassion is often the best apologetic against opposition, the final theme to which we now turn.

---

35 This bifurcation is more common in worldviews most affected by Greek dualism. For helpful discussions on keeping word and deed together, see Harvie M. Conn, *Evangelism: Doing Justice and Preaching Grace* (Grand Rapids, MI: Zondervan, 1982); Lesslie Newbigin, *The Gospel in a Pluralistic Society* (Grand Rapids, MI: Eerdmans, 1989), 128–40; A. Duane Litfin, *Word versus Deed: Resetting the Scales to a Biblical Balance* (Wheaton, IL: Crossway, 2012).

36 It is also important that this debate on the relationship of word and deed does not distract us from doing what God's word clearly commands (1 John 3:16–18). See also Jonathan Edwards, "Christian Charity: or, The Duty of Charity to the Poor, Explained and Enforced" in *The Works of Jonathan Edwards*, vol. 2 (Edinburgh: Banner of Truth, 1974), 163–73; Tim Chester, *Good News to the Poor: Social Involvement and the Gospel* (Wheaton, IL: Crossway, 2013); and Timothy Keller, *Ministries of Mercy: The Call of the Jericho Road*, 3rd ed. (Phillipsburg, NJ: P&R, 2015), 113–27.

Persecution: Witness in Suffering

Parallel to the story of gospel witness is the historical theme of Christian suffering due to persecution that results from social opposition to God's truth. In Acts 4, the apostolic church started to experience this opposition, which they immediately interpreted in light of Scripture and committed to the sovereign Lord in prayer (Acts 4:24–30). Christ had predicted this opposition, linking it with Old Testament persecution (Matt. 5:10–12; 10:16–25). Stephen echoed the same before he was martyred (Acts 7:52). Opposition against God and his word is the norm: the true church is always hated by the world (John 15:18–20).

Christian witness in suffering continues today with an unbroken procession of persecuted saints: the Old Testament prophets, the righteous one, the apostolic fathers, and now a long line of faithful believers since Pentecost who follow Christ in suffering. This fact is depicted by the two witnesses in John's Revelation: "Their dead bodies will lie in the street of the great city that symbolically is called Sodom and Egypt, where their Lord was crucified" (Rev. 11:8). This happened very literally in Rome when Christian martyrs were burned as torches to light up garden pathways. It continues to happen today all around the world when suffering Christians stand as shining lights in crooked and perverse generations (Phil. 2:15–16). It is no surprise, therefore, that in most world civilizations since Pentecost many Christians have been publicly persecuted.

Opposition to Christian witness is complex and variegated, with Satan behind the scenes constantly recycling and refining his malevolent tactics. There have been many antichrists in the world, some directly empowered by the beast and the false prophet (1 John 2:18; 2 John 7; Rev. 16:13). Even religious organizations that masquerade as the church can become "drunk with the blood of the saints, the blood of the martyrs of Jesus" (Rev. 17:6). Church history also tells the story of many false teachers, much apostasy, numerous heresies, and many other false gospels, like the constantly mutating assortment of Christian cults today. Indeed, wherever God's Spirit is building his true church, there Satan is also building a synagogue of syncretism.[37]

Witness through suffering during times of persecution is a sad but beautiful history, the bittersweet story of many who have followed Christ through painful shame into the joy of glory. We have no space here even to list many who died for the faith; their names are recorded in heaven where they enjoy an audience with the King (Rev. 6:9–11).[38] Consider only a few examples from Africa: the many martyrs in the first three centuries whose blood was seed for future churches; those who gave their life for the faith during the seventh-century Muslim conquest; the Muslim apologist Ramon Llull (1232–1316); and more recent stories like those of the Malagasy Martyrs of Madagascar (1831–1865),[39] the Buganda Martyrs (1885–1887), and faithful martyrs today in Nigeria and elsewhere along the bloody borders of Islam.

God has used this history of persecution and suffering to mature his church and motivate their endurance (Rom. 5:3; Heb. 10:32–36). The church is called to be sojourners and exiles in the world, with times of peace and sociopolitical protection being the exception and not the norm. It is especially in times of persecution that the church has learned to witness "with gentleness and respect" (1 Pet. 3:15). Though historical studies of apologetics have often focused on the defense of the faith by Christians and churches in positions of power and influence, there is also much to learn from the church's defense in times of marginalization and persecution.

Christ's Preservation of His Church

These historical themes summarize two thousand years of Christian witness (fig. 8). They are not exclusive or exhaustive; at many times,

---

37 As Luther wrote: "For, where God built a church, there the devil would also build a chapel. . . . In such sort is the devil always God's ape." See volume 2 of *Colloquia Mensalia* (1566), trans. Henry Bell as *Martin Luther's Divine Discourses* (1652).

38 For a list of 2,550 martyrs, see Barrett and Johnson, *World Christian Trends*, 247–64.

39 This inspiring story of tragedy and triumph is told by F. Graeme Smith, *Triumph in Death: The Story of the Malagasy Martyrs* (Hertfordshire, UK: Evangelical Press, 1987).

multiple themes work concurrently. There are also many other motifs that could be highlighted, such as the ever-present activities of the church's evangelistic proclamation and evangelistic worship, to be considered systematically in part 3.

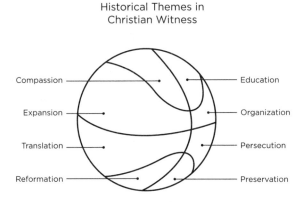

Figure 8. Historical themes in Christian witness.

One more historical theme must be mentioned before we conclude this chapter: Christ's preservation of his church. This eighth theme is behind the scenes, not scientifically observable in human history. Yet it is equally significant, and a great comfort to all Christian witnesses. From his position of power in heaven, Christ is building his church (Matt. 16:18). He is opening the successive times and seasons of church history, directing various combinations of these historical themes while preserving his people through it all, not allowing the powers of hell to prevail against them (Rom. 8:31–38; 2 Pet. 2:9). Christ's preservation of his church will continue, until the last day when he returns at the end of mission to bring this history to its grand conclusion.

This chapter is a concise overview, like looking at the landscape from an airplane window. It is impossible from this perspective to identify the details or finer points, but we can see the major motifs and reoccurring patterns. Such high-level study is helpful for seeing the whole, and for reflecting on how the church should engage in gospel witness for the future until Christ returns.

The study of Christian witness across church history is a valuable exercise. Through it, we learn how God used various methods of witness to advance Christ's kingdom. We also learn from those who have gone before us, trying to avoid their errors and excesses while emulating their devotion and methods suitable for our own context. The study of this history helps us praise God for his wonderful works, giving him glory for the ways he has used imperfect men and women across the centuries to accomplish his perfect plan.

Discussion Questions

1. Briefly describe each of the seven major historical themes of Christian witness.

2. Reflect on this statement: church history is a long sequence of failures and successes in gospel translation for indigenous witness. How is your church a part of this history, and what can you learn from those who have gone before?

3. How does the historical theme of reformation compare with and complement the theme of expansion in Christian witness?

4. What lessons can your church learn from the historical themes of education and compassion as your church learns to faithfully follow Christ today?

5. Imagine a map of the world with the areas of persecution shaded in red. How has the picture of this map changed over the course of history during the past two thousand years?

PART 3

OUR WITNESS IN AN
UN-CHRISTIAN WORLD

7

Christian Witness as Gospel Presence

WHAT SHOULD CHRISTIAN WITNESS look like in practice? Evangelistic ministries, both local and global, are perhaps the most obvious examples of Christian witness. Many other examples are common among churches today: the support of missionary families and international gospel partnerships; various activities such as church planting, church member discipleship and training, and church-based community outreach; an assortment of apologetic ministries in diverse forms; and a host of other effective activities by faithful Christians both with and alongside the church.

Christian witness, however, is much more than simply the sum of all these separate ministry activities. It is easy to think that our churches are faithful in witness when our church community as a whole is busy doing some of these activities at specific times and in particular places. But witness as merely ministry activity is not enough. The witness of the church is deeper and more comprehensive; Christian witness is essential to the identity and calling of the church.

The first part of this book studied the biblical story of God's mission to learn how Christian witness is grounded in God's word and located within God's mission. Then we surveyed church history briefly in part 2 to learn from the various methods of witness used by those who have gone before us. Now we are ready to reflect on several essential aspects of Christian witness in the un-Christian world. Our goal in part 3 is to reflect theologically on the church's witness in contemporary practice. Informed discussion about contemporary methods and principles for witness in today's world today will help us make relevant applications for our own churches and ministries. We start in this chapter by focusing specifically on the church's identity and calling in society, beginning with a fuller definition of Christian witness.

Aspects of the Church's Witness

Christian witness[1] is a comprehensive biblical concept, like the *new covenant* or *history of redemption*, making it impossible to define with several exegetical studies or a few biblical examples. We started to define Christian witness in the introduction, distinguishing between God's mission and the church's witness. Then, based on our study of biblical theology, we expanded this definition in chapter 5: the role of the church after Pentecost is to bear witness to Christ by participating in God's mission through evangelism, apologetics, global gospel partnerships, church planting, compassion ministries, biblical counseling, cultural engagement, gospel worship, gospel suffering, and the many other related aspects of Christian witness. Having briefly surveyed the more common methods of witness in church history, I now suggest a more precise definition.

Table 4. Biblical and historical aspects of witness

Showcase Community	Gospel Living	Expansion
Loving Confrontation	Gospel Speaking	Reformation
Expectant Worship	Gospel Defense	Translation
		Organization
Discipleship	Gospel Increase	Education
Compassion	Gospel Suffering	Compassion
		Persecution

---

1   As indicated in the introduction, I use the terms *Christian witness* and *the witness of the church* somewhat interchangeably. However, the first term often accents the personal practice of all believers, whereas the second term usually highlights the corporate testimony of the local gathering of God's people.

The concept of *Christian witness* encapsulates the many ways in which God's church is empowered by God's Spirit to give testimony in the world about God's redemption in Christ. It includes a multifaceted array of the many different biblical and historical aspects of bearing witness to Christ (table 4). In the Old Testament, God's people participated in God's mission by living as a showcase community, by the loving confrontation of error, and by expectant worship of the only true God. In the New Testament, God's people bore witness to Christ by gospel living, gospel speaking, gospel defense, gospel increase, and gospel suffering. Since Pentecost, the church has borne witness to Christ by practicing these ten aspects of witness within various contexts, and by engaging in this witness with a variety of methods and strategies. Our definition of Christian witness, therefore, is determined by Scripture and guided by church history. Several observations help clarify this definition.

First, the church's witness is defined by and practiced within God's mission. This is the reason we began our study with the biblical story of God's redemption. The witness of the church serves within the Father's mission and is a continuation of the ongoing mission of Christ. The church's witness, built on the foundation of witness in the Old Testament, is continued and expanded in the New Testament. This witness is empowered by and cooperates with the Spirit's mission to glorify Christ. Thus, the witness of the church must always seek to participate in and advance God's mission, or else it is not mission at all but—at best—a postscript in God's plan. Bearing witness to God's promise in Christ continues to be the role of the church in the world.

Second, Christian witness is not everything.[2] Witness is distinct from the doxology of God's people: "Missions exist because worship

2   This statement echoes discussions in missiology: Stephen Neill (1964) said, "If everything is mission, nothing is mission," though in practice he limited it to a broad scope of Christian activities. David Bosch (1991) wrote, "Ultimately, mission remains undefinable," which is the logical conclusion if Scripture is viewed as merely contextual. John Stott (1975) is more guarded, saying mission is "everything the church is sent into the world to do." These quotes come from DeYoung and

doesn't. Worship is ultimate, not missions. . . ."[3] Witness is also distinct from the creational calling of all people to cultivate and preserve God's world, though often the work environment is a wonderful way to bear witness to how Christ is transforming our whole beings (Gen. 2:15; Rom. 12:1–2). Additionally, we distinguish between the inward facing ministry of the church and the outward facing witness of the church, while recognizing that churches with mature internal ministries are best suited to be mature witnesses in society. Furthermore, as noted in previous chapters, our witness must be distinguished from God's redemptive mission, Christ's unique mission, and the mission of God's Spirit in the world. The church's witness, though essential and wide-ranging, is only a part of God's plan.

Nevertheless, Christian witness is a comprehensive concept in Scripture, spanning the whole history of God's redemption. Furthermore, as part of the church's identity, it must not be segregated from other essential characteristics of the church, relegated to a small compartment of Christian living, or briefly mentioned at the end of the theological encyclopedia. It is most helpful, therefore, to define this broad concept—as we have done—by looking specifically at the many aspects of witness in Scripture and church history. We have answered the question, What is Christian witness? by examining how the church has always engaged in witness as participants in God's mission. With this fuller definition, we now can reflect further on various contemporary issues related to the theory and practice of Christian witness. We start in this chapter by considering the identity and calling of the church for witness.

The Church's Spiritual Identity

Suppose that you were a Greek-speaking citizen living in the pluralistic society of Syria during the first century. How would you describe the

Gilbert who advance the discussion but do not fully answer it. Kevin DeYoung and Greg Gilbert, *What Is the Mission of the Church?* (Wheaton, IL: Crossway, 2011), 15–27.

3   John Piper, *Let the Nations Be Glad* (Grand Rapids, MI: Baker, 1993), 11.

new sect of religious devotees who were beginning to get attention all over the Roman world? They were not Jews, though many of their leaders were Jewish and they held similar beliefs. They were not Barbarians, nor were they only North Africans or Hellenists. They did not worship the gods; they did not follow the philosophers; they abstained from the immoral practices of most people in society. They were not exclusively slaves, nor were they exclusively merchants or fishermen. Rather they were a diverse mixture of all nationalities and languages, people from all walks of life and economic classes.[4] What social label should be given to this new united multiethnic religious community?

This new religious movement was given a new name in society: *Christian*, since adherents were disciples of Christ (Acts 11:26). Their new social identity set the church apart as an eclectic group of people who followed "the Way" (Acts 19:9, 23; 24:14, 22). Even outsiders recognized the powerful witness of their unique identity and their unity in Christ (Acts 4:21; 5:13), which was a preliminary answer to Christ's prayer (John 17:21). Their new identity and name in society, though perhaps pejorative at first, expressed the essence of their community: a diverse community of people who were united in Christ and learning to follow him.

The church's identity, however, was more than just a unique social label or distinct cultural characteristic in the first-century Roman world. It was also, more importantly, a new spiritual identity in Christ. For example, Paul gives considerable attention to how people of all nations are united with ethnic Jews in Christ; though formerly strangers and foreigners, they are now "fellow citizens with the saints and members of the household of God" (Eph. 2.19). Peter also highlights this new spiritual identity: "Once you were not a people, but now you are God's people" (1 Pet. 2:10).

---

4   The *Epistle to Diognetus* states, "For Christians are not distinguished from the rest of mankind either in locality or in speech or in customs." See Joseph Barber Lightfoot, *The Apostolic Fathers* (Grand Rapids, MI: Christian Classics Ethereal Library, 1956), 193.

This is a significant fact: the church itself, as a new sociospiritual community united in Christ, is itself a public testimony to the truth of Christ's reconciliation. Their deep united fellowship was itself a message to society, not only of social harmony but especially of spiritual peace with God through the atoning blood of Christ (Acts 4:32–33; Eph. 2:13–17). While the social activity of each church member is important, the very essence of a strong church community is itself a powerful witness. Therefore, the witness of the church's presence in society precedes any of its witnessing activities of word or deed.

The witness of the church in society is not evidenced merely by *what* we say or do, but—more importantly—by *who* we are; the sociospiritual *identity* of the church is even more of a witness to truth about Christ than is our *activity*. Jesus did not say, "You must stay busy with various witnessing activities." He did not even say, "Do the work of an evangelist." Rather, Christ said, "You will be my witnesses" (Acts 1:8). Actions speak louder than words, but appearance and character speak the loudest.

All true believers "are witnesses" of Christ (Acts 2:32; 3:15; 5:32; 10:39). The identity of being a witness (noun) precedes the activity of witnessing (verb). We must start our theological reflection on the church's witness by noting this important reality: the church is a witness in essence and nature, which should then result in the church's many activities of witnessing in practice. Furthermore, the church's identity as witnesses of Christ is also more than a mere calling or function they must perform in the world (as considered later). Their identity flows from being in spiritual union with Christ, and consequently being indwelt and empowered by the Spirit of Christ.[5]

Lord's Day 12 of the Heidelberg Catechism provides a starting point and framework for understanding this important truth as it relates to the

---

5   As Henry Martyn wrote, "Tell them to live more with Christ, to preach Christ, to catch his spirit, for the spirit of Christ is the spirit of Missions. The nearer we get to Him the more intensely missionary we become." Quoted in Lettie Cowman, *Charles E. Cowman: Missionary Warrior* (Los Angeles, CA: Oriental Missionary Society, 1939), 116.

witness of all believers (table 5). Question 31 is structured around the threefold office of Christ as prophet, priest, and king, which is a helpful way to summarize his multifaceted ministry as it was typified and anticipated in the Old Testament.[6] Question 32 then famously applies the pattern of Christ's threefold ministry to all who have been united in Christ, describing the groundwork for the office of all believers. Consider several observations drawn from these catechism questions.

Table 5. Heidelberg Catechism, Lord's Day 12

Question 31	Question 32
Why is he called "Christ," meaning "anointed"?	But why are you called a Christian?
Because he has been ordained by God the Father and has been anointed with the Holy Spirit to be	Because by faith I am a member of Christ and so I share in his anointing. I am anointed
our chief prophet and teacher who fully reveals to us the secret counsel and will of God concerning our deliverance;	to confess his name,
our only high priest who has delivered us by the one sacrifice of his body, and who continually intercedes for us before the Father;	to present myself to him as a living sacrifice of thanks,
and our eternal king, who governs us by his Word and Spirit, and who guards and keeps us in the deliverance he has won for us.	to strive with a free conscience against sin and the devil in this life, and afterward to reign with Christ over all creation for eternity.

6   This threefold office framework was recognized in the early church. For example, fourth-century writer Eusebius of Caesarea developed Christ's threefold office of prophet, priest, and king from Luke 4:18–19 (cf. Isa. 61:1–4). Most theologians view all the other roles of Christ as falling under one of these three distinctions. John Calvin uses this framework to explain Christ's work and ongoing ministry; see *Institutes of the Christian Religion*, ed. John T. McNeill, trans. Ford Lewis Battles (Philadelphia: Westminster Press, 1960), 2.15.1–6. Other classic examples include William Perkins, *The Works of William Perkins*, vol. 1 (Grand Rapids, MI: RHB, 2014), 169; Francis Turretin, *Institutes of Elenctic Theology*, vol. 2 (Phillipsburg, NJ: P&R, 1994), 393; Westminster Larger Catechism, q. 42–45; Westminster Shorter Catechism, q. 23–26; and the London Baptist Confession, 8.9–10.

First, as taught by question 31, Christ's threefold ministry is not limited to his completed mission of redemption as the suffering servant but continues today in his ongoing mission as the exalted sender, as we considered in chapter 2. Christ's ongoing ministry works *within* each believer personally and also corporately *for* and *with* the church. As our prophet, he has perfectly revealed God to the world, and he now continues to teach and guide the church by means of his word and Spirit (Matt. 11:27; Luke 24:45; John 1:14). As our high priest, he has made atonement with God for all his people, and he now "always lives to make intercession for them" (Heb. 7:25; cf. John 17:9). As our king, he has conquered the power of death, and he continues to deliver and preserve his church until the last day (Rom. 8:37; Heb. 2:14–15).

Second, question 32 teaches how each believer participates individually in Christ's ongoing threefold ministry by public confession, holistic Christian living, and spiritual warfare. This answer is personal and experiential, the great strength of the Heidelberg Catechism. Yet this truth is not limited to the inward-facing personal spirituality of salvation but must also be extended to the corporate life of the church community. In union with Christ, the whole church community together confesses gospel truth in society. In thankful worship of Christ, the whole church is transformed for priestly gospel service in society. In obedient submission to Christ, the whole church seeks first the gospel of the kingdom and its righteousness in society. This threefold office of all believers includes the church's outward-facing spirituality of gospel witness.[7]

Third, "by faith I am a member of Christ and so I share in his anointing." This phrase in answer 32 highlights two conjoined doctrines that have great importance for the witness of all believers today. Being in

7   Considerable attention has been given to the ministry of Christ and his Spirit *in* the believer personally. Less attention has been given to this ministry *through* and *with* the church, a distinction we noted in chapter 3: the Spirit's ministry *for our salvation* and *with God's people*. Yet the Reformers and Puritans did not overlook this important area.

union with Christ, we are mystically united in him as spiritual members of his body (1 Cor. 12:12–13; Eph. 1:3–14). As spiritual members of Christ's body by faith, we live and move in him, and thus his ministry shapes and guides our ministry.

Being partakers of his anointing, we are clothed with power by Christ's Spirit for this threefold office of ministry. As Christ was anointed by the Spirit for his mission (Luke 4:18–19; cf. Isa. 61:1–4), so all believers are also anointed, sharing together in fellowship with the same indwelling Spirit and being empowered for ministry (Luke 24:49; Acts 2:17; 2 Cor. 1:21; 1 John 2:27). As seen in chapter 3, the Holy Spirit ministers in us and through us to accomplish his mission of proclaiming Christ to the world. We are anointed with and empowered by Christ's Spirit for the threefold office of all believers, including the outward-facing ministry of Christian witness.

The Witness of All Believers

The office of all believers is a beautiful doctrine that was revived during the European Reformation. Luther taught that each individual believer has direct access to God, without human mediation through the clergy, and that every believer shares in the whole ministry of the church. Calvin further developed this doctrine: Christ is the perfect office bearer and he "also admits us into this most honourable alliance."[8] The threefold office, though in a special way applied to church leaders, is not limited to the clergy alone but can be applied generally to the laity as well, to all members of Christ's spiritual body.[9]

---

8 As John Calvin says, "Christ now bears the office of priest, not only that by the eternal law of reconciliation he may render the Father favourable and propitious to us, but also admit us into this most honourable alliance. For we, though in ourselves polluted, in him being priests (Rev. 1:6), offer ourselves and our all to God, and freely enter the heavenly sanctuary, so that the sacrifices of prayer and praise which we present are grateful and of sweet odour before him" (*Institutes*, 2.15.6).

9 For example, Wilhelmus à Brakel, a theologian of the Dutch Second Reformation, applies practically the doctrine of Christ's office of prophet with an exhortation to engage in evangelism. Brakel, *The Christian's Reasonable Service*, vol. 2 (Ligonier, PA: Soli Deo Gloria Publications, 1993), 2.534–37.

One specific application of this Protestant doctrine is especially important for Christian witness: flowing from their union with Christ, all believers are witnesses in the world, anointed by Christ's Spirit, in order to serve in his threefold office.[10] Similar to God's covenant people in the Old Testament, the church today has a holy identity and calling to serve in society as prophets, priests, and kings.

A Holy Company of Prophets

In the Old Testament, God's people were keepers of his covenant, called to live within society according to his truth, as a witness to the surrounding nations. The prophets proclaimed God's word, as his advocates among Israel and the nations, confronting disobedience and calling people to live according to God's truth. Samuel, Elijah, and many sons of the prophets to follow continued in the prophetic tradition of Moses who looked forward to the coming of God's final prophet (Deut. 18:15; Acts 3:22–26). Then Christ took on flesh as God's final Word, perfectly fulfilling the Old Testament prophetic office (John 1:18; Heb. 1:2; 2 Pet. 1:18–19). Now Christ the exalted sender continues to direct God's global mission, primarily through the agency of his Spirit and his church.

The Holy Spirit indwells all believers and at times anoints them, empowering them to serve in Christ's continuing prophetic ministry today. Moses's wish that all God's people would be prophets is now fulfilled after Pentecost since even the lowliest servants in the church have received Christ's Spirit in order to communicate his word with boldness (Num. 11:29; Acts 2:17–18).[11] Consider for example the wit-

10 Unfortunately, this doctrine has been abused in many ways. Consider, for example, the overabundance of self-appointed "superanointed" leaders with their cults of personality, or the hyperindividualism of "Bible experts" who, though untaught and out of step with the Spirit of truth, assume their own interpretations are infallible. The frequent abuse of this doctrine, while also requiring corrective action, especially calls for a renewed focus on its proper use, tested within the orthodox church community, based on God's word alone and for God's glory alone.

11 Christ's prophetic ministry continues in this limited way, not with new revelation (Rev. 22:18–19) but in his continued activity through his people. For example, the whole church is called to engage in evangelism as they are filled by the Spirit to repeat his word, bearing witness to Christ and telling

ness of a godly young woman studying in a secular university. There will inevitably be opportunities for witness as she interacts with her classmates and other unbelievers. But she need not fear, since according to the truth we confess in the Heidelberg Catechism, she is a spiritual member of Christ and thus a partaker of his anointing. By faith, she can confess Christ boldly, knowing that the Spirit has promised to empower her to speak God's word with power (Luke 12:11–12). Believers today speak prophetically at times when Christ's Spirit powerfully repeats God's truth through them to illumine and convict people around them who are living in sin.

Scripture also pictures the prophetic presence of the church in society as a city on a hill that is an example for all human civilization (Matt. 5:14; 1 Thess. 1:7–8; Rev. 21:10; contra Gen. 11:4), as light to illumine ethically, and as salt to preserve morally many societies in a world of darkness and decay (Matt. 5:13–16; Phil. 2:15; Col. 4:6). God's people, dispersed across all social strata, can serve as a leavening influence for good within the whole (Matt. 13:33).

As God's prophetic messenger to the world, the church is a herald greater than John the Baptist, called to lovingly convict all peoples with the truth of God's law by displaying this truth in ethical examples and by calling sinners back to ethical living. The church is "the aroma of Christ to God" among all nations, which becomes for some people a pleasant fragrance of spiritual life, but for others the smell of the death that is quickly approaching (2 Cor. 2:14–16). The church is also a harbinger of hope in this broken world, warning of coming judgment while also proclaiming God's gracious overtures of mercy to repentant rebels.

As a holy company of prophets, all believers in the church collectively are God's pastor-teachers as they together serve one another by mentoring and shepherding all the people of God. Many believers are gifted by the

---

all nations the good news about him. See Brakel, *Reasonable Service*, 2.534–37; cf. Iain M. Duguid, "What Kind of Prophecy Continues?" in *Redeeming the Life of the Mind* (Wheaton, IL: Crossway, 2017), 126–28.

Spirit of wisdom to live as God's sages in influential places, like Daniel, in order to display and declare the true source of wisdom. The church often functions as God's advocates in society, like Amos or Ezekiel, who warn all people about the outcomes of rebellion, calling society back to God's law "whether they hear or refuse to hear" (Ezek. 2:5; cf. Amos 5:23–24).

A Holy Community of Priests

The Old Testament showcase community was consecrated to be a kingdom of priests. This identity and office, however, was only partially realized by Israel in the Old Testament since their unethical living and spiritual idolatry hindered their priestly witness. Christ perfectly fulfills the biblical office of priest (Heb. 7). Christ's atoning sacrifice was once for all, by which the church is being made a spiritual kingdom of priests to God in preparation for perfected worship (Rev. 1:6; 5:10; 20:6). Other aspects of Christ's priestly ministry continue today, both within each believer personally and through the church collectively (John 10:16; 17:20; Rom. 10:14; Heb. 7:25). Paul's gospel witness to the nations was a priestly service (Rom. 15:16; cf. Isa. 61:6; Mal. 1:11; 3:4), and the church today is called to follow Paul as he followed Christ (1 Cor. 11:1). Thus, in union with Christ and anointed by his Spirit, all believers are called to serve in this spiritual priesthood.

How can members of your church serve as a spiritual priesthood in your own context? Consider, for example, the conduct of a godly businessman in a work environment. He prays for his colleagues and occasionally has opportunities to pray with them for their needs. His genuine compassion and generosity toward others is noticed and appreciated. He is known as a wise counselor and a peacemaker who heals broken relationships. The Spirit empowers him to be a godly example in order to attract unbelievers to glorify God (1 Pet. 2:12). Though unbelievers despise our message, they cannot ignore the good deeds that God produces in and through us (Eph. 2:10; Col. 1:10; Titus 2:7–8). Consider how we can serve in each of the following areas.

Believers participate in the priestly *service of intercession*. God's people are a kingdom of priests in society with the official responsibility of praying for all people in the world (1 Tim. 2:1–10; cf. Gen. 8:21; Jer. 29:7; Ezra 6:10). We also pray for our own consecration in this spiritual priesthood so that we may better serve in this broken world.[12]

Believers share in the priestly *service of consecration*. The church community is called out of the world and set apart for holy service, not only as individuals in personal sanctification but also collectively by the purification of Christ's spiritual body, the whole church and temple of the living God (1 Cor. 5:7; 2 Cor. 6:14–7:1). Thus, believers are often urged by the Holy Spirit to increase in holiness, to live separate from defilement, and to flee worldliness (Phil. 2:15; 1 Pet. 2:11; 1 John 5:21), since the spiritual consecration of believers greatly expands and amplifies their witness in society (Isa. 56:7; Ezek. 20:41; Mal. 3:4).

Believers embody the priestly *service of compassion*. As Christ perfectly personified God's loving mercy for all lost sinners in this broken world, so we must also demonstrate tangible acts of mercy in society as an indelible witness to God's truth (Heb. 13:16; 1 Pet. 2:12; 1 John 3:17). James calls all believers to action: the best way to prove the genuineness of our faith alone in Christ alone is by visibly displaying Christ's gospel through our good works (James 2:14–26). We know our actions of compassion will never eradicate poverty or eliminate suffering; these noble desires are not the ultimate goal of our witness.

---

12 As John Calvin prayed after explaining Malachi 3:4: "Grant, Almighty God, that since Thou hast been pleased to choose us as priests to Thyself, not that we may offer beasts to Thee, but consecrate to Thee ourselves, and all that we have, O grant, that we may with all readiness strive to depart from every kind of uncleanness, and to purify ourselves from all defilements, so that we may duly perform the sacred office of priesthood, and thus conduct ourselves towards Thee with chasteness and purity; may we also abstain from every evil work, from all fraud and all cruelty towards our brethren, and so to deal with one another as to prove through our whole life that Thou art really our Father, ruling us by Thy Spirit, and that true and holy brotherhood exists between us; and may we live justly towards one another, so as to render to each his own right, and thus show that we are members of Thy only-begotten Son, so as to be owned by Him when He shall appear for the redemption of His people, and shall gather us into His celestial kingdom. Amen." Calvin, *Commentaries on the Twelve Minor Prophets*, vol. 5 (Louisville, KY: Westminster John Knox, 2006), 586.

Rather, as priestly witnesses of Christ, we desire to embody his gracious character and display his tender compassion to all people, not only to prove the genuineness of our faith but especially as further confirmation of the authenticity of his gospel (Mark 16:20).

Believers today symbolize the priestly *service of benediction*. In worship the church approaches God in intercession for society, and then in work and witness the church returns to society to share God's blessings with society. Indeed, all families of the earth are now being blessed by the spiritual children of Abraham, who in Christ have become a kingdom of priests within the whole of creation. The church's presence in society is like leaven that influences the whole: by grace, God's people are not overcome by evil since they live in such a way as to overcome evil with good (Rom. 12:21). The church demonstrates God's goodness to society, so that the world will praise God when they see the church's good deeds (Gal. 6:9–10; 1 Thess. 5:15; Titus 2:7–8; 1 Pet. 2:15).

Finally, believers are a foretaste of the priestly *service of restoration*. Christ's ministry announced the beginning of jubilee. Now the church's presence in society is living proof of this spiritual liberty that is already being experienced by many in this present age, and also a sign of the final liberation that is still coming (Luke 4:19; Rom. 8:23). As God's priests in society, the church is given a ministry of reconciliation in which they implore sinners to find spiritual peace with God through Christ, while they also promote peace on earth as much as possible this side of heaven (2 Cor. 5:17–20). The church also demonstrates and promotes the restoration of all social relationships (Eph. 5:1–2). God's holy community is both a counterexample to the world's self-destructing societies, and also a foretaste of the future perfected community in glory, the restored creation in which even the wolf will lie peacefully with the lamb (Isa. 65:17–25).

A Holy Lineage of Princes

How are believers anointed by the Spirit to serve as kings? We could describe the church as those who by spiritual adoption are members of the royal family of Christ to reign as kings. But this title is premature for the present time. We are kings, but for now we are merely kings in preparation and humiliation; only later will we reign with Christ in exaltation (Dan. 7:18; Heb. 12:28; Rev. 22:5). Our captain and fore-runner has gone ahead, and we anticipate the joy of this glory (Heb. 2:10; 6:20; 12:2), even while we are called to suffer a little longer in this valley of tears (Rom. 8:14–18; 1 Pet. 4:12–16).[13] Hence, before the final return of the King, the regal presence of the church in the world is best described as a holy lineage of princes and princesses.

Through Christ's blood and victory over death, all believers have been adopted into the royal family of the messianic King, who now sits as almighty sovereign on his throne in heaven. Yet we are still living on earth, as churches under the cross in suffering. By faith, we confess our spiritual lineage, even though our true identity is not yet fully realized nor recognized by the rebellious world.

First, as the King's children, we are presently *spiritual exiles* in a world that rages against God and his anointed one. Scripture often describes God's people as a minority group in a hostile environment; they are so-journers and foreigners (1 Pet. 2:11) and a remnant of refugees among the nations (Isa. 1:8; 10:20–23). The church is a people pursued by evil into the wilderness (Rev. 12:6). Christ's own prayer summarizes the church's presence in society: "sent into the world" but "not of the world" (John 17:14–18). As spiritual exiles, however, the church's witness is far from silenced. As Paul's witness while in chains gave him a greater audience to proclaim Christ, so the church in exile often has a greater witness

---

13 This truth is confessed beautifully in question 49 of the Heidelberg Catechism on the benefits of Christ's ascension. As Charles Simeon said, "We must not mind a little suffering for Christ's sake [our Head]. When I am getting through a hedge, if my head and shoulders are safely through, I can bear the pricking of my legs. Let us rejoice in the remembrance that our holy Head has surmounted all His suffering and triumphed over death. Let us follow Him patiently; we shall soon be partakers of His victory." H. C. G. Moule, *Charles Simeon* (London: InterVarsity, 1948), 155–56; quoted by John Piper in "Brothers, We Must Not Mind a Little Suffering: Meditations on the Life of Charles Simeon," Desiring God website, April 15, 1989, https://www.desiring god.org/.

within the world while living faithfully in a position of sociopolitical weakness. The church continues to witness through the doxology of expectant worship, even if the gospel message is proclaimed by songs of lament in a strange land (Ps. 137:4). Thus, God's people in exile learn to display a message of hope, living with expectation for a better country (Heb. 11:10, 13–16) while seeking the welfare of the society in which, by God's providence, they are placed (Jer. 29:4–7; Matt. 6:33).[14]

Second, we are *spiritual pilgrims* traveling toward a better country. We live simultaneously in two realms, citizens both of this world by natural birth and of God's holy nation by spiritual rebirth. We are also on pilgrimage between two cities, fleeing the city of destruction and journeying toward the glorious city of God. The witness of gospel community, therefore, is both a warning message against the idolatry in this natural realm and also a hopeful message about the imminent spiritual reality of Christ's kingdom.

Third, as the King's children, we are *spiritual soldiers* who are engaged in a spiritual warfare. Though this warfare includes cosmic dimensions (2 Cor. 10:3–6; Col. 1:13), it begins with spiritual battles against personal sin as we put on the whole armor of God to abstain from fleshly lusts and to remain steadfast in trial.[15] Like Christ, we openly confess that our kingdom is not of this world (John 18:36). Yet we must fight against the devil's lies while living as countercultural examples of God's truth in the often ambiguous battle zone between good and evil. By

---

14 As Samuel Zwemer (1867–1952) noted, many faithful witnesses of former years "had this 'inverted homesickness,' this passion to call that country their home which was most in need of the Gospel. In this passion all other passions died; before this vision all other visions faded; this call drowned all other voices. They were the pioneers of the Kingdom, the forerunners of God, eager to cross the border-marches . . ." ("The Glory of the Impossible" in *The Unoccupied Mission Fields of Africa and Asia* [New York: Student Volunteer Movement, 1911], 222).

15 See the Heidelberg Catechism, q. 123: "What does the second petition mean? 'Your kingdom come' means: Rule us by your Word and Spirit in such a way that more and more we submit to you. Preserve and increase your church. Destroy the devil's works; destroy every force which revolts against you and every conspiracy against your holy Word. Do all this until your kingdom fully comes, when you will be all in all" (*CCC* 330).

grace, the church militant makes spiritual conquest, sometimes while as refugees or prisoners of war, living as spiritual soldiers in the trenches for the present time.

Finally, as the King's children, we are *spiritual ambassadors* for Christ as we live within enemy territory. The church has been officially appointed and anointed to represent Christ, speaking on his behalf as ambassadors of his kingdom hope, and imploring all people to seek reconciliation with the triune God of heaven (2 Cor. 5:14–20). The church, as God's covenant community and spiritual society, continues to publicly reveal the mystery of Christ's spiritual kingdom (Eph. 3:10; 6:20). We join with the church of all ages to echo Christ's word as we publicly proclaim the year of jubilee that has come and the day of judgment that is coming.

Consider the testimony of Polycarp of Smyrna (69–155), who lived and died faithfully as a spiritual prince in the royal family of Christ. When urged by the governor to curse Christ, Polycarp replied: "For eighty-six years have I served him, and He has done me no wrong, and how can I blaspheme my King who saved me?"[16] For this confession he was condemned to death. Like Polycarp, we also are called to live and die as witnesses of the King who has saved us, and who has gone before us into glory.

The Church's Renewed Calling

Christian witness, therefore, is embodied in the church's spiritual identity, as expressed through the witness of all believers. It is also central to the spiritual calling of the New Testament church, as we will now consider. This truth is concisely expressed in 1 Peter 2:9–12:

> But you are a chosen race, a royal priesthood, a holy nation, a people
> for his own possession, that you may proclaim the excellencies of

---

16 Eusebius Pamphili, *Ecclesiastical History* (Washington, DC: Catholic University, 1953), book 4.15, 237–38.

him who called you out of darkness into his marvelous light. Once
you were not a people, but now you are God's people; once you had
not received mercy, but now you have received mercy.

Beloved, I urge you as sojourners and exiles to abstain from the
passions of the flesh, which wage war against your soul. Keep your
conduct among the Gentiles honorable, so that when they speak
against you as evildoers, they may see your good deeds and glorify
God on the day of visitation.

The apostle Peter wrote this epistle to the Christian dispersion, the
various communities of believers scattered across the Roman world. Many
of these believers were beginning to suffer for their faith in Christ, an
experience that caused discouragement and confusion about their place in
society. Peter wrote to give renewed hope, exhorting the believers to spiritual endurance and obedience in Christ, and grounding their experience
in the identity and calling of God's church within an opposing world.

Peter's teaching here reinforces what we have been considering: in
their union with Christ, God's people have a new spiritual identity in the
world. Peter highlights the contrast between what these believers once
were and what they have now become in Christ. Though "sojourners
and exiles" in an un-Christian society, in Christ they are a new spiritual
community enjoying their special covenant relationship with God.

Yet the essence of God's church is not new; it is deeply rooted in and
continues from Old Testament history. Peter deliberately grounds his
doctrine of the church in the story of God's Old Testament covenant
people, quoting from Exodus and Hosea to prove this point. His quote
of Exodus 19:6 (cf. 1 Pet. 2:9) is most significant since this passage, as
considered in chapter 1, is foundational to Israel's calling to be witnesses
as God's showcase community.

Therefore the Spirit, speaking through Peter, links God's Old and New
Testament people, identifying them both as objects of God's redemptive
mission who also are called to be agents in God's mission as witnesses

among the nations. The following analogies concisely express this biblical reality. As God's people in the Old Testament were set apart from the nations and given a new identity in God's covenant community, so the New Testament church is distinguished from society and given a new spiritual identity in Christ. As God's covenant people were called to be a showcase community and a light to the nations, so the New Testament church is described with the same spiritual identity and calling, in order that they "may proclaim the excellencies of him who called you out of darkness into his marvelous light" (1 Pet. 2:9). Thus the church today, following Christ's coronation and the Spirit's empowerment, continues to participate in God's mission, but now in a much grander way and with a much broader scope.

This doctrine of the church—which some have labeled *missional ecclesiology*—is foundational for our understanding and practice of Christian witness.[17] The identity and calling of God's church is defined by and rooted in God's mission. The very presence of God's church in the world is itself a gospel witness to the world. Indeed, the witness of the church begins with its spiritual calling to preserve and promote this gospel presence in society.

This passage, like much of 1 Peter, defines the church's gospel presence in society. Through Peter, the Spirit teaches all churches how to live in relation to the world, especially when society is hostile to their gospel identity and witness. As objects of his mercy, God's people have been called out of sinful society and into holy fellowship in Christ. As such, the very presence in society of this new identity is a powerful witness of gospel truth.

The church is *called to preserve* this gospel presence in order to be faithful witnesses in society. Note the sharp contrast: darkness versus light and

---

17   I hesitate to use the adjective *missional* to describe Peter's doctrine of the church for several reasons. As noted previously, the word *missional* has become ambiguous since it is used in various and sometimes conflicting ways, and since it comes with some unbiblical baggage. Also, this passage clearly teaches about the church's witness in the world, regardless of whether or not it is described with this adjective; so the adjective may say more about the person using it than about what the Spirit through Peter is teaching here. However, I strongly affirm what many have used this label to describe: namely, that God's church and its witness are defined by and rooted in God's redemptive mission. Lesslie Newbigin has been influential in this area; see especially *The Household of God: Lectures on the Nature of the Church* (Carlisle, UK: Paternoster Press, 1953).

mercy-less versus mercy-full. The church's gospel presence is most observ-able in situations with the greatest contrast between sin and grace.[18] God's people, therefore, are urged to abstain from fleshly lusts; they must be careful to avoid anything that will confuse or compromise their spiritual identity in Christ. Maintaining holy consecration, especially in the midst of much spiritual opposition and great temptations to worldliness, may be the most important way for a local church to witness of Christ in society. For example, consider Daniel's witness in Babylon: he did not need to launch a campaign to influence the whole city, though presumably he could have used his position for this purpose. Instead, he simply prayed three times a day before an open window, "as he had done previously" (Dan. 6:10). Daniel's faithful presence was itself most important and greatly used by God as a powerful witness to the entire society.

The church is also *called to promote* this gospel presence in society with honorable conduct. In response to evildoers who speak against them, God's people are called to display character and conduct that is praiseworthy. The church's witness is authenticated by this honorable behavior and the good deeds among all peoples that complement it. Thus Peter implies the church's witness in society begins not with various evangelistic activities, but first and foremost with honorable conduct before a watching world.

My Church's Gospel Presence

Christian witness includes many activities; there are many tangible ways in which God's church is empowered by God's Spirit to give testimony in the world about God's redemption in Christ. In previous chapters we

---

18 Though closely related, there is not space here to consider the complex relations of Christ to culture and the church to the world. It is interesting to note, however, that much of what is promoted under the banner of contextualization overlooks the sharp contrast that Peter implies between the church and the world. Unfortunately, the motive of some contextualization is to get as close as possible to the world in order to win the world. But Scripture's focus, here and elsewhere (John 17:15–19), is on preserving a spiritual identity separate from the world in order to witness of Christ to the world. See Brian A. DeVries, "Contextualisation within Context: A Pedagogical Spectrum of Six Methodologies" in *In die Skriflig* 55, no. 1 (Oct. 2021), 1–8.

considered seventeen biblical and historical aspects of witness. As previously considered, the witness of the church is an extension of Christ's mission, the activity of Christ exercised with his church. The Spirit of Christ has anointed us to bear witness to Christ and participate in his evangelistic ministry. Christ's prophetic ministry continues through us today as we display and declare his truth within gospel community. Christ's priestly ministry continues through his church today as we defend the gospel and speak his truth with loving conviction. Christ's kingly ministry continues through us today as we seek gospel increase, even at the cost of gospel suffering, all the while confessing his truth in expectant worship. Each of these seventeen aspects of witness should be viewed as an expansion of Christ's ministry with and through his church (see fig. 9).

Furthermore, as stated at the start of this chapter, Christian witness is more than a combination of all the various evangelistic activities performed by churches and faithful Christians. These evangelistic activities are merely the consequence of a deeper reality: the church's spiritual identity and calling in Christ. Christian witness is embodied by the church's gospel presence in society. It is also demonstrated by the church's gospel message, gospel response, and gospel community in the world, as we will consider in the next three chapters.

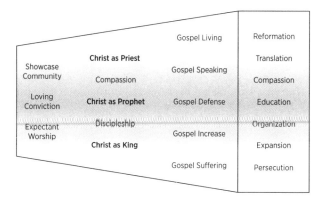

Figure 9. Christ's threefold office and our witness.

Our church may be tempted to think that we are faithful in Christian witness if we are supporting a few global missionaries, or if members of our church are at certain times of the week busy in one or another local evangelistic ministry. But this definition of witness leads to many incomplete and superficial forms of ministry today. Such thinking misses the point of this chapter: Christian witness is essential to the identity and calling of the church; it is not simply an activity the church performs at specific times. Just as there is no golden key that will unlock massive evangelistic results or any other shortcut to success in spiritual witness, so also there is no way to short-circuit genuine Christian witness by promoting a flurry of activities which give only an illusion of the holistic embodiment of gospel presence in society.

Our church must strive to witness *coram Deo*, to live our entire lives as witnesses of Christ in God's presence, under his authority, to his glory. Like spiritual worship, the witness of our church should not merely be an activity that we engage in occasionally or at certain times of the week. When our witness is genuine and faithful, then our church—both as individual members and corporately—will be witnesses of Christ at all times and in all places. Of course, the perfection of witness is impossible this side of heaven; but faithful gospel witness remains the high calling of the church.

Discussion Questions

1. Give a concise definition of Christian witness in your own words, based on our study in previous chapters of biblical theology and church history.

2. How is the witness of all believers rooted in the doctrine of the church as a member of Christ and partaker of his anointing?

3. Describe a way in which your church witnesses of Christ as prophets, as priests, and as princes. What are several other ways in which your church could witness of Christ in your local society as prophets, as priests, or as princes?

4. How does the gospel presence of the church's identity and calling precede and undergird all the activities of the church's witness in the world?

5. Why is Peter's doctrine of the church especially relevant for post-Christian and pluralistic societies that are increasingly common in the world today?

8

Christian Witness by Gospel Message

COMMUNICATION OF THE GOSPEL MESSAGE is the epicenter and passion of all Christian witness. Each of the four Gospel writers describe this message, and proclaiming it is their motivation (Mark 1:15; John 20:31; Acts 1:1). Gospel communication is also the foremost activity in the book of Acts.[1] Indeed, communicating the good news about Jesus Christ is the heart of Christian witness in the New Testament. The same is true for most of church history. As Christ's earthly ministry is the center of God's mission, so the gospel message and its communication is the center of Christian witness.

Many evangelistic theories focus on strategies, methods, motives, and other matters related to Christian witness.[2] Such study is not un-important, but it cannot be the starting place for understanding evan-gelistic communication. We must start further back, especially given all the present confusion and conflicting methodologies available today.

---

1 Communication words dominate the discourse of the books of Acts: speaking, teaching, proclaim-ing, exhorting, reasoning, appealing, urging, convicting, testifying, and so on. See David B. Barrett and Todd M. Johnson, *World Christian Trends* (Pasadena, CA: William Carey, 2001), 22.

2 For a few of many excellent studies, see Will Metzger, *Tell the Truth* (Downers Grove, IL: InterVarsity, 1981); William J. Abraham, *The Logic of Evangelism* (Grand Rapids, MI: Eerdmans, 1989); and Ryan Denton, *Even If None: Reclaiming Biblical Evangelism* (Dublin, CA: FirstLove Publications, 2019).

Communication of the gospel message must be grounded in God's mission and informed by the history of the church's witness. It must also flow directly from the church's presence in society and be shaped by theological reflection on evangelistic communication in contemporary contexts.

Christian witness begins with gospel presence. All true believers are witnesses in essence, by virtue of their spiritual identity and calling, which then results in the activity of witnessing through words and actions. Yet, gospel presence in society should always lead—sooner than later, ideally—to a verbal proclamation of the gospel message. Therefore, the next step in our study of Christian witness is to reflect theologically on this message and its communication.

What Concisely Is the Message of the Gospel?

As a major theme in Scripture, the gospel message has great significance and also great complexity, which has caused a great deal of discussion about it.[3] Unquestionably, it is central to the activity of evangelism and closely related to other major biblical themes of proclamation, salvation, and kingdom.[4] While recognizing this complexity, my intention here is to outline ten truths about the gospel in order to concisely summarize the message of Christian witness.

The gospel message is *personified, literally and fully, in the person of Christ* and the historic event of his ministry, death, and resurrection. Peter's sermon to the Gentile Cornelius in Acts 10:34–43 is one of Scripture's clearest gospel presentations:

> Truly I understand that God shows no partiality, but in every nation anyone who fears him and does what is right is acceptable to him.

---

3   Helpful reviews include D. A. Carson, "What Is the Gospel?—Revisited" in *For the Fame of God's Name* (Wheaton, IL: Crossway, 2010), 147–69; Kevin DeYoung and Greg Gilbert, *What Is the Mission of the Church?* (Wheaton, IL: Crossway, 2011), 91–113; and Tim Keller, *Center Church* (Grand Rapids, MI: Zondervan, 2012), 29–37.

4   For helpful reflection on these themes in relation to the gospel message, see Lewis A. Drummond, *The Word of the Cross: A Contemporary Theology of Evangelism* (Nashville: Broadman Press, 1992), 203–86.

As for the word that he sent to Israel, preaching good news of peace through Jesus Christ (he is Lord of all), you yourselves know what happened throughout all Judea, beginning from Galilee after the baptism that John proclaimed: how God anointed Jesus of Nazareth with the Holy Spirit and with power. He went about doing good and healing all who were oppressed by the devil, for God was with him. And we are witnesses of all that he did both in the country of the Jews and in Jerusalem. They put him to death by hanging him on a tree, but God raised him on the third day and made him to appear, not to all the people but to us who had been chosen by God as witnesses, who ate and drank with him after he rose from the dead. And he commanded us to preach to the people and to testify that he is the one appointed by God to be judge of the living and the dead. To him all the prophets bear witness that everyone who believes in him receives forgiveness of sins through his name.

Scripture speaks best for itself; yet several points can summarize Peter's sermon. The gospel is the "good news of peace" embodied by the person of Christ the Word, whom God sent first to Israel and then to "every nation." The historic gospel event tells the story of Jesus Christ: his divinely empowered earthly ministry, his death on the cross, and his resurrection by God. The apostles are divinely appointed eyewitnesses of this historic event who must proclaim it publicly and testify to its truth, like the Old Testament prophets. Thus Christian witness is, first and foremost, the public proclamation of the historic event of Christ and his ministry. Witness is, in its most basic form, the repeating of the truth about the Christ who is attested to by Scripture and the apostolic eyewitnesses. Giving a personal testimony about how God's gospel has changed us can be very powerful in evangelism, but our experience of the gospel is ancillary to the Spirit's inspired witness through the authors of Scripture. We don't add to the truth by our personal testimony; we only echo and affirm it.

The gospel message is *central to the whole history of God's redemptive mission*. As such, the gospel unifies the many major themes that run through the Old and New Testaments, giving meaning to the whole.[5] Accordingly, Christian witness is amplified by the telling of God's story of ancient promises and their fulfillment in Christ (1 Pet. 1:10–12).

The gospel message is *singular and holistic*, though described variously in Scripture and nuanced in close relation with other biblical doctrines. We can emphasize one aspect of the gospel over against others, such as the spiritual dimension of Satan's defeat[6] or the social dimension of human justice. But there is one gospel message that holistically expresses the message of Christ and our redemption through him. Many evangelistic methods have tried to reduce this message into a simple set of propositional truths; yet while these summaries can be helpful at times, they can never perfectly express the gospel in its fullness.

The gospel message is *transformative, both individually and communally*. It is more than simply a fact that must be repeated. Rather, it is the truth which, when received, affects and transforms us.[7] As such, believing the gospel is a very personal, spiritual experience. Paul even calls it "my gospel" (Rom. 2:16; 16:25). But it is also a communal experience since receiving Christ, the truth, also transforms the whole church, a collective spiritual experience that John wants many others to enjoy with him (1 John 1:1–4).

The gospel message is *most clearly highlighted in contrast with the sinful world*. The Bible's history relates how God has spoken his good news

---

5   The whole story is held together by the gospel message: sin and salvation; creation, fall, redemption, and restoration; relationship broken and restored; etc. Keller, *Center Church*, 41.

6   Some versions of spiritual warfare distort the gospel with less biblical views of Christ's atonement, by overemphasizing material power, or with many other popular distractions. For helpful corrections, see Frederick S. Leahy, *Satan Cast Out: A Study in Biblical Demonology* (Carlisle, PA: Banner of Truth, 1975), 160–70; and Keith Ferdinando, *The Triumph of Christ in African Perspective* (Carlisle, UK: Paternoster, 1999), 396–407.

7   Lesslie Newbigin writes: "The Christian story provides us with such a set of lenses, not something for us to look *at*, but for us to look *through*." Newbigin, *The Gospel in a Pluralist Society* (Grand Rapids, MI: Eerdmans, 1989), 38.

of peace in the context of sinners who are rebelling against him. The bad news context of sin and its deadly consequences, therefore, starkly outlines the good news of God's amazing grace. Thus Christian witness should never try to ignore or minimize the badness of the present context, but instead seek always to display the light of God's gospel in clear contrast against this dark background.[8]

The gospel message *gives hope by anticipating the consummation of Christ's kingdom.* At the start of his earthly ministry, Jesus proclaimed "the gospel of God" by announcing that "the kingdom of God is at hand" (Mark 1:14–15; cf. Matt. 4:23; 9:35; 24:14). As God's good news, Christ began to fulfill Old Testament hopes for God's coming kingdom of shalom. This kingdom, though already now present in part, has not yet fully come. Christian witness is an announcement and message of hope that anticipates all aspects of the final coming of God's kingdom.

The gospel message *must be communicated contextually.* Gospel communication requires that God's word, which has been spoken, be faithfully repeated by God's witnesses in each local context. God's final word was proclaimed by Christ at the fullness of time in his particular context (Heb. 1:2). We now seek to understand this message, within our own contexts, in order to communicate it to other people in their contexts, a communication process that requires faithful hermeneutics and contextualization. We will give further attention to gospel communication at the end of this chapter.

The gospel message is *universal, inclusive, and particular.* The proclamation of this message is universal: this "eternal gospel" must be

---

8   Likewise, God's gospel cannot be isolated from God's law, just as the Spirit's work of illumination is not separate from his work of conviction. Since "through the law comes knowledge of sin" (Rom. 3:20), preaching the law must accompany preaching the gospel. As John Owen wrote, "Let no man think to understand the gospel, who knoweth nothing of the law." Owen, "The Doctrine of Justification by Faith," *Works* (London: Banner of Truth, 1965), 5:189. See also Herman Bavinck, *Reformed Dogmatics: Holy Spirit, Church, and New Creation,* vol. 4 (Grand Rapids, MI: Baker Academic, 2008), 441–60.

proclaimed "to every nation and tribe and language and people" (Rev. 14:6) and "to the whole creation" (Mark 16:15; cf. Rom. 8:19–22). The audience of this message is radically inclusive: as Peter preached, God does not discriminate but sends his gospel to every nation (Acts 10:34–35).[9] Yet the promise of the gospel is effectual only for God's particular people as all others refuse to obey this gospel (2 Thess. 1:8; Heb. 4:2; 1 Pet. 4:6).

The gospel message is *never spiritually neutral*. It is so much more than merely a repeated fact, "for it is the power of God for salvation" and, by implication, for damnation too (Rom. 1:16; cf. 2 Cor. 2:16; 1 Pet. 2:8). The hearers of this message are always spiritually changed upon hearing it, either toward good or toward evil. This gospel is an invitation that expects an answer, a truth claim that requires acceptance, a command that demands obedience. Christian witness, therefore, is a spiritually weighty task: as heralds and ambassadors of the sovereign Lord, we make passionate appeals to sinners, on Christ's behalf, imploring them to be reconciled with God, before it is too late (2 Cor. 5:20–6:1). Our gospel is the message of God's good news of peace.

Finally, the gospel message is *exclusive and essential* in Christian witness. It is not enough to show acts of generic love, to pray publicly to a generic god, or to promote generic acts of kindness for the good of humanity in general. Christian witness requires the communication of God's exclusive message of Christ alone. Furthermore, a living relationship with Christ is prerequisite for all gospel witnesses. Reformed experiential witness requires active faith and gospel transformation, both individually and communally, as well as the verbal proclamation of the exclusive message of Christ.

---

9   As confessed in the Canons of Dort, head 2, art. 5: "Moreover, it is the promise of the gospel that whoever believes in Christ crucified shall not perish but have eternal life. This promise, together with the command to repent and believe, ought to be announced and declared without differentiation or discrimination to all nations and people, to whom God in his good pleasure sends the gospel" (*CCC* 150). See also Geerhardus Vos, "The Biblical Basis for Missions," *Kerux NWTS* 24, no. 1 (2009): 5.

How Is the Gospel Communicated Effectually?

In Luke 4:18–19, Jesus publicly announced the mission statement of his earthly ministry:

> The Spirit of the Lord is upon me,
>> because he has anointed me
>> to proclaim good news to the poor.
> . . . to proclaim liberty . . .
> to proclaim the year of the Lord's favor.

These verses are often used to highlight the holistic character of the gospel message, as previously considered. But there is much more. This announcement also hints at the answer to our second reflection question: How can we communicate this message better, both effectually and effectively?

It is helpful, at this point, to clearly distinguish between *effective* and *effectual* communication. With effective communication, the focus is on the best manner to achieve a desired result, which is related to communication theory and contextual applications. We will give more attention to the manner and modes of gospel communication at the end of this chapter. With effectual communication, however, the focus is on the required power to produce a desired result, which is directly related to the salvation doctrine of effectual calling. The act of gospel communication is performed by human witnesses. But the power in effectual communication is divine, since only the Spirit of Christ can produce the desired result of new spiritual life in once-dead sinners (John 6:63).

A study of *effectual* communication, therefore, must logically come before a study of the human manner and modes of *effective* communication. To this end, consider the following five aspects of witnessing with the Holy Spirit.

First, effectual gospel communication is *the direct result of the Spirit's anointing upon human witnesses.* As Jesus was anointed by the Holy Spirit to proclaim the gospel, so also Christian witnesses are anointed by Christ's Spirit to proclaim the gospel. As the Holy Spirit came upon Jesus to empower him during his earthly mission, so the Spirit also empowers all believers after Pentecost to be witnesses in the world.

The Spirit's anointing for gospel proclamation is a wonderful doctrine that brings together many of the themes we already considered in chapters 2, 3, and 7. Christ the anointed evangelist was empowered by the Holy Spirit during his earthly ministry, in order to proclaim the good news of God's shalom. Then after his resurrection, Christ the exalted sender poured out his Spirit into the church, in order to empower God's people to continue proclaiming this gospel message. The Holy Spirit, as God's empowering presence, now ministers in God's church, and he continues to witness with the church as well. All believers, in spiritual union with Christ, share in Christ's anointing, in order that they may, as prophets, priests, and princes, effectually communicate the gospel. We are cowitnesses with the Spirit of Christ, empowered by him for evangelistic and apologetic witness.

Second, effectual gospel communication is *a trialogue, not merely a dialogue as it is often conceived.*[10] Most evangelistic methods focus on the human-to-human level of communication between the evangelist and the unbeliever. Such communication is dialogical, a conversation between two parties. But effectual gospel communication always involves three parties, since the person of the Holy Spirit is also involved in this conversation along with the human evangelist and the unbeliever (fig. 10).

---

10 Here, as throughout this book, I use the word *dialogue* to describe a rational communication between two parties often involving persuasion, similar to the Greek word *dialegomai* (Acts 17:2, 17; 18:4, 19; 19:8, 9; 20:7, 9; 24:12, 25). Dialogue of this kind is distinguished from interreligious dialogue that usually starts with a premise, which, at least in essence, denies the exclusivity of salvation in Christ alone, a starting point that is unacceptable for faithful Christians.

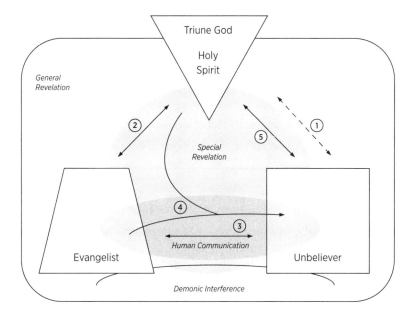

Figure 10. The evangelistic trialogue.

The evangelistic trialogue involves communication between three parties, among which are five distinct relationships.[11] Each relationship in this trialogue can also be described within communication theory as a distinct channel for communicating God's truth.

The relationship between God and an unbeliever (arrow 1 in fig. 10) is described by Scripture as a broken relationship: a sinner running away from God (Rom. 1:19–25). The triune God has already spoken, at least by means of general revelation that includes innate knowledge and the human conscience. But the unbeliever is busy suppressing God's truth in unrighteousness while exchanging it for a lie, as we will consider in the next chapter.

The relationship between God and the evangelist (arrow 2) has been restored in Christ. There is open communication between them, by

11   Brian A. DeVries, "The Evangelistic Trialogue: The Holy Spirit and Gospel Communication," *Calvin Theological Journal* 44 (2009): 49–73.

means of the inspired word, the internal witness of the Spirit (Rom. 8:14–27), and the ordinary means of grace. The Spirit indwells and empowers the evangelist to witness of Christ to unbelievers.

The relationship between the evangelist and the unbeliever (arrow 3) depicts communication on the human-to-human level. This dimension of communication is the focus, often exclusively, of most evangelistic methods. Our discussion later about effective communication focuses on improving this relationship.

The fourth relationship is the precise location for evangelistic trialogue (arrow 4). This divine-human cowitness of the word is the crux of effectual gospel communication. On this dimension, Christ's Spirit anoints the evangelist to witness together with him in order to make an earnest gospel appeal to an unbeliever. By this relationship, the unchanging word of God is prophetically spoken again by the Spirit, through the evangelist as his mouthpiece, to the ears and heart of a sinner.[12]

The final relationship results from the reconciliation of an unbeliever with the triune God (arrow 5). This is the desired outcome of our evangelism (arrow 3). More precisely, it is the consequence of effectual gospel communication, the result of the Spirit's divine power working through the human evangelist (arrow 4).

This evangelistic trialogue is a useful framework for understanding Paul's teaching on gospel communication in 2 Corinthians 5:20–6:1: "Therefore, we are ambassadors for Christ (arrow 2), God making his appeal through us (arrow 4). We implore you (arrow 3) on behalf of Christ, be reconciled to God (arrow 5). . . . Working together with him (arrow 4), then, we appeal to you (arrow 3) not to receive the grace of God in vain." Christ also anticipated this cowitnessing ministry: "But when the Helper comes . . . he will bear witness about me. And you also will bear witness . . ." (John 15:26–27). Likewise, the apostolic church was often filled with the Spirit for bold gospel witness (Acts 4:31; 5:32).

---

12 "Ministers knock at the door of men's hearts, the Spirit comes with a key and opens the door." Thomas Watson, *A Body of Divinity* (London: Banner of Truth, 1958), 154.

This joint divine-human witness is especially important in light of the spiritual confrontation that must take place between God and a sinner in every gospel encounter.

Third, effectual gospel communication *always includes the Spirit's work of conviction.* In John 16:8, Jesus describes the Holy Spirit's preliminary evangelistic work: "When he comes, he will convict the world concerning sin and righteousness and judgment. . . ." The key word in this verse is *convict (elenkho),* which can also be translated as *convince.*[13] It carries the ideas of exposing, by bringing someone's wrongdoing to light, and summoning to repentance before the truth. The method of elenctics in Christian witness gets its name from a transliteration of this Greek word.[14]

Elenctics describes the Spirit's work of unmasking the deception of all idolatry and human false religions as sin against God, and the calling of unbelievers to genuine repentance before the only true God. As J. H. Bavinck writes, it is the Spirit who "awakens in man that deeply hidden awareness of guilt. He convinces man of sin, even where previously no consciousness of sin was apparently present. The Holy Spirit uses the word of the preacher and touches the heart of the hearer, making it accessible to the word."[15]

Elenctics and illumination are the Spirit's evangelistic works, a general gospel calling that sometimes leads to effectual calling and spiritual

---

13 D. A. Carson, "The Function of the Paraclete in John 16:7–11," *Journal of Biblical Literature* 98 (1979): 558.

14 Only a few theologians and missiologists have given attention to this crucial doctrine for Christian witness, most notably J. H. Bavinck, *An Introduction to the Science of Missions* (Phillipsburg, NJ: Presbyterian & Reformed, 1960), 221–46. See also John R. W. Stott, *Christian Mission in the Modern World* (Downers Grove, IL: InterVarsity, 1975), 69–71; and Daniel Strange, "An Apology for Elenctics" in *Ruined Sinners to Reclaim,* eds. David Gibson and Jonathan Gibson (Wheaton, IL: Crossway, 2024), 821–43.

15 Bavinck, *Introduction,* 229. Elenctics "does not in the first place refer to arguments which show the absurdity of heathendom. Its primary meaning refers to the conviction and unmasking of sin, and to the call to responsibility" (226). "We can never employ philosophical argumentation to build a bridge from a non-Christian religion to the Christian faith, a bridge which would make an inner change unnecessary, and would thus make superfluous the call to repentance. . . . You do not then need to begin with endless rational argumentation in order to break the webs of his thoughts. In the grace of Jesus Christ you possess a more powerful means" (229–30).

regeneration. Its focus is on divine agency, not the activity of the human evangelist. Yet this divine work is usually mediated through the person of the human evangelist in the evangelistic trialogue.[16] Thus divine elenctics (arrow 4) and human dialogue (arrow 3) work together.[17]

Many Christians consider conviction of sin to be an unpleasant task in evangelism, a task that is often avoided or minimized for being much too negative and unloving.[18] But divine elenctics is a compassionate confrontation. It is not merely a series of rude, probing questions in a human-to-human relationship (arrow 3), questions that can sour or irreversibly harm the relationship between the human evangelist and unbeliever. Rather, the probing questions in elenctics are the Holy Spirit's gracious overtures (arrow 4), spoken through the compassion-ate evangelist, and spoken with divine love for the helpless sinner. Like the Lord's apologetic conversation with Adam and Eve (Gen. 3:9–13), the Spirit's questions are designed to gently expose the terrible sin of rebellion against God and to convince an unbeliever of his or her need for a gracious Savior.

Fourth, understanding the theology of effectual gospel communica-tion *helps to precisely focus our gospel witness.* As confessed at the end of chapter 3, we are merely witnesses of Christ and dependent upon his Spirit. Our evangelistic efforts, therefore, must always strive to keep in step with the Holy Spirit, supporting his work and echoing his word. We must carefully examine our methods and strategies to ensure they

---

16 The works of the divine Spirit and the human evangelist have different starting points. Both are evangelistic agents of Christ, and both speak the same revealed truth. But the Spirit has direct access to the spiritual domains of the heart and the deep structures of worldview, while the evangelist must start with the surface structures of worldview, culture, and external manifestations of the heart in life.

17 Brian A. DeVries, "Evangelistic Dialogue: Reflection on a Personal Encounter," *Haddington House Journal* 18, no. 1 (2016): 89–113.

18 Many evangelistic methods place very little attention on the need for a radical conviction of sin. A few missiologists deal with the method of elenctics, but they frame it on an ethical level and not as a more radical spiritual confrontation that is necessary to produce evangelical repentance (2 Cor. 7:10). For example, see the otherwise excellent contribution of Robert J. Priest, "Mis-sionary Elenctics: Conscience and Culture" *Missiology* 22 (1994): 291–315.

do not in any way contradict his way of working or create distractions to the gospel message of Christ, as also noted in chapter 3. Knowing how the Spirit works also helps us precisely shape our communication modes and evangelistic methods in order to enhance gospel witness, as we will consider at the end of this chapter.

Finally, the fact of the Spirit's sovereign power in effectual gospel communication *does not minimize the importance of human agency in evangelism.* Though God can speak to sinners through angels and donkeys, he has sovereignly chosen normally to speak through human witnesses (Rom. 10:14). God works salvation by means of his word and Spirit, usually mediated through his church community of Christian witnesses.

For example, we may be tempted to question God's wisdom in selecting the Old Testament people of Israel as his witnesses (Isa. 43:9–12). Why did God choose to use this stubborn nation, a people who were constantly distracted by surrounding idolatries? Was the agency of Israel the best way for God to showcase his grace and mercy among the nations? A similar point could be made about many instances of the church today. Why does God use these people who often get it wrong? Why use a church that is often powerless and despised in society?

However, God often uses unlikely means to accomplish his purposes; he often chooses the weak things of the world in order to more powerfully showcase his great grace. It is part of the gospel mystery that God's sovereign power is made known to the world by means of the church's gospel message (Eph. 3:10). So let us not despise the church, since it is God's chosen agent for gospel witness in the world today. Let us rather work to equip and mature our churches for this noble task of being Christ's witnesses

Why Must the Gospel Message Be Proclaimed?

Why do you share the gospel message with others? What motivates your witness? Our immediate answer to these questions may be to list several biblical motives: a personal conviction (Acts 4:20; Rom. 1:16;

1 Cor. 9:16); an obedience to Christ (Mark 16:15; Phil. 2:15–16a); seeing the desperate need around us (Luke 19:41; Jude 22–23); knowing the love of God (John 3:16; 2 Cor. 5:14); or even eschatological urgency (Matt. 20:6; 24:14; Luke 10:2).[19] Other factors may also motivate our evangelistic activity. For example, many Christians are motivated by feelings of guilt for not sharing the gospel with neighbors. Others may be moved to activity out of self-righteous superiority or condescending pity. Unfortunately, even our best motives are often mixed with impure and misguided passions. Furthermore, the focus is often placed only on personal and ethical motives for witness. The motive of God's glory, however, raises our focus to a higher level.[20]

Keeping God's glory in view helps us reformulate our thinking on the question of motivation. It is not unhelpful to ask the question from a personal and ethical perspective: Why should I share the gospel in this instance? It is more helpful, however, to see the matter from God's perspective: What is God doing in the world today, and how is the witness of our church helping or hindering his mission?

It is easy to become distracted by details. What is the irreducible kernel of the gospel? How are deed-based ministries related to word-based evangelism? By what means can we most effectively communicate this message to others? Stepping back to see God's big-picture plan, however, helps us focus on what is most important. It also motivates us to participate with God in a way that will give him greater glory.

With this in view, consider again two Old Testament realities that we observed in chapter 1: the two globalisms and God's international

---

19 See Johannes Verkuyl, *Contemporary Missiology* (Grand Rapids, MI: Eerdmans, 1978), 163–75; and Gailyn Van Rheenen, *Missions: Biblical Foundations and Contemporary Strategies*, 2nd ed. (Grand Rapids, MI: Zondervan, 2014), 107–24. We will give further attention to missionary motivation in the conclusion.

20 The triune God is the first cause of mission (Gen. 3:9), and his glory is the ultimate goal of mission (Phil. 2:10–11). Gisbertus Voetius believed that the glorification of God and the manifestation of his divine grace is the ultimate motive for mission. See Jan A. B. Jongeneel, "The Missiology of Gisbertus Voetius: The First Comprehensive Protestant Theology of Missions," *Calvin Theological Journal* 26, no. 1 (1991): 68.

courtroom. The Bible portrays world history as a tale of two globalisms: humanistic globalism is trying to make a name for itself, starting with the failed Tower of Babel project (Gen. 11:1–9). But gospel globalism is God's plan for his covenant people to become a blessing to all nations, for his Son to achieve global dominance, and for his name to be glorified throughout the perfected global community (Gen. 12:1–3; 2 Sam. 7:23; Phil. 2:9–11; Rev. 7:9–10). In this polarized context, the prophets served as God's advocates in his international courtroom, speaking his truth publicly in contrast to the idolatry and opposition of the nations. The presence of God's people, as his own witnesses, was public evidence of his truth, mercy, and power (Isa. 43:9–12).

The vision of Revelation 11 underscores and magnifies these Old Testament realities. Here we see a global context in which God's place of worship is being desecrated. During this fixed period of time, however, God gives great authority to his two witnesses, symbolic of the Spirit-anointed church and its witness in the world.[21] God's witnesses are killed at the end of this period, and the celebration of their death unites the society of humanistic globalism. But then God resurrects his witnesses and sends great judgment upon the earth. The application of this vision is clear: though rejected by the world, God's witnesses play an important role in his mission, especially in this period after Pentecost.

It is necessary, therefore, to view our gospel communication from God's perspective. The Holy Spirit tells the story of God's mission since Pentecost against this background of rebellious nations and competing plans for global dominance. Like in the Old Testament, God's people, as his trophies of grace, are public evidence within the international courtroom of God's sincere offer of mercy to all nations. The church's presence, now dispersed among the nations and usually despised in the world, is a public witness to the gospel of Christ's kingdom: their words confirm and their lifestyles affirm the gospel message. The specific

---

21 See G. K. Beale, *The Book of Revelation* (Grand Rapids, MI: Eerdmans, 1999), 556–620.

instances in which we share this message today are important, especially because all these instances are tiny parts of a much greater and grander story of how God will get all the glory in the end.

Our success in gospel witness is not measured merely by numerical results or other social factors that may be deemed important to the world. Rather, as already implied several times, our success is usually counterintuitive to the world's way of thinking: our loss is great gain, the sweet fragrance of our witness is a putrid stench to the world (2 Cor. 2:16); final glory is reached by way of suffering (Mark 8:35; Heb. 12:2). Success in gospel communication must be measured by the extent to which our witness advances God's mission objective. Therefore, with these realities in view, we can briefly examine four reasons why we communicate the gospel message.

Evangelism is *a public declaration of God's exclusive truth*. The church serves as God's spokespersons among the nations, declaring his incomparability and making an official announcement of his impending judgment. Through us, God calls all peoples to give an account of their actions: Will they believe his truth and worship him, or will they continue worshiping idols in unbelief? As God's witnesses, we proclaim his truth in the context of idolatry and the fact that the day of judgment is coming (Acts 17:31).[22]

Evangelism is *a public declaration of God's justice and mercy*. We also declare the gospel message because "in it the righteousness of God is revealed." God is just both in punishing unbelieving sinners and in saving undeserving sinners (Rom. 1:17; 3:26). The gospel is proof of how God's justice and mercy are perfectly magnified together in Christ. We passionately and extravagantly declare God's sincere gracious offer to the worst of rebelling sinners (Ezek. 33:11; cf. Matt. 11:28; John 3:16–17).

Evangelism is *a public declaration of God's sovereign power*. The gospel message is the story of how Christ crushed Satan's opposition: Jesus's

---

22 The gospel message of God's exclusive truth is especially important in postmodern contexts. For a helpful study in this area, see Nancy R. Pearcey, *Total Truth* (Wheaton, IL: Crossway, 2004).

death defeated death, and his resurrection proved his victory publicly. As Christ's witnesses, we proclaim God's power over all so-called gods by simply declaring our faith in Christ who already holds all power in the universe. When strong in Christ, the church stands in spiritual warfare against Satan's opposition, declaring God's absolute omnipotence over all forces of evil.[23]

Finally, and perhaps most obvious, evangelism is *the means by which God has chosen to work salvation* (Rom. 10:14–15). The Spirit usually speaks through human agents to effectually communicate the gospel message. Thus we proclaim Christ and his kingdom during this day of salvation. We declare the whole counsel of God: the precious gospel in context with the convicting law, the promises of grace against the curses of nature, and the hope we have of a better city "whose designer and builder is God" (Heb. 11:9–10).

Why must our churches communicate the gospel message? It is necessary, in God's bigger story, that this gospel be "proclaimed throughout the whole world as a testimony to all nations" (Matt. 24:14; Luke 13:33). The church is God's witness in the world to declare the fame of Christ's name to all peoples, and to publicly vindicate God's truth, mercy, and power among all nations.

Effective Gospel Communication to All Peoples

How should we communicate the gospel with maximum effectiveness? So far, we have described the gospel concisely, considered how it is communicated effectually by the Spirit in and through us, and reflected on why it must be communicated within the bigger story of God's mission. We now conclude this chapter with several brief reflections on effective gospel witness.

---

23 Much of what has been written about evangelism and spiritual warfare is of questionable value. For several helpful studies, see Leahy, *Satan Cast Out*; Ferdinando, *Triumph of Christ*; David Powlison, *Power Encounters* (Grand Rapids, MI: Baker, 1995); and Iain M. Duguid, *The Whole Armor of God* (Wheaton, IL: Crossway, 2019).

For effective communication, we focus on contextualization as the application of the gospel message within diverse contexts.[24] Our purpose here is not to focus on theories of indigenization,[25] or on how culture may influence biblical interpretation,[26] but instead on the practical choice of means for gospel communication to be most effective in a specific context. By *effective*, as stated above, we mean the best manner to achieve a desired result. Our focus is on improving the communication channel between the evangelist and the unbeliever (arrow 3 in fig. 10). To this end, we can learn from communication theory and the social sciences in order to contextually apply the gospel message in each situation.

First, communication theory helps us understand the process of gospel witness. Paul's gospel ministry demonstrates his knowledge and skill of the communication process (Acts 13:16; 17:22; 22:1; 26:1). It is true that he carefully avoided using rhetoric in a way that might influence his audience with human technique rather than the power of God (1 Cor. 2:1–5). But Paul could not avoid communication, since "faith comes from hearing" (Rom. 10:17). Hence we should carefully study valid theories for communicating in order to improve our knowledge and skill in this task that is the epicenter and passion of all Christian

24 As Richard Muller writes, "In order for the gospel to become meaningful to us in our own present life-situation and to others in different places and different cultures in their distinctive life-situations, it must be brought into the diverse contexts of the modern world. It must be contextualized." Muller, *The Study of Theology: From Biblical Interpretation to Contemporary Formulation* (Grand Rapids, MI: Zondervan, 1991), 202.

25 *Indigenization*, like the newer term *contextualization*, includes gospel translation, cross-cultural communication, and intercultural ministry. These terms need further clarity to be used effectively, since they are often taken in many diverse directions, with much ambiguity caused by different underlying theologies and ministry contexts. Timothy Keller summarizes this discussion well in *Center Church*, 194–232; see also Brian A. DeVries, "Contextualisation within Context: A Pedagogical Spectrum of Six Methodologies" in *In die Skriflig* 55, no. 1 (October 2021): 1–8.

26 For studies on hermeneutics and culture, see Harvie M. Conn, *Eternal Word and Changing Worlds: Theology, Anthropology, and Mission in Trialogue* (Grand Rapids, MI: Academie Books, 1984); William J. Larkin Jr., *Culture and Biblical Hermeneutics* (Grand Rapids, MI: Baker, 1988); and Brian A. DeVries, "Towards a Global Theology: Theological Method and Contextualisation" in *Verbum et Ecclesia* 37, no. 1 (2016): 7–12.

witness.[27] It is especially important to study how we witness together with the Holy Spirit, as considered above, and how to cooperate with God's ancillary witnesses, as we will consider in the next chapter.

Second, the social sciences give us helpful tools to understand the context of gospel witness. The gospel message is unchanging, and it is always relevant for all peoples. The various contexts into which the gospel must be communicated, however, are diverse and constantly changing. Indeed, it is impossible not to contextualize, since all communication takes place within a unique context—the message is always affected by the medium, culture, and location.[28] Thus these tools should be used to better understand a specific context in order to best package our precise applications of the gospel message. Yet these tools and their valuable inputs must never replace our clear declaration of the gospel message or our dependence upon the Spirit to make its communication effectual.[29]

Third, understanding the process and context helps us contextualize our gospel witness for each particular situation. The history of Christian witness gives us many excellent examples that can guide our own gospel communication in contemporary contexts. The New Testament records

27 "As in the planting of the seed or the rearing of the child, the more we know of natural law—the divinely ordained order of the universe—the more effectively we can work within its structure.... It is precisely because he believes that language and the human mind are both products of God's creation and because he believes that God has deliberately chosen to communicate with men through the medium of human language that the minister is rewarded by study of the communication process." Leslie Sargent, "Communication and the Spirit," *Christianity Today* 7 (1 Feb. 1963): 15.

28 As D. A. Carson states, "Every truth from God comes to us in cultural guise: even the language used and the symbols adopted are cultural expressions. No human being living in time and speaking any language can ever be entirely culture-free about anything." Carson, "A Sketch of the Factors Determining Current Hermeneutical Debate in Cross-Cultural Contexts," in *Biblical Interpretation and the Church: The Problem of Contextualization*, ed. D. A. Carson (New York: Thomas Nelson, 1984), 20. See also David J. Hesselgrave, *Communicating Christ Cross Culturally: An Introduction to Missionary Communication*, 2nd ed. (Grand Rapids, MI: Zondervan, 1991), 95–189.

29 This caution is expressed well by Paul Hiebert: "In recent years in evangelical missions, we have been so fascinated by the power of the social sciences that we are in danger of leaving our biblical foundations, and, in the process, of losing the heart and soul of mission. We need to return to the Scriptures to lay the foundations for a theology of mission for the next century." Hiebert, "The Social Sciences and Missions" in *Missiology and the Social Sciences*, ed. Edward Rommen and Gary Corwin (Pasadena, CA: William Carey, 1996), 202.

many different modes of evangelistic speech: exhorting, speaking, rebuking, dialoguing, and so forth. There are also many different methods of evangelistic ministry, such as preaching, counseling, church planting, and apologetics. Furthermore, we have studied seventeen aspects of Christian witness as found in Scripture and church history (see table 4).

Our gospel communication today should learn from all these, mixing and modifying various combinations to best serve the context and audience of our specific ministry. For example, Jesus's discipleship model, as employed in the early church's schools of theology, can be modified with mentorship models of the Puritans and aided by modern technology to create new forms of theological education that are more effective in Southeast Asia today. There are countless combinations of these methods for the contemporary application of the gospel message. This choice of means and methods should be guided by both faithfulness and functionality. Faithfulness to the gospel's content and the purpose of witness is essential.[30] Yet functionality is also important, since with Paul we desire to engage the minds and hearts of all people (1 Cor. 9:22), and since God "desires all people to be saved and to come to the knowledge of the truth" (1 Tim. 2:4; cf. Acts 17:30).

Finally, we pray for the Spirit's guidance as we use these tools to more effectively communicate the gospel message. Only he can make this message effectual, so we depend upon him while using all suitable means to make our witness more effective. In this way as well, we strive to bring greater glory to God as we declare his truth, mercy, and power to all peoples.

Discussion Questions

1. What is the gospel message? Answer this question concisely by describing ten truths about the gospel as explained in this chapter.

---

30 The criteria for faithfulness is defined by several questions: (1) Is it biblical? Is it faithful to God's word and biblical hermeneutics? (2) Is it ethical? Does it promote Christian witness and Christian values? (3) Is it effective? Does it support the cause of my specific calling within God's mission?

2. Explain the difference between effectual communication and effective communication.

3. How do we as human evangelists witness together with the Holy Spirit? Use the evangelistic trialogue model to explain what happens when we share the gospel message with others.

4. Explain four reasons, from the perspective of God's global mission, why your church today should communicate the gospel message in your own local setting.

5. The apostle Paul became "all things to all people" with the desire that God would save some (1 Cor. 9:19–23). How does knowledge of the Spirit's witness in effectual communication guard us from unfaithful extremes as we seek to contextualize our evangelistic ministry in order to more effectively communicate the gospel to people in our local community?

9

Christian Witness by Gospel Response

PICTURE IN YOUR MIND a biblical church that is a faithful witness in your vicinity. Does this church display publicly its identity and calling as a witness of Christ? Yes, it does. Does it communicate the gospel, both internally to its members and externally within society? Yes, by God's grace. Does this church also defend the gospel in response to the lies and opposition of unbelievers? Yes, it should. Each of these three aspects of witness are vital parts of this picture. In fact, it would be difficult to be faithful in one of these areas alone, since they all are interrelated.

Christian witness intrinsically involves gospel presence, gospel message, and gospel response. These three aspects are integrally braided together in the threefold cord of the church's ministry in the world. Though gospel message (evangelism) and gospel response (apologetics) can be studied separately, the church engages in both activities as the spontaneous expression of its identity and calling within society. In addition to witness by gospel presence and gospel message, the church must also be prepared to give a gospel response to the idolatry and opposition of the world (1 Pet. 3:15).[1]

---

1   In this chapter, I present apologetics as *gospel response* since it is inherently an answer to untruths and objections. This does not mean it is only a defensive reaction or retreat, since we must also respond proactively and persuasively. Though this gospel response is integrally intertwined with

What should the church say in response to the assortment of false religions, unbiblical ideologies, and popular untruths in the world today? How should the church live in response to challenges and opposition from an unbelieving society? These questions are answered by apologetics, the defense of the Christian faith. Resources for gospel response have multiplied abundantly,[2] often after their kind.[3] We now stand on the shoulders of giants: there is a huge collection of excellent apologetic resources available today, as well as many excellent examples in history of faithful apologetic response.[4]

The purpose of this chapter is not to duplicate what has already been published or to defend a particular methodology. More modestly, we will simply describe the activity of gospel response (apologetics) that must be defined within God's mission as an essential aspect of Christian witness.

How Should Adam Have Responded?

Genesis 3 sets out many foundational truths for Christian witness. As considered in the introduction, we see the beginning of God's mission and his comprehensive plan of redemption in the context of a cursed world. We also see a preview of Christ's mission and the first hints

---

evangelism, we look at them separately to aid study: evangelism in the conclusion and now apologetics. Both evangelism and apologetics are humans means through which the Spirit works.

2   For resources related to the theory of apologetics, see John V. Fesko, *Reforming Apologetics* (Grand Rapids, MI: Baker Academic, 2019); K. Scott Oliphint, *Covenantal Apologetics* (Wheaton, IL: Crossway, 2013); and Cornelius Van Til, *Christian Apologetics*, 2nd edition, ed. William Edgar (Phillipsburg, NJ: P&R, 2003). It is clear in what follows that I stand with those who have been influenced by Van Til's thinking in this area, as well as by J. H. Bavinck's theology of religions, *The Church between Temple and Mosque: A Study of the Relationship between the Christian Faith and Other Religions* (Grand Rapids, MI: Eerdmans, 1966); and James W. Sire's worldview evangelism, *The Universe Next Door* (Downers Grove, IL: InterVarsity, 2004).

3   For views on different methods, see Steven B. Cowan, ed., *Five Views on Apologetics* (Grand Rapids, MI: Zondervan, 2000) and Brian K. Morley, *Mapping Apologetics: Comparing Contemporary Approaches* (Downers Grove, IL: IVP Academic, 2015).

4   For example, see Benjamin K. Forrest, Josh Chatraw, and Alister E. McGrath, eds., *The History of Apologetics: A Biographical and Methodological Introduction* (Grand Rapids, MI: Zondervan, 2020); and L. Russ Bush, ed., *Classical Readings in Christian Apologetics* (Grand Rapids, MI: Academie Books, 1983).

of God's gospel promise to sinners. Yet there is more we must learn from this foundational history, now specifically regarding the origin of idolatry and the church's response to it.

Genesis 3:1–7 explains the beginning of human sin in the world. We all know the main points of this history: Satan, in the form of a serpent, deceives and tempts the first humans. His lie was the first antithesis to God's truth. Eve then listens to Satan's lie and is tempted to eat the forbidden fruit. Adam should have defended God's truth and protected his wife from temptation, but instead he also is tempted by Satan's lie. Consequently, Adam chooses sin and rebellion against God instead of a life of faith and obedience to God.

What should Adam have said to Satan? We know the result of his failure, but we can also learn from reflecting on how he *should* have responded. Scripture describes Adam as the federal head of humanity; his choice was not simply personal, since it brought eternal consequences upon the entire human race.[5] In his original state of innocence, Adam could have responded with a flawless apologetic defense of God's truth. He could have exposed Satan's lie: No, Satan, your words are twisting God's truth. But Adam failed to uphold God's truth; rather, he chose to follow Satan's lie.

As a result, sin entered the world and death through sin (Rom. 5:12). Adam, with all his posterity, fell from his state of innocence into the fallen state of depravity. Here we see the origin of false religion; this is the start of human rebellion against God, the point at which human society first began living in opposition to God and his truth. Instead of standing against Satan's antithesis, Adam and his children became part of a community that followed the lie, consequently being separated from God and exchanging God's truth with this lie (Rom. 1:25).

Yet, thankfully, the story does not end here! The Son of God, Christ the divine evangelist, came to his garden, calling out to sinners: Adam,

---

5   See Romans 5:12–21. This point has been made by many, including John Murray, *The Imputation of Adam's Sin* (Phillipsburg, NJ: P&R, 1977).

where are you hiding? Then many years later, the Son took on human flesh in order to make atonement for sin and to correct the mess that Adam had made. Christ the Son, the divine apologist came to destroy the works of the devil and to expose every lie raised against the knowledge of God (2 Cor. 10:4–6; Heb. 2:14). Accordingly, Paul rightly describes Christ as the last Adam (1 Cor. 15:22, 45).

How did Jesus Christ respond to Satan's lie? Christ's entire life was an apologetic against Satan's lie. More specifically, he was tempted by Satan—not in a perfect garden but in a wilderness, when experiencing human weakness (Matt. 4:1–11). Yet Christ corrected Satan's Scripture-twisting with biblical truth. He destroyed Satan's lie and made the perfect defense of God's truth. Concisely stated, Christ came to manifest God's righteousness and display God's truthfulness (Rom. 3:20–26; 15:8–9).

The church is called to follow Christ our Lord, always being prepared to make a defense of his gospel (1 Pet. 3:14–17; cf. 2:20–21). This calling is seen faintly in the Old Testament: as we considered in chapter 1, the prophets acted as God's advocates; they declared and defended God's truth in the context of idolatry and opposition. The New Testament church continues this task, now with the great benefit of full gospel light and being empowered by the divine apologist who works with and through us, as previously considered in chapters 3 and 8. The church, even when suffering, is called to make a gospel response: to expose Satan's lie by repeating God's truth.

The main points in a concise biblical theology of gospel response are clear: God's truth has been revealed, both through general revelation and Scripture. Satan's lie is an antithesis to this truth, not as a direct opposite being entirely different, but rather as a counterfeit truth being mostly similar. Adam's response to Satan's lie was an apologetic failure, resulting in rebellion and running away from God. All those who follow the first Adam are thus part of a rebellious community that is defined by willful unbelief and the idolatry of false religion.

Conversely, Christ the last Adam is God's gospel response to human sin and Satan's lie. All those who follow Christ—those who by faith are in spiritual union with him—are thus part of his church, a community of redeemed sinners who are defined by faith in God's truth and the worship of true religion. The church, therefore, is called to follow Christ as a gospel response to all rebellious sinners in the world who are still running away from God. In the end, Satan's lie will be completely refuted and God's truth fully vindicated.

Christian apologetics explains how the church should make this gospel response: What should the church say in response to untruths and idolatry? How should the church live in response to unbelief and opposition? As such, apologetics must be defined within God's mission of redemption and guided by God's own triune acts to refute Satan's lie.[6] Biblical history relates both the effects of Adam's failure and also God's answer to the question of what Adam should have done instead. The church must serve in God's mission, therefore, not only by their gospel presence and gospel message, but also through their gospel response to the world as witnesses of Christ the last Adam.

A Context of Idolatry and Opposition

Gospel response presupposes gospel opposition, just as an answer presupposes a question. As Christian witnesses, the church is called to respond to rebellious opposition against God and his truth. In the process, we must also respond to unbelieving society and the challenging questions instigated by their untruths and idolatry.

We know the answer that the world needs—his name is Jesus. But the rebellious world is still raising the wrong questions, so our gospel response must often begin by correcting the questioners and exposing their idolatry and opposition. For example, you may have a coworker

---

6 John Calvin insightfully starts with Scripture and the theology of religions: *Institutes of the Christian Religion*, ed. John T. McNeill, trans. Ford Lewis Battles (Philadelphia: Westminster Press, 1960), 1.1–12.

or neighbor who is offended when you openly confess your faith in Christ alone. This unbeliever may object, questioning why your lifestyle is intolerant and unloving. But the real issue is not the question of this objection: Are you intolerant? Rather, the problem is the questioner's unbelief: What has he done with God's truth? So we must find a compassionate way to unmask his unbelief and rebellion against God. Correcting the questioners and presenting the only answer, however, requires a better understanding of the context in which these questions are raised.

The context of apologetics is often hostile: because Satan's lie is opposed to God's truth, human society following this lie is inherently opposed to God's church built upon his truth. The book of Acts relates how opposition arose against the church soon after Pentecost. As considered in previous chapters, the witness of the church has often been matured in times of persecution and great suffering. This opposition was not new; the Old Testament had already chronicled the story of growing hostility toward the holy seed (Gen. 3:15; 4:25; Ex. 1:22; Ps. 14:4; Est. 3:6; cf. Rev. 12:17). Furthermore, Scripture also describes a deeper form of opposition: not merely social enmity among humans, but spiritual enmity expressed in humanity's flight from and revolt against God (Ps. 2:1–3; Rom. 1:28–32; 8:7; James 4:4).

The theology of religions helps us explain this flight away from God and his truth.[7] When Adam suppressed God's truth to follow Satan's lie, he began to experience God's wrath that is revealed against all human sin (Rom. 1:18). Immediately Adam began to experience guilt for sin, shame of sin, and fear of God's righteous judgment against sin. Rather than returning to God in repentance, however, the first sinners tried to hide themselves from God (Gen. 3:7–8).

Likewise, all unbelieving sinners today are still trying to cover the consequences of sin with idolatrous fabrications. They exchange God's

---

7   See Bavinck, *Church between Temple and Mosque*, 11–34; and Daniel Strange, *Their Rock Is Not Like Our Rock: A Theology of Religions* (Grand Rapids, MI: Zondervan, 2015).

truth for Satan's lie, resulting in further spiritual blindness. They worship created things rather than the Creator, running further from the light of God's truth. This is the vortex of false religion, a falling from natural depravity ever deeper into utter depravity (Rom. 1:21–32). All sinners are busy fleeing from God and his truth, even while also responding to him in willful unbelief and opposition.

Human religion at the heart level is, simply put, humanity's response to God's revelation.[8] Thus false religion can be described as the many divergent responses of sinners who all are running away from God in different directions, while fabricating an assortment of idolatrous ways to shield oneself from God's righteous wrath against sin. Conversely, true religion is described as biblical worship of God as true knowledge, righteousness, and holiness is restored, having been rescued from the vortex of deception and being drawn ever closer to God in Christ. In essence, there are only two spiritual orientations: the revolt and flight away from God, and the repentance and faith in Christ.[9]

Adherents of false religion are the primary audience of the church's apologetic witness. Though originating from one spiritual orientation, false religion in the world is extremely diverse, since there are many directions in which sinners can run away from God.[10] The result is a

8   God created Adam to respond to him rightly: the response of true religion with covenantal worship in perfect knowledge, righteousness, and holiness. But Adam's sin resulted in false religion, the response of idolatry and opposition defined by willful unbelief and untruth. As Bavinck writes, "Religion is by its very nature a communion, in which man answers and reacts to God's revelation. This definition implies that there is a divine revelation, an act of self-disclosure on the part of God. It also implies that there is a human response to this self-disclosure, either in a negative or in a positive sense. Religion can be a profound and sincere seeking of God; it can be a flight from God, an endeavor to escape from His presence, under the guise of love and obedient service. At the bottom of it lies a relationship, an encounter." Bavinck, *Church between Temple and Mosque*, 19.

9   Peter Jones describes the stark dichotomy of spiritual orientations as "the only two timeless, mutually contradictory ways to think about the world." Jones, *The Other Worldview* (Bellingham, WA: Kirkdale Press, 2015), 12.

10 It has been popular in much of Western philosophy for the past two centuries to picture the historical development of religion as an evolutionary process from the so-called primitive traditional religions to the more advanced expressions of human religiosity, like Buddhism or Christianity,

countless number of human religiosities today, classified in many different ways: world religions, religious cults and movements, unbiblical
ideologies and worldviews, sinful sociocultural traditions, and popular
untruths in the world.[11] Satan's original lie and ongoing demonic deception is the root system of the gnarly old tree of human religiosities with
many distorted branches bending out in separate directions shrouded
by various aberrant growths of all kinds.[12]

Apologetic witness should carefully seek to understand the specific
religiosity of each audience for our gospel response. We don't need to
know all the details of their deceptions and revolt against truth, but
it is very helpful to know the direction in which a particular sinner is
running away from God and some facts about how he is masking the
consequences of his sin with idolatrous fabrications.

Consider several sad realities in light of this context of opposition
and idolatry. First, all adherents of human religion are *hopelessly lost in
unbelief.* Scripture states this emphatically:

> None is righteous, no, not one;
> > no one understands;
> > no one seeks for God.
> All have turned aside; together they have become worthless;
> > no one does good,
> > not even one. (Rom. 3:10–12; cf. Pss. 14:1–3; 53:1–3)

---

usually with humanism at the pinnacle. But the theory of original monotheism more closely
aligns with biblical theology, since the historical development of religion is better pictured as a
devolutionary flight away from God and his truth. See Winfried Corduan, *Neighboring Faiths*
(Downers Grove, IL: InterVarsity, 1998), 32–35.

11 For example, there are substitute gods, which replace the Creator with nature, and counterfeit
gods, which redefine God or replace the only mediator with an antichrist. There is also the worship of man, which replaces God with self, following Satan's original lie that man will become
like God. The Heidelberg Catechism (q. 80) denounces the "condemnable idolatry" of one type
of false religion (*CCC* 315). This pronouncement is an apt description, not only of the prevailing
false religion when the catechism was written, but for all religious opposition to God's truth.

12 Compare 1 Corinthians 10:19–22. See Strange on demonic deception: *Their Rock Is Not Like Our
Rock*, 237–73.

Though they clearly perceive the reality of God, they remain without excuse since they have fled from him and exchanged his truth for the lie (John 3:18; Rom. 1:20). As a result, all humans by nature are both in darkness, having run away from the light, and also blinded, having deliberately put out their eyes in order not to see.[13] Even the human quest for answers to the big questions of life is futile, since the presence of untruth and idolatry misleads this quest from the start.[14]

Second, there is *no place of neutrality* in the world, or even in human reason. At the core, there are only two spiritual orientations: either hostility or repentance toward God. There is also "not a square inch" of this universe that God cannot rightly claim as his own.[15] Our gospel response, therefore, in both message and method, must always confess God's sovereignty and Christ's exclusivity. There is no so-called neutral space in which faithful Christian witnesses can discuss terms of agreement with unbelieving sinners. Seeking this kind of common ground compromises our confession of faith from the start.

Third, it is not possible to construct a man-made bridge across *the great gulf between unbelief and Christian faith*. There are, of course, some points of contact for Christian witness, since all humans were created in the image of God, still have some knowledge of general revelation, and share many cultural and social experiences. But these

---

13 Scripture often uses the metaphor of human blindness, also when describing the sorry state of covenant children who have turned from the truth (Isa. 6:10; 44:18; Matt. 13:15; John 12:40; 1 Cor. 2:14; 2 Cor. 4:4; Eph. 4:18; and so on). This has been called the *noetic effects of sin*: due to sin, human ability to think and reason is clouded, resulting in doubt and unbelief concerning the things of God (1 Cor. 2:14), despite that fact that humans still retain aspects of the image of God. As Paul states, "For although they knew God, they did not honor him as God or give thanks to him, but they became futile in their thinking, and their foolish hearts were darkened" (Rom. 1:21).

14 John Calvin describes human reason as "a traveler passing through a field at night who in a momentary lightning flash sees far and wide, but the sight vanishes so swiftly that he is plunged again into the darkness of night before he can take even a step—let alone be directed on the way by its help." Calvin, *Institutes*, 2.2.18.

15 Abraham Kuyper, inaugural lecture at the Free University of Amsterdam, October 20, 1880, quoted in *Abraham Kuyper: A Centennial Reader*, ed. James D. Bratt (Grand Rapids, MI: Eerdmans, 1998), 488.

contact points are only starting places for gospel response; they cannot even serve as bridgeheads upon which human religion can be built.[16] Unbelieving sinners are in revolt against God. "No one seeks for God" until the divine apologist exposes their lies and destroys their idols. He must work with divine power to tear down their opposition and completely humble their human pride. The Holy Spirit must open their blinded eyes and shine the glorious light of Christ into their darkness.

The Church's Apologetic Response

Christian apologetics is the church's response to the sad reality of idolatry and opposition in the world, as described in the preceding sections. In this context, gospel response is a counterantithesis:[17] as Satan's lie was posed in opposition to God's revealed truth, so the church's witness is positioned in opposition to the world's unbelief and idolatry. The church responds with gospel truth in order to correct Adam's incorrect response to Satan's lie, and especially in order to proclaim the gospel message of Christ to Adam's wayward children.

Apologetic witness is *an authoritative declaration against idolatry and opposition.* The Old Testament prophets were anointed to speak with authority on God's behalf as his advocates among the nations. The apostolic eyewitnesses of Christ also spoke with an authority that came from the truth of the word itself, not from their own power or

---

16 J. H. Bavinck writes, "We can never employ philosophical argumentation to build a bridge from a non-Christian religion to the Christian faith, a bridge which would make an inner change unnecessary, and would thus make superfluous the call to repentance. . . . You do not then need to begin with endless rational argumentation in order to break the webs of his thoughts. In the grace of Jesus Christ you possess a more powerful means." Bavinck, *An Introduction to the Science of Missions* (Phillipsburg, NJ: Presbyterian & Reformed, 1960), 229–30.

17 The concept of *antithesis* in apologetics can refer to both (1) Satan's lie in response to God's truth, and (2) the church's gospel response to the world's untruths and opposition. It is helpful, therefore, to conceive of gospel response as a double or counterantithesis, since Christian witness does not turn "the world upside down" (Acts 17:6) but rather it turns an upside-down world back right-side-up again.

piety (Acts 3:12). Though the canon of Scripture is closed, Christian witnesses today are still empowered by the Spirit to speak this word with authority as ambassadors of Christ (2 Cor. 5:20).

Paul's concept of ambassador, however, is more than merely a messenger who presents facts or opinions, like a peddler who tries to convince customers to buy a product (2 Cor. 2:17). Rather, Christ delegates special authority to the church, so that his word, spoken by its officially appointed gospel witnesses, has divine power to destroy Satan's strongholds, even having authority to open or close the doors of heaven (2 Cor. 10:4–6; cf. Matt. 16:19; John 20:23).[18] Thus the official gospel response of the church must not be dismissed as impotent or inconsequential, even though human society today mocks and marginalizes the church. God still speaks with divine power today, and the final judgment in his controversy with the nations is still pending (Ps. 2:9–10; Jer. 25:31; Acts 17:31; Rev. 19:15).

Apologetic witness is *inherently intertwined with evangelism.* Gospel message and gospel response witness together, the faithful apologist always aiming to be evangelistic and the evangelist often responding with apologetics to objections. Apologetics often precedes evangelism in order to prepare the way for the gospel message, and apologetics must also follow evangelism in order to disciple those who have believed in Christ. Unfortunately, evangelism and apologetics have at times been treated as separate, even competing disciplines.[19] However, it is better to employ them as complementary aspects of the same activity with similar goals, which is consistent with the New Testament theology of Christian witness outlined in chapter 4. As suggested at the start of

---

18 As confessed by Lord's Day 31 of the Heidelberg Catechism, especially in answer 84: "God's judgment, both in this life and in the life to come, is based on this gospel testimony" (*CCC* 317).

19 Apologetics is often studied under systematic theology and it can become a highly philosophical exercise, while evangelism is located under practical theology and often becomes a highly pragmatic exercise. But these complementary witnesses should not be bifurcated across different departments of study and practice. Rather, we should define both activities of Christian witness as expressions of the church's gospel presence in the world.

this chapter, both should flow spontaneously from the faithful gospel presence of the church in the world.

The apologetic witness is *multifaceted and variegated*. Scripture uses many words to describe gospel response: Christ's witnesses speak in defense of the gospel (Acts 22:1; 2 Cor. 12:19; Phil. 1:7, 16). They reason and dialogue with unbelievers (Acts 17:2, 17; 18:4, 19). They correct false teaching and persuade objectors (Acts 19:8–9; 28:23–24). They expose and rebuke false teachers (Eph. 5:11; 1 Tim. 5:20; Titus 2:15). They contend for the faith (Jude 3) even in order to tear down gospel opposition (2 Cor. 10:4–6), all the while acting with wisdom and grace (Col. 4:5–6; 1 Pet. 3:13–17).

Apologetics is *both what the church says* in response to idolatrous religiosities (active ministry) *and how the church lives* in response to unbelieving society (passive identity). We can distinguish between gospel defense and gospel offense.[20] It is also helpful to distinguish between evangelistic apologetics, which precedes and complements evangelism, and discipleship apologetics, which follows spiritual regeneration to aid sanctification. Additionally, we can study apologetic approaches to a spectrum of different audiences, from individual sinners resisting God's truth to maturing disciples on the way to glory, and a vast array of different topics, from archeological studies defending the Bible's historicity to counter-cult ministries in specific areas.

Apologetic witness *must be personal and relational*. Our goal is much greater than winning arguments; we desire to be used by the Spirit in his work of winning souls for Christ. J. H. Bavinck explains this fact poignantly:

---

20 There are many other nuances and similar distinctions. John M. Frame adds rational proof as a third category in *Apologetics: A Justification of Christian Belief* (Phillipsburg, NJ: P&R, 2015). Kenneth D. Boa and Robert M. Bowman Jr. add persuasion as a fourth category and then argue for an integrative approach in *Faith Has Its Reasons: An Integrative Approach to Defending Christianity* (Colorado Springs, CO: NavPress, 2001). Harold A. Netland separates theoretical apologetics as problem-solving from applied apologetics as persuasion: "Apologetics" in *Evangelical Dictionary of World Mission* (Grand Rapids, MI: Baker, 2000), 70–72.

In practice . . . I am never in contact with Islam but with a Moslem and his Mohammedanism. If I seek to take a man by storm with general rules and norms derived from books, it is possible that I may miss the mark, and what I say may go over his head, because what he himself finds in his own religion, and the way in which he lives it, is something entirely different from what I had originally thought. . . . As long as I laugh at his foolish superstition, I look down upon him; I have not yet found the key to his soul. . . . As soon as I actually stand next to him, I can in the name of Christ stand in opposition to him and convince him of sin, as Christ did with me and still does each day.[21]

Often our apologetic posture of love and humility is more powerful than any human ingenuity or intellect. We must remember that gospel response is ultimately a coworking with the divine apologist who witnesses through us.

Cowitnessing with God's Witnesses

How should the church respond to Satan's lie? How must we refute the false teaching and opposition that surrounds us in society? As considered above, the church living between idolatry and opposition is called to respond apologetically with Christian witness. We now turn our attention to the way in which we conduct this apologetic witness.

By what means should the church engage in gospel response? There are many apologetic helpful "how-to" guides; but which means are most faithful to Scripture? Which tools are both valid and useful in our contemporary context? We must reflect theologically, therefore, on the specific ways by which the church makes a faithful gospel response within the world.

First, we cowitness with the divine apologist. In the previous chapter, we examined the cooperation of human and divine agency as a framework for gospel communication in the evangelistic trialogue (arrow 4

---

21 Bavinck, *Introduction*, 240–41 and 242–43.

in fig. 10). Ultimately, the Holy Spirit is the apologist who convicts rebellious idolaters of their sinfulness, but he usually chooses to work through human agency.[22] We as human apologists, therefore, are merely the means that he uses; he speaks *mediately* through us and *immediately* into the hearts of sinners, to convince them to repent before the one true God.[23] Thus our apologetic witness, working with the Spirit, is simply standing next to unbelievers and politely commanding them, in Christ's name, to be reconciled with God (2 Cor. 6:1; 5:20).

Second, we always join a prior religious conversation. It is crucial to remember that all sinners are already in a conversation with God (arrow 1 in fig. 10). Many are, as it were, shouting at God over their shoulder, as they run away from him. Others are fabricating idolatrous false religiosities to shield themselves from God's righteous wrath. With others, the Spirit is striving, through general revelation or the general call of the gospel. We enter into this dialogue between God and a sinner, becoming the third party in the conversation.

How is God already communicating with sinners? A number of related ways must be noted. Paul describes humanity's innate knowledge of God: unbelievers "clearly perceive" God's "eternal power and divine nature," though they suppress this truth (Rom. 1:18–20). Paul also mentions humanity's conscience and the internal law "written on their hearts" (Rom. 2:14–15). The Canons of Dort speak of the "light of nature" which is enough to convict of sinfulness but not enough for salvation.[24]

22 On the role of the Holy Spirit in apologetics, see K. Scott Oliphant, *The Battle Belongs to the Lord* (Phillipsburg, NJ: P&R, 2003), 179–93.

23 As J. I. Packer explains, the Spirit works both mediately with the word on the mind and immediately with the word in the heart, and thus his work is both moral by persuasion and physical by power. Packer, "Puritan Evangelism," in *A Quest for Godliness* (Wheaton, IL: Crossway, 1990), 294–95.

24 Canons of Dort, heads 3/4, art. 4. "There is, to be sure, a certain light of nature remaining in man after the fall, by virtue of which he retains some notions about God, natural things, and the difference between what is moral and immoral, and demonstrates a certain eagerness for virtue and for good outward behavior. But this light of nature is far from enabling man to come to a saving knowledge of God and conversion to him—so far, in fact, that man does not use it rightly even in matters of nature and society. Instead, in various ways he completely distorts this light, whatever its precise character, and suppresses it in unrighteousness. In doing so he renders himself without excuse before God" (*CCC* 156). See also the Belgic Confession of Faith, art. 14.

John Calvin describes these concepts as a sense of deity[25] and seed of religion;[26] J. H. Bavinck describes them as an ineradicable intuition[27] and the five magnetic points of religious consciousness.[28]

God has also spoken to all people through his creation. The heavens declare the glory of God, a speechless "voice" that communicates "words to the end of the world" (Ps. 19:1–4). The theological category of general revelation, distinct from God's special revelation, includes both intuitional knowledge and acquired knowledge from the book of creation.[29] Human cultures today also contain "a dim and distorted memory" of God's truth, the traces of what was once clearly known by Adam.[30] Furthermore, we must not overlook the importance of human reason and wisdom, human experience and emotions, and other influential witnesses to the truth.[31] In all apologetic witness, we should seek to understand how the unbeliever is already listening to this prior conversation.

Third, we cooperate with God's ancillary witnesses. The apostle Paul strengthened his gospel response in this way. For example, Paul

---

25 "That there exists in the human minds and indeed by natural instinct, some sense of Deity, we hold to be beyond dispute, since God himself, to prevent any man from pretending ignorance, has endued all men with some idea of his Godhead, the memory of which he constantly renews and occasionally enlarges, that all to a man being aware that there is a God, and that he is their Maker, may be condemned by their own conscience when they neither worship him nor consecrate their lives to his service." Calvin, *Institutes*, 1.3.1.

26 "But though experience testifies that a seed of religion is divinely sown in all, scarcely one in a hundred is found who cherishes it in his heart, and not one in whom it grows to maturity so far is it from yielding fruit in its season." Calvin, *Institutes*, 1.4.1.

27 "There is in man an ineradicable intuition that there exists a Higher Being, a God, and that this God is concerned about his life. There is in him a realization that this blind and dazzled world with its whirl of tragic happenings forms an impenetrable curtain, behind which is concealed the mystery of God's majesty. There is in man a vague sense of his own dependence on this invisible Power. He cannot grasp it, but he feels an impulse to seek it and to worship it." J. H. Bavinck, *The Riddle of Life* (Grand Rapids, MI: Eerdmans, 1958), 15.

28 Bavinck, *Church between Temple and Mosque*, 29–34. See also John Bolt, James D. Bratt, and Paul Visser, eds., *The J. H. Bavinck Reader* (Grand Rapids, MI: Eerdmans, 2013), 145–99.

29 Belgic Confession of Faith, art. 2; See Bruce A. Demarest, *General Revelation: Historical Views and Contemporary Issues* (Grand Rapids, MI: Zondervan, 1982), 228–47.

30 Demarest, *General Revelation*, 227–28; See Strange, *Their Rock Is Not Like Our Rock*, 254–55.

31 Consider, for example, the contemporary phenomena of dreams and visions in the Muslim world that are at times instrumental in bringing unbelievers into contact with Christian witnesses, like the vision of Cornelius in Acts 10 that God used to bring the word of the gospel to him.

appealed to God's witness of general revelation when preaching against idolatry in Lystra: God "did not leave himself without witness," proving this by giving rains and fruitful seasons (Acts 14:17). Likewise, when preaching to Greek philosophers in Athens, Paul appealed to human reason, to cultural proverbs of their own poets, and even to their own false forms of religiosity (Acts 17:22–31). In other places of Scripture, we find appeals to human reason (Prov. 8:1), zoology (Isa. 1:3; Jer. 8:7), and natural biology (Rom. 1:26–27). Though only ancillary to special revelation, God already has many witnesses in the world to his truth, which can be powerful means in our gospel response.[32]

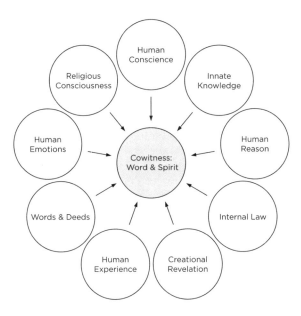

Figure 11. God's ancillary witnesses.

32 As Herman Bavinck summarizes: "There is not an atom of the universe in which his everlasting power and deity are not clearly seen. Both from within and from without, God's witness speaks to us. God does not leave himself without a witness, either in nature or history, in heart or con-science, in life or lot. This witness of God is so powerful, accordingly, that almost no one denies its reality. All humans and peoples have heard something of the voice of the Lord." Bavinck, *Reformed Dogmatics: God and Creation*, vol. 2 (Grand Rapids, MI: Baker Academic, 2004), 90. See also David VanDrunen, *Natural Law: A Short Companion* (Brentwood, TN: B&H Academic, 2023), especially 112–39.

Our apologetic task, following our Lord in Genesis 3, is to call out to sinners who are running away from God's truth: Adam, where are you hiding? How are you busy suppressing God's truth in unrighteousness? What idols have you fabricated to shield yourself from God's wrath? What have you done with God's revelation? But unbelievers have deliberately put out their eyes, refusing to see the truth of God's word. As a result, these ancillary witnesses are often strategic places to begin our apologetic dialogue with unbelievers (fig. 11). In fact, when the truth of special revelation is ignored and rejected, even forged and distorted, we must then cooperate with these witnesses that still linger. Indeed, as the common ground of a shared Judeo-Christian worldview erodes in most Western cultures, we are forced to start "further back," beginning our dialogue with unbelievers at the starting points of God's ancillary witnesses.[33]

Fourth, we maintain the priority of God's word and exclusivity of Christ. This God declares emphatically: Christ is the only mediator between God and men; there is salvation in no one else, for there is no other name than Jesus Christ, the only way back to God (John 14:6; 1 Tim. 2:5; Acts 4:12). Furthermore, though God has many ancillary witnesses, the witness of Christ by word and Spirit are God's ordained means for effectually working salvation.[34] Our evangelistic and apologetic methods must be careful to maintain this truth, both in theory and practice.

Our goal in gospel response is to answer objections and defuse opposition in order to clearly present the gospel truth of Christ to unbelievers; we want them to come face-to-face with God's Son, their Creator and Judge. We especially desire that they will be encountered by his compassionate conviction and gracious forgiveness. Our passion in apologetics is to preach Christ; we only start with ancillary witnesses,

---

33 D. A. Carson states, evangelism, especially in contexts of religious pluralism, "means starting further back. The good news of Jesus Christ . . . is simply incoherent unless certain structures are already in place. . . . We cannot possibly agree on the solution that Jesus provides if we cannot agree on the problem he confronts." Carson, *Telling the Truth: Evangelizing Postmoderns* (Grand Rapids, MI: Zondervan, 2000), 386.

34 See Canons of Dort, heads 3/4, art. 6 and Westminster Confession of Faith 10.1.

if helpful, in order to make way for "the light of the gospel of the glory of Christ" (2 Cor. 4:4). The faint glimmerings of these natural lights are no longer needed—indeed, scarcely discernable—in the full light of the glorious gospel of Christ. Therefore, while recognizing God's ancillary witnesses and contextually employing them where useful in our gospel response, we strive to bring Christ's word to sinners, knowing that this word is the means the Spirit will use to convince and convert sinners.

Fifth, we engage sinners within their own culture and society. Here we focus again on human-to-human dialogue in the evangelistic trialogue (arrow 3 in fig. 10). As the third party in this conversation, our apologetic witness can be greatly strengthened by understanding the specific sociocultural setting of our audience. Careful sociocultural analysis is also valuable for identifying ancillary witnesses—like Paul's use of Greek poets—and for contextualizing our specific apologetic approach. Many helpful resources are now available to guide us in understanding the worldview and culture of unbelievers.[35] As in evangelism, our goal in apologetics is to collaborate with all of God's witnesses, by all acceptable means (1 Cor. 9:22; 10:33), in order to most effectively respond to idolatry and opposition with faithful gospel witness.

Always Being Prepared to Respond

We must always be ready to make a gospel defense to everyone, even in contexts of opposition to the gospel and suffering for righteousness' sake

---

35 In the past century, considerable attention has been given to sociocultural analysis that aids the gospel encounter of world religions. See J. H. Bavinck, *Church between Temple and Mosque*, and Harvie M. Conn, "Conversion and Culture" in John R. Stott and Robert T. Coote, eds., *Down to Earth* (Grand Rapids, MI: Eerdmans, 1980), 147–72. There is also growing attention to the witness of the gospel in Western culture and society, such as Lesslie Newbigin's *Foolishness to the Greeks* (Grand Rapids, MI: Eerdmans, 1986) and *The Gospel in a Pluralist Society* (Grand Rapids, MI: Eerdmans, 1989), and many following Newbigin such as George R. Hunsberger and Craig Van Gelder, eds., *The Church between Gospel and Culture* (Grand Rapids, MI: Eerdmans, 1997). Other thoughtful reflections on apologetics within cultural context include Benno van den Toren, *Christian Apologetics as Cross-Cultural Dialogue* (New York: T&T Clark, 2011) and Paul M. Gould, *Cultural Apologetics* (Grand Rapids, MI: Zondervan, 2019).

(1 Pet. 3:13–15). Thus, we conclude this chapter with five general reflections on the mode and manner of our gospel response, which apply to both believers individually and especially to God's church collectively.[36]

We are called *to represent Christ as his witnesses*. Let the significance of this reality saturate our thinking and define our public conduct; this, indeed, is a high calling, an impossible task without grace and the Spirit's guidance. As considered above, our gospel response is an authoritative declaration on behalf of Christ (2 Cor. 5:20), so we represent him in both word and deed. Not only must we repeat his words of loving invitation to rebellious unbelievers, but we must also display his gracious compassion for sinners (Matt. 9:36; 20:34; Luke 10:33; 15:20). Our apologetic witness must be done "with gentleness and respect" (1 Pet. 3:15) and opposition should be defused "by the meekness and gentleness of Christ" (2 Cor. 10:1). Our goal is not merely to win arguments. No, we sincerely desire to be used by the Spirit to win souls for Christ. So we present Christ to everyone—by both our speech and conduct—with the prayer that the Spirit will draw them to Christ.

We are called *to compassionately confront all unbelievers*. As stated above, apologetics includes the oftentimes unpleasant task of stating truths that are hard to hear (Acts 28:28; Jude 3).[37] Yet we must always keep in mind how Christ graciously evangelized us when we were still living in unbelief; we remember how the Holy Spirit graciously convicted us, and how he still continues to lovingly draw attention to our own remaining sins. Therefore, in this same gracious way, we also stand next to unbelieving sinners in order carefully to expose their idolatrous fabrications and

36 Regrettably, there is no space here to develop contextually sensitive methods for an apologetic response within the framework of a biblical theology of religions and the evangelistic dialogue, and aided by ancillary witnesses and sociocultural awareness, as outlined above. For one helpful book in this regard, see Daniel Strange, *Making Faith Magnetic: Five Hidden Themes Our Culture Can't Stop Talking About . . . And How to Connect Them to Christ* (Epsom, UK: Good Book, 2021).

37 "Elenctics as a science, in other words, can never make superfluous the sensitive probing of the hidden religious depths of a person, a probing of his inner existence. And it can never replace the true desire to serve a person by calling him to repentance and by opening his eyes to the light of life." J. H. Bavinck, *Introduction*, 241.

rebellion against the one true God: Adam, where are you hiding? How are you responding to God's revelation? We desire to serve our fellow sinners by compassionately bringing God's truth to bear upon their conscience and finding ways to repeat Christ's gracious promises, with the prayer in our hearts that they will repent and return to God for forgiveness.

We are also called *to dialogue evangelistically with sinners*. Indeed, gospel dialogue and gospel confrontation work best together.[38] The prophet Nathan in 2 Samuel 12 gives us an excellent example. His calling was to confront King David for his deception and adultery, a dangerous task considering that the king had just killed one of his best men. So with great wisdom, Nathan tells David a captivating story. This story proved to be an ideal mode of communication for the situation, not only to maintain dialogue between the meek prophet and the mighty king, but especially as a relationship through which God's Spirit spoke his word into the heart of David, in one moment exposing his months of wickedness and effectually convicting him of his sinfulness (2 Sam. 12:7, 13; Ps. 51:1–4).

Like Nathan, we also carefully enter into a dialogue with fellow sinners. Like the apostle Paul, we ask probing questions, trying to understand why sinners are hiding behind idolatry and Satan's lie: "Men, why are you doing these things?" (Acts 14:15).[39] It is not a roundtable interreligious dialogue in which we seek a common "truth" together; nor is it merely a discussion about God's truth, as if we are not speaking with divine authority on Christ's behalf but making only suggestions to sinners. Rather, gospel response takes place within the relationship between two fellow humans, as gospel witnesses find creative ways to understand unbelievers in their own situations and to engage with them evangelistically.

---

38 As John Stott writes, "Only those who see the need for elenctics can also see the need for dialogue and can understand its proper place." Stott, *Christian Mission in the Modern World* (Downers Grove, IL: InterVarsity, 1975), 71.

39 "The disenchantment of the unbeliever with his way of thinking comes about as the Christian effectively shows him that his rejection of Christ is based on a self-contradicting and self-frustrating perspective which can therefore never lead to true knowledge of himself, the world, or God." Richard L. Pratt Jr., *Every Thought Captive* (Philipsburg, NJ: P&R, 1979), 92–93.

We are called *to give testimony within sinful society* to God's truth, mercy, and power. There is also a public aspect to apologetic witness, which we will consider in the conclusion. Our goal and great desire, of course, is to present Christ to sinful men with the hope they will be saved. But even if we are rejected, our witness was not without purpose. For example, the prophet Ezekiel was sent to sinful people who had rebelled against God. Yet he was commanded to speak on God's behalf: "Whether they hear or refuse to hear . . . [so] they will know that a prophet has been among them" (Ezek. 2:3–5). In the same way, the church is called to be an apologetic witness in the public square. Whether people around us "hear or refuse to hear," it cannot be said that God has been left without a witness within our sinful society today. The church must shine as lights in the midst of a crooked and twisted generation, even though most men love darkness rather than the light (John 3:19; Phil. 2:15).

We are called *to respond with humble boldness*, in dependence upon the Holy Spirit. This was the response of the New Testament church when they first began to experience gospel opposition: they confessed God's sovereignty and prayed for boldness to continue speaking the word. God immediately answered this prayer by filling them afresh with his Spirit and with boldness for gospel witness (Acts 4:24–31). Likewise, our apologetic response—even in the face of much opposition—should be filled with humility and boldness, since our confidence lies not in ourselves or in the affirmation of our audience but exclusively in our trust of Christ's truth and our dependence upon his Spirit. Thus our gospel response is conducted in a posture of dependent prayer, and it is characterized by an attitude of divine compassion and humble boldness.

Discussion Questions

1. What should Adam have said to Satan in Genesis 3:1–7? Answer this question by explaining how Jesus Christ responded to Satan in Matthew 4:1–11.

2. John Calvin wrote, "Man's nature is . . . a perpetual factory of idols."[40] Use this statement and our discussion in this chapter to explain the global context of false religion and opposition against God's truth.

3. What is Christian apologetics, and how is it an important part of the church's witness?

4. Describe how we can use the ancillary witnesses of general revelation, the human conscience, and shared experience as we dialogue with unbelievers.

5. What should be our attitude and posture as we engage in apologetic witness?

---

40 Calvin, *Institutes*, 1.11.8.

10

Christian Witness in Gospel Community

HOW CAN YOUR CHURCH become a more faithful witness within society? Suppose you are planning a meeting of church members to discuss ways to grow in Christian witness. You could address questions such as: How should we get involved with neighborhood evangelism or partner with a local ministry? What should be done to multiply the number of members serving in our outward-facing ministries? How can our church leaders motivate involvement or set up structures to manage these activities effectively? In such meetings, the focus is often on what we can do, or what we should do better, or even on how much we are failing to obey the Great Commission. Sadly, these discussions often evoke strong feelings of guilt and do little to produce lasting results.

It is more helpful to start by stepping back to view the church's public witness from the perspective of God's mission. The story of mission does not start with the church, since the church is an object of God's mission before it becomes an agent in it. Thus, seeing the church's role in the bigger picture of God's plan helps us define more clearly the church's witness in society: What is God's purpose for our church in society? What is the social status of our church in the world? How should our church model its witness in society? We consider each of these questions in this conclusion, concluding with practical reflections about how our churches can be more faithful witnesses in society. But first we must define the biblical concept of gospel community.

Communion of Saints on Public Display

What is witness in gospel community? A community is a group of people with common characteristics or interests who are living together within a larger society. A *gospel community* can be defined as a congregation of Christians, spiritually united in Christ and guided by his Spirit, who are living together as a witness to the surrounding society. The collective witness of a faithful church—a public display of gospel community—is itself a powerful witness of Christ within a local society.

We considered the church's spiritual identity and calling to witness as a gospel presence in chapter 7. As witnesses of Christ, all Christians are called to live within society as prophets, priests, and princes whose very presence testify to the glories of Christ. Christians also fulfill this calling by means of gospel message and gospel response (chaps. 8–9). Here, our focus shifts from the personal and vocational to the social and practical aspects of Christian witness. We now focus more directly on the church living in gospel community not merely as many separate individual witnesses who each engage in evangelism and apologetics, but as a corporate community that collectively is itself a witness within contemporary society.

Witness in gospel community is beautifully described by Luke's inspired account of the post-Pentecost church in Acts 2:42–47 and 4:32–34. The whole church was devoted to worship, prayer, fellowship, and the apostle's teaching. All believers were united in heart and soul, sharing all things in common. They witnessed to Christ's resurrection with great power, and great grace was upon them all. They praised God with glad and generous hearts, providing for all needs among them and having favor with all people in society. They gathered daily in public worship and household fellowship. Luke repeatedly highlights a consequence of this gospel community: "The Lord added to their number day by day those who were being saved" (Acts 2:47; cf. 5:14; 6:7; 9:31; 11:24; 12:24; 19:20). Several aspects of this gospel community can be further explained in logical progression.

Gospel community is grounded in *spiritual communion with the triune God* in Christ. The doctrine of the communion of saints confesses all believers "are united to Jesus Christ their Head, by his Spirit and by faith" and thus "have fellowship with him"[1] Likewise, John desired "that you too may have fellowship" with all the saints, confessing that "our fellowship is with the Father and with his Son Jesus Christ" (1 John 1:3). Conversely stated, it is not possible to be a gospel community without genuine spiritual communion with God as defined by his word and produced by his Spirit.

Gospel community is a *consequence of the church's spiritual unity* in Christ. The closer each believer is living to Christ, the closer each believer will be with other believers who are living close to Christ. Since all Christians are spiritually united to Christ by faith, we each together can enjoy spiritual fellowship with all other believers worldwide, and even solidarity across all eras of church history (Eph. 6:18).[2] Hence our public display of spiritual unity is itself a powerful witness of the inner gospel reality of our new life in Christ (John 17:21).

Gospel community is an *inner spiritual reality also expressed outwardly* in society that should be stronger and deeper and more precious than all other kinds of social cohesion. The Greek word *koinonia*, translated

---

1   Westminster Confession of Faith, 26.1.

2   John Edwards wrote, "They sympathize with the condition of all distressed saints, wherever they are, and thereby hold communion with all saints in the world . . . they feel an ineffable pleasure and satisfaction . . . whenever they hear of . . . the success of the family of God, the prosperity of his people, and the spreading of his kingdom in the world." Edwards, *Theologia Reformata* (London: Lawrence & Wyat, 1713), 747.

"fellowship" or "communion," attempts to describe this sweet spiritual experience that is much more than merely time together each week: "Being united to one another in love, they have communion in each other's gifts and graces, and are obliged to the performance of such duties, public and private, as do conduce to their mutual good, both in the inward and outward man."[3] Thus, we do not merely try to find ways to show compassion in order to conform to a Christian standard in this area. Rather our compassion to others is the spontaneous consequence of our union and communion with Christ. Genuine expressions of charity are the unstoppable overflow of the lavish love we are experiencing in Christ. True believers are not able not to love others (1 John 3:16–18). True churches are not able not to share the compassion of Christ.

Gospel community is *covenantal*, cultivating and preserving the spiritual relationship that believers enjoy with the triune God in Christ and also with one another. God's people have always been a covenant community (Ex. 19:5–6; 1 Pet. 2:9–10), a spiritual family with a shared heritage and a mutual outlook. This covenantal fellowship creates a strong sense of common belonging and purpose, while also guarding against widespread social extremes like individualism, communalism, and tribalism.

Gospel community *encompasses the many witnessing activities of the church*, such as evangelistic outreach, ministries of compassion, cultural engagement, global partnerships (Phil. 1:5), financial support (2 Cor. 8:4), and even gospel suffering (Phil. 3:10; 2 Tim. 1:8; 2:3). As the witnessing activity of each believer is the result of their identity and calling to be Christ's witness, so also the whole church itself, as a gospel community in constitution and calling, is the environment in which the fellowship together engages in many activities that collectively add to the church's public witness. In this way, each faithful church

---

3 Westminster Confession of Faith, 26.1.

community will be involved in various methods and means of gospel ministry that all add to its collective witness within its society.

Gospel community is *synergistic*: the collective witness of a faithful church community is much more than only the sum of all the evangelistic activities. The glowing coals of a fire stay warm longer when gathered together, and the individual strands of straw when bound tightly together make the whole broom stronger yet still flexible. In the same way, the spiritual community of God's people is much stronger together and stirs up each other to serve longer, when closely bound together by union and communion in Christ.

Gospel community *reproduces Christian witnesses*. A faithful church community is the ideal environment for the multiplication of faithful witnesses. As Jesus discipled his followers and sent them as witnesses, so the church today must be like a vocational school for Christian discipleship. Gospel communities are like greenhouses for planting, nurturing, training, and maturing the next generation of gospel witnesses.

Therefore, the gospel community of a faithful church is itself the strongest witness of Christ within a local society. As a public expression and extension of Christ's compassion, it is living and authentic, which is vital in societies today that despise hypocrisy and desire authenticity. As a winsome community of genuine love and sharing, it is beautiful and attractive. As a powerful testimony that speaks above the noise of conflicting messages, confused opinions, and the uncertainty of postmodern relativity, the faithful church is clear and bold. And even in societies that willfully reject God's truth in exchange for Satan's lie, the public witness of gospel community is undeniable and irrefutable.

The Great Commission is a clear and unquestioned instruction to the whole church. Yet there are few direct references to this command in Scripture, while there are many passages throughout the New Testament commanding and motivating Christian witness in gospel community (Phil. 2:15; Titus 2:12; 1 Pet. 2:12; 1 John 4:20–21). Thus the witness of the church is not primarily the task of organizing and coordinating various forms of gospel ministry in obedience to the Great Commission. Rather, the first and most enduring aspect of the church's witness is to become and remain a faithful gospel community. The public testimony of the communion of saints is the most powerful human witness to Christ on earth.

Making Known God's Manifold Wisdom

What is God's purpose in the world for the church as a gospel community? This question focuses our attention on the cosmic significance of the church's public witness. This was Paul's perspective as he marveled at the mystery of the gospel revealed: God's plan, once hidden but now publicly proclaimed, is "that through the church the manifold wisdom of God might now be made known to the rulers and authorities in the heavenly places" (Eph. 3:10; cf. 1:9–10). It is "through the church" as a gospel community in society that the triune God's wisdom is made known to the whole creation.

First, the church is *God's covenant community*, the family of God founded on the foundation of prophets and apostles (Eph. 2:19–20). God the Father's plan from the beginning was to make a name for himself by forming a people to declare his praise (2 Sam. 7:23; Isa. 43:21). God's purpose was never limited to a particular ethnic group. The Father's plan was always universal in scope: that through his people all families of the earth would be blessed. This is the mystery, now fully revealed by the coming of Christ and his Gentile mission, which Paul celebrates in Ephesians 3.

In the Old Testament, God purposefully placed his people among the nations to be a showcase community, to live within pluralistic societies as witnesses of his exclusive sovereign grace (Isa. 43:8–12; 44:6–8). The collective presence of this community was a light for the nations. Their identity and calling as a consecrated nation was to be a royal priesthood responsible for promoting God's exclusive praise among all nations, as considered in chapter 1. The dominant focus of

Old Testament witness is not on specific evangelistic activities but on the collective witness of God's covenant community that exemplified his gracious blessings among the nations.

The New Testament church, in the same way, is a collective gospel fellowship living within broader international societies. As the Old Testament showcase community was God's trophy of sovereign grace, placed on public display among the nations, so the church today is God's trophy of grace, kept in the world to make known God's manifold wisdom to the whole creation (Ex. 19:5–6; 1 Pet. 2:9–10). The church, in union with Christ and anointed by his Spirit, is a holy company of prophets, a holy community of priests, and a holy lineage of princes. This priesthood of all believers, as considered in chapter 7, is not limited to occasional activities of particular Christians; it also includes the collective witness of the church community.[4]

How should your church, as a local gathering of God's covenant community, make known God's manifold wisdom within your specific context? Each local church has a significant role in society, though it is only a small part of God's universal plan. Your church should be a fellowship of prophets who "shine as lights" within "a crooked and twisted generation" (Phil. 2:15), and who counteract rebellious culture with biblical living (2 Cor. 10:5–6). Your church should be a fellowship of priests, with a ministry of intercession and reconciliation (2 Cor. 5:18–6:1; 1 Tim. 2:1–4), who exemplify within broken societies God's gracious blessings and Christ's tender compassion (Ps. 67:1–3; Titus 2:11; Jude 22–23). Your church should be a fellowship of princes and princesses who seek first God's kingdom, humbly promoting true peace and biblical justice in society (Jer. 29:7; Matt. 6:33; Rom. 12:18; 2 Cor. 13:11). Our church communities today must be

---

4   More attention has been given recently to collective aspects of the priesthood of all believers; see Andrew S. Malone, *God's Mediators: A Biblical Theology of Priesthood* (Downers Grove, IL: IVP Academic, 2017), 179–85; see also Uche Anizor and Hank Voss, *Representing Christ: A Vision for the Priesthood of All Believers* (Downers Grove, IL: IVP Academic, 2017); and Stefan Paas, *Pilgrims and Priests* (London: SCM Press, 2019), 187–204.

light, salt, and leaven in society, acting as minority agents that affect positive changes within the majority, thereby making known publicly God's manifold wisdom.

Second, the church is *Christ's new humanity*, a "new race" community of renewed identity and restored relationships.[5] This aspect of witness is especially important in societies today that are tragically divided by open hostility, enshrined racism, or persistent violence. In Ephesians 2, Paul describes God's antidote to social conflict: "For [Christ] himself is our peace, who has made us both one and has broken down in his flesh the dividing wall of hostility . . . that he might create in himself one new man in place of the two, so making peace" (Eph. 2:14–15). Christ's atonement makes peace, reconciling humans with God and with each other, by creating a new gospel community.

This gospel community has a new spiritual identity. Spiritual deadness and darkness are replaced with spiritual life and light. Personally, believers put on the new self, being recreated into God's image and renewed in their minds; and collectively, the church is a new humanity, recreated in Christ after the likeness of God for good works (Eph. 2:1–10; 4:17–24). This gospel community also has a unique social identity. As noted in chapter 7, the spirit-filled community of believers after Pentecost was soon recognized in society as a diverse but closely united community of Christ followers: both males and females, from all ethnicities and all economic strata (Acts 11:26; Gal. 3:28–29; 1 Pet. 2:10). As such, this new sociospiritual community is itself a powerful witness in the world; it is the primary human agent of Christ's mission post-Pentecost.

Christ's gospel community is a place of reconciliation. Not only does Christ's atoning work restore peace with God, but his atonement also kills the monstrous hostilities of former social offenses and tears

---

5 The *Epistle to Diognetus* calls believers "this new race." Likewise, Clement of Alexandria wrote: "We who worship God in a new way, as the third race, are Christians." Quoted by R. Kent Hughes who adds, "Jesus didn't Christianize the Jews or Judaize the Gentiles. He didn't create a half-breed. He made an entirely new man." Hughes, *Ephesians: The Mystery of the Body of Christ* (Wheaton, IL: Crossway, 1990), 93.

down all barriers that create social divisions.[6] As Christ's new humanity, this gospel community is the ultimate message of peace. Christ, who is "our peace," "came and preached peace" to Jew and Gentile (Eph. 2:14, 17). The church continues Christ's mission of preaching this amazing message of sociospiritual peace in all ethnic groups and all societies. This gospel message of reconciliation with God (2 Cor. 5:18–6:1), when guided effectually by God's Spirit, will also produce restored social relationships among all peoples.

In Christ's gospel community, social exclusion and distance are replaced with social inclusion and belonging. Though still "sojourners and exiles" in the world (1 Pet. 2:11), believers from all ethnic groups are "no longer strangers and aliens" but are "fellow citizens with the saints and members of the household of God" (Eph. 2:19). As previously stated, the covenantal fellowship of gospel community is the antidote to individualism, communalism, and tribalism. Racism is replaced with restored relationships, with mutual love and sharing, and with sociospiritual communion, since we "are all one in Christ Jesus" and "Abraham's offspring, heirs according to promise" (Gal. 3:28–29; cf. Col. 3:11).

Biblical worship in a multiethnic church is a beautiful expression of Christ's new humanity, a foretaste of perfect worship in heaven (Rev. 7:9–10). We know how a faithful multiethnic gospel community, as tangibly evidenced by genuine cross-cultural friendships and holistic multicultural fellowship, is itself a powerful witness within societies tragically divided by discrimination and conflict. We also know how the church's witness is greatly hindered by persistent racism even within Christ's body, his new humanity. So we bow our knees with Paul, praying that all our churches will comprehend this mystery and will continue to mature in this gospel community. Indeed, Christ himself is praying for multiethnic unity in gospel community (John 17:21) and, by this means of witness, God's manifold wisdom is publicly made known in all societies.

---

6   Brian A. DeVries, "Christ Kills Hostility: Peace and Love for an Angry World," *Joy! Magazine*, October 2020, 46–47.

Third, the church is *the Spirit's temple of praise*, the place on earth of God's empowering presence among his people. The public witness of the Spirit's temple is an important theme across Scripture.[7] In Ephesians, Paul describes the construction of this spiritual structure: "You also are being built together into a dwelling place for God by the Spirit" (Eph. 2:21–22; cf. 4:12–16). Believers are "living stones" in this structure and a "holy priesthood," offering themselves as a "living sacrifice" in sacred service (1 Pet. 2:4–5; Rom. 12:1–2). As a living witness, the church points back to Christ's finished work, points upward to the reality of new life in Christ, and points forward to Christ's coming kingdom. The Spirit's temple stands in society as a signpost of God's truth, grace, and power.[8]

The Spirit's temple is a harbinger of Christ's coming kingdom. As our multiethnic worship is a small foretaste of perfected worship in heaven (Rev. 7:9–10), so the whole church is a foretaste of perfected community and society in Christ. In gospel community, we anticipate the *not yet*, the coming reality when God's glory will fill the whole earth (Num. 14:21; Ps. 72:19; Isa. 11:9; Hab. 2:14). However, this temple is *already now* erected as a colossal monument across all lands. God's global church is a spiritual monument, being built up "to the praise of his glorious grace" (Eph. 1:6; cf. Isa. 66:19; Mal. 1:11), publicly making known God's manifold wisdom.

Living Between the Clash of Globalisms

We must now descend, however, from the lofty heights of spiritual communion and God's cosmic purpose for the church into the abysmal

---

7   G. K. Beale, *The Temple and the Church's Mission* (Downers Grove, IL: InterVarsity, 2004), 395–402.

8   "John Calvin said it is the task of the church to make the invisible kingdom visible. We do that by living in such a way that we bear witness to the reality of the kingship of Christ in our jobs, our families, our schools, and even our checkbooks, because God in Christ is King over every one of these spheres of life. The only way the kingdom of God is going to be manifest in this world before Christ comes is if we manifest it by the way we live as citizens of heaven and subjects of the King." R. C. Sproul, *The Prayer of the Lord* (Lake Mary, FL: Reformation Trust, 2009), 39–51. See also Paas, *Pilgrims and Priests*, 106.

present reality of the church's social status in the world. Social status is defined as the level of social value a person is considered to possess. More precisely, it refers to the relative level of respect and value given to people, groups, or organizations in a society. The church's social status can be viewed from two distinct perspectives: the world's assessment and God's description.

How does the world describe the social status of God's church? Throughout history, the church has been labeled by the world with various social statuses: occasionally *exalted*, as during Christendom; frequently *supplanted* by counterfeits; at times *exiled* to the margins of society; and often *persecuted*, as in the early church and now in many places. It can be helpful to analyze the church's status in different global societies, but it remains difficult to know which status on this spectrum is better for Christian witness since each comes with its own challenges.

How does God's word describe the social status of the church? This question focuses widely on the eschatological context of the church's public witness. Consider several realities concerning the conceptual location of Christian witness within the present age.

First, the church community *lives in the context of clashing globalisms*. As already noted in chapters 1 and 8, humanistic globalism is trying to build a name for itself (Gen. 11:1–9). In contrast, gospel globalism is built on God's higher plan for his church to become a blessing to all nations, for his Son to achieve global dominance, and for his name to be glorified universally (Gen. 12:1–3).[9] The Bible's storyline relates how these competing globalistic ideologies are often twisted together and even at times confused. We also get occasional glimpses of the ominous presence of evil that empowers humanistic globalism (Rev. 12:13–17).[10]

Second, the church community *witnesses of Christ within ungodly society*, publicly testifying against the world's idolatries, ideologies, and

---

9   Brian A. DeVries, "A Tale of Two Globalisms," *The Messenger* 70, no. 5 (May 2023), 10–11.
10   See J. H. Bavinck, *And On and On the Ages Roll* (Eugene, OR: Cascade Books, 2019), 1–25.

infidelities. God's people are called both to be separate from the world and also to live honorably within the world. They are called both to cultivate and preserve what is good in culture, and also to refute and correct the sinful ideologies of society. Yet often the church's witness is confused with the world's ideologies. God's own people can even, at times, be influenced by wicked thinking, addicted to sinful ambitions leading to infidelity and destruction. Furthermore, the world often mimics the church and parrots fake news; it pretends to speak the truth but, actually, it has accepted Satan's lie from the beginning and replaced God with an idol. So the church must flee idolatry while witnessing of Christ's truth, grace, and power.

Third, the church community *moves forward as a fellowship of pilgrims*, traveling through this present age toward Christ's consummated kingdom. God's people are sojourners and exiles in this world, living simultaneously in two realms and on pilgrimage between two cities (1 Pet. 2:11).[11] The church is not at home in this present reality but only passing through it, while anticipating its future destination, the reality of which is already experienced in part. Consequently, the gospel community contains an unavoidable tension, a restless mixture of both temporary and eternal. Our public witness will be simultaneously indigenous and contextual, still being citizens of this world, while also transcendent and foreign, already being citizens of Christ's kingdom.

Fourth, the church community *stands as a countercultural contrasting fellowship*.[12] God's church is a counterwitness in the context of humanistic globalism since the attractive beauty of gospel fellowship disproves Satan's lie. The very existence and presence of a faithful church is an offense to a society that is rejecting God's exclusive sovereignty and trying to suppress his undeniable truth. As such, the

---

11 Noted briefly in chapter 7; see also John Bunyan's *The Pilgrim's Progress* and Augustine's *The City of God*.

12 Timothy Keller, *Center Church* (Grand Rapids, MI: Zondervan, 2012), 260–61.

church's united consecration and exclusive confession of Christ is foundational for and central to the church's faithful witness in society. The gospel community stands amidst global upheaval and social destruction, like a lighted billboard or flashing signal that directs the gaze of society from scenes of increasing desolation to the higher reality of reconciliation in Christ and the perfect society that will soon descend from heaven.

Finally, the church community *serves faithfully while anticipating what will soon come.* By faith, the church looks above the present clash of globalisms to see the higher truth of God's mission soon to be finalized. For the present time, God allows humanist globalism to have influence, but soon Christ's kingdom will be consummated and every knee will bow before him. The church lives like diligent laborers working while it is day, like wise stewards investing God's resources profitably, and like pure virgins longing for the final wedding feast (Matt. 20:1–16; 25:1–13, 14–30). In hope, the church faithfully witnesses within the present reality while firmly guided by God's promise of a glorious future reality.

Being in the World but Not of the World

What is the church's posture to the world? Having described God's purpose for the church and its social status in the world, we now study several practical models for the approach and attitude of the church's public witness. As already noted in different ways, the church as a gospel community is a fellowship of people who are kept separate from the world while being sent into the world (John 17:14–18). This requires the church to be in the world but not of it, which raises complex questions about the relationships of Christ and culture, gospel and society, general and special revelation, and Christian living within the clash of globalisms. Without getting distracted by the details, we will briefly reflect on five practical areas in which the church should model its witness in the world (fig. 12).

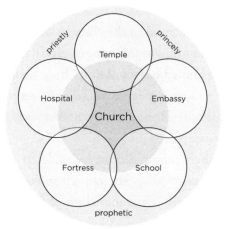

Figure 12. The church's posture in the world.

The church is like a *hospital*, sharing Christ's compassion within a hurting world. As a place of specialized spiritual care, the church reaches out to sin-sick people, inviting them to experience Christ's healing, therapy, and restoration (Jude 22–23). The church is a global network of localized institutions that each demonstrate Christ's tender compassion for all who are poor, suffering, disabled, or oppressed (Luke 4:18).[13] The church's posture is characterized by a holistic hospitality that welcomes social strangers into community and belonging, a stark contrast to xenophobia and racism common to broken societies across the world today.[14]

The church's public witness, however, can be diluted with humanitarian objectives or distracted by dreams of mere social improvement and liberation theology. Though noble desires, the ultimate goal of Christian

13 Expressions of Christian compassion are highly contextual. For several examples, see Bryant L. Myers, *Walking with the Poor* (Maryknoll, NY: Orbis, 2011); Tim Chester, *Good News to the Poor* (Wheaton, IL: Crossway, 2013); and Timothy Keller, *Ministries of Mercy* (Phillipsburg, NJ: P&R, 2015), 113–27.

14 Note that the Greek word for hospitality (*philoxenia*) in Hebrews 13:2 is the opposite of xenophobia. For more on the witness of hospitality, see Rosaria Butterfield, *The Gospel Comes with a House Key* (Wheaton, IL: Crossway, 2018).

witness is not the eradication of poverty, the elimination of suffering, the increase of human flourishing, or any other form of overrealized eschatology that loses sight of the future glories of Christ's kingdom not yet consummated. The church's witness as a hospital must continue to communicate the gospel, in both word and deed, and to demonstrate Christ's compassion in this sin-sick world until Christ returns to wipe away every tear (Rev. 7:16–17).

The church is like a *fortress*, standing strong above the conflict as a place of refuge. The church is to be a showcase community and a standard of truth within society, as a refuge and city on a hill (Ps. 46; Matt 5:14). It is a stronghold in society that defends sound teaching and practice, while promoting social reconciliation and biblical justice (Ps. 72:12–14; Jer. 9:24). It is also a place of safety amidst the disorder and conflict common to human society, like the cities of refuge that God established in Israel's economy (Josh. 20). The church is a weekly haven of sabbath rest, reaffirming and rejuvenating weary pilgrims and keeping God's creational rhythm as a counterwitness, within a restless and weary world, of the eternal rest that awaits the people of God (Ex. 31:13–17; Matt. 11:28; Heb. 4:8–9).

We should not reject this fortress metaphor, overlooking the fact that the church's separateness from the world is essential for its witness to the world. Yet we must guard against the myopic fortress mentality that has often hindered the witness of the church. The church is not a hermitage for a secluded life of personal improvement, nor is it a lavish resort for an indulgent life that disregards those suffering just outside the gate. This metaphor can also be misapplied to promote a militant or triumphalist mentality that appropriates Christ's spiritual victory to our present social state instead of humbly following in Christ's suffering this side of heaven.

The church is like a *school*, discipling the next generation of Christian witnesses. As previously considered, discipleship ministries have always been central to the church's witness in the world, encompassing a wide range from neighborhood Sunday school programs, to mentorship at urban campuses, to theological education in global partnerships (Matt. 28:20; Acts 18:24–28; 2 Tim. 2:2). The church is also an equipping community where believers are mentored and prepared for public witness (Eph. 4:11–16). It is a protected learning environment for new witnesses, like a seedbed or greenhouse for growing young flowers. It is the center of wisdom from which Christian witnesses are sent into society as agents of transformation to demonstrate and apply God's truth. This model of public witness can be compromised, however, by false teachers with "silly myths" (1 Tim. 4:7; Titus 1:14), by academic pursuits divorced from the church's ministry,[15] or by other objectives that distract from the gospel purpose of Bible education.[16]

The church is like an *embassy*, representing Christ and his truth in a foreign land. Throughout history the church has often been called to live in exile, as strangers in a foreign land, worshiping Christ while living in the presence of people with different allegiances (Ps. 137:4; Jer. 29:4–7; 2 Tim. 1:8). The embassy model of witness is especially helpful in such times.[17] The church is a heavenly outpost on earth, a place where Christ is worshiped as the universal King within a society that rejects him. It is a community of Christ's representatives, who are called to demonstrate their faith through good deeds and public actions that authenticate and amplify the truth of their confession (Titus 3:1; James 2:17; 1 Pet. 2:12). It is a temporary residence of Christ's ambassadors who, on his behalf, implore sinners to be reconciled with God, promote justice in society,

15 Biblical literacy devoid of gospel repentance can become a seedbed for social apostasy. As Martin Luther cautioned, "Every institution that does not unceasingly pursue the study of God's word becomes corrupt. . . . I greatly fear that the universities, unless they teach the Holy Scriptures diligently and impress them on the young students, are wide gates to hell." Luther, "To the Christian Nobility" in *Luther's Works*, vol. 44 (Minneapolis, MN: Fortress Press, 1966), 207.

16 For example, many excellent mission schools in the African continent were eventually taken over by postcolonial governments in the second half of the twentieth century, often for political purposes completely contrary to biblical truths and gospel purposes for which they had originally been founded.

17 See Paul S. Williams, *Exiles on Mission* (Grand Rapids, MI: Brazos Press, 2020), 99–114.

and convey official declarations from heaven. The church community is Christ's sovereign territory, a place of love and restored relationships, a harbinger of peace and hope in a chaotic world.

As an embassy, the church must strive to maintain allegiance to Christ, rejecting competing loyalties, ungodly associations, and compromise with sinful ideologies that contradict the church's spiritual identity. The church's public witness is greatly hindered when Christians bring shame on the gospel's image in a society through personal moral failures, bitter discord among churches, or endorsement of public sin.

The church is like a *temple*, maintaining God's worship within the idolatrous world. A common metaphor across Scripture, the church is the place where God dwells with and is worshiped by his covenant people.[18] The church is commanded to maintain its consecration and purity, not only to promote true worship but also in order to be witnesses within the sinful world that worships idols in place of God. Unbiblical forms of worship are idolatry that compromises the church's spiritual identity (2 Cor. 6:14–7:1). Association with the world's ideologies and infidelities must be avoided since drinking with the Lord while also drinking with demons provokes God to holy jealousy and thwarts faithful witness (Deut. 32:21; 1 Cor. 10:14–22). Like Daniel living in Babylonian society, the church must remain undefiled and maintain true worship as Christ's prophets, priests, and princes in an ungodly land. A danger of this temple metaphor, however, is giving too much attention to church structures and worship performances, thereby taking focus from the witness of exclusive worship in a world of opposing idolatries.

These five practical models for the church's posture in the world are held up here to aid contemporary reflection. Many other models, and combinations thereof, can be developed from Scripture and church history. We are also painfully aware of the fact that the church and its leaders often do not live up to these ideals. We know that society's

---

18 See G. K. Beale, *The Temple and the Church's Mission* (Downers Grove, IL: InterVarsity, 2004).

scorn of the church is often due to our own failures (2 Kings 17:7–23; Ps. 137:1–4). With Daniel, therefore, we confess our collective sin and plead with our gracious Lord for his reviving mercy (Dan. 9:4–19).

Furthermore, the public witness of each local church community is varied and diverse, each with its own strengths and weaknesses. Which two or three models best characterize the public posture of your church community? Preferably, a church should pursue several models of witness within society simultaneously, and some combinations are more suitable within specific contexts. For example, it may be better to avoid the fortress-school combination and instead promote the hospital-school for a more balanced approach that remains ministry focused and is not merely an ivory tower for polishing abstract ideals. While important principles shape each of these models, contextual factors will influence the best way for your local gospel community to be an effective witness. Therefore, it is not a conceptual question about which model is most biblical, but a practical question of which foci are best for your church in your unique social context.

Our Gospel Community in God's Mission

How should our churches become more faithful witnesses in society? We answered this question by looking at God's purpose for the church, God's perspective of its social status, and several biblical models of the church's posture within the world. The starting point is not what activity we must perform or which task we must complete, but rather who we are and what we are called to become as God's people in this world. The church is called to be a gospel community and, being such, to witness publicly of its fellowship in Christ and of his truth, grace, and power.

We are witnesses of Christ, called to live in this world as a community of his prophets, priests, and princes. This is God's plan for how his church's witness should advance his mission. In light of this truth, we can reframe the question: How can what we are doing better display who we are becoming?

- How can our church's evangelistic activities be a clearer and more convincing message of who we are as Christ's witnesses in the world?
- How can our discipleship ministries better mature and equip Christ's witnesses for holy conduct and good deeds in the local community?
- How can our church's public acts of compassion best display God's gracious generosity and Christ's self-giving love?
- How can our church community better stir up one another to love and good deeds, and to overcome evil with good?
- How can our apologetic witness more effectively correct and defend the authentic presentation of Christ's truth to those in society who oppose us?
- How can our church community support church planting and church revitalization to grow faithful gospel witness both locally and globally?
- How can our church fellowship better witness of Christ in public through hospitality, intercession, and social justice?
- How can our church members be more intentional and effective in engaging cultural values and patterns that are contrary to God's truth?
- How can our church's honorable conduct and good deeds better shine the light of Christ in this sin-darkened world?
- How can our church's suffering for the gospel better embody Christ's truth, grace, and power through our weakness?

What is your church becoming? Children often ask the question, "What should I be when I grow up?" If wise, they then act in ways that align with a vision of what they will become. What will your church be when it has matured, and how should it act now in preparation? God's word gives us the answer: "In [Christ] you also are being built together into a dwelling place for God by the Spirit" (Eph. 2:22). The triune

God has a plan for the church, and his Spirit is managing the building project. He gathers believers into gospel community and binds them together in Christ. He also empowers all believers with spiritual abilities so that they all strive together "to excel in building up the church" (1 Cor. 14:12). It is a great comfort that the Holy Spirit is still working to mature the witness of our churches. He greatly desires our gospel communities to be better witnesses of Christ. Our task as churches is, simply, to align with the vision of God's mission and to keep in step with the Spirit who is busy building us according to God's sovereign plan.

Discussion Questions

1. Why is our public display of the communion of saints a powerful witness of Christ?

2. Explain three tangible ways in which the triune God makes known his manifold wisdom in the world through his church.

3. How should your church, as a local expression of Christ's new humanity, intentionally promote gospel reconciliation in your local region?

4. Describe the social status of your church from two perspectives: according to the narrow assessment of your society and according to the wider description of God's word.

5. Which two models of the church's posture in the world best describe your own church community? In which three areas should your church strive to witness in your society?

6. How can your church be more faithful in witness and more aligned with God's mission?

Conclusion

Motivating Christian Witness

WHAT SHOULD WE DO to motivate our churches to become better Christian witnesses? Our task has been to understand the church's witness within God's mission. We have developed a biblical definition for the multifaceted concept of mission, tracing God's story of mission through redemptive history (part 1), briefly reviewing historical aspects of the church's witness (part 2), and building on these with theological reflection about contemporary Christian witness (part 3). Our goal for this book, however, is much more than merely academic: we passionately desire to see growth and maturity in Christian witness, as individuals and as churches. How does this biblical theology of God's mission help us guide our church communities to become more faithful witnesses of Christ?

We conclude our study, therefore, on a practical note: How can we motivate God's church—our own local community along with all churches everywhere—to more faithful service in God's mission? The answer to this question must be grounded in our theology, authenticated by our experience, and animated with practical activity, which are the three main sections of this conclusion, following a comprehensive definition of Christian witness within God's mission.

Mission and Witness

Mission is God's work; witness is how Christians participate in it. As noted in the introduction, *witness* is the best term to describe the church's role in a way, consistent with Scripture, which does not combine, obscure, or disconnect God's work from ours. Based on this assumption, we have carefully unpacked the interrelated aspects of the triune mission and the witness of God's people encompassed by it. In chapter 5, we considered the relationship of mission, church, and witness. Now we conclude by concisely defining God's mission, the witness of church, and Christian witness.

God's mission is comprehensive and sovereign. Before creating the world, God the Father planned to redeem fallen sinners. The history of his mission of redemption began directly after the fall. Sinful humanity responded to God's revelation with unrighteousness and suppression of the truth, leading to idolatry and opposition against God. But the Father's plan from the beginning was to bless those whom he had elected from all the families of the earth, all to the praise of his glorious grace (Eph. 1:5–10).

God the Son was sent by the Father to fulfill the Old Testament promises and advance God's universal plan of redemption. This was accomplished when Christ made full atonement for his people's sin by his death, and then instituted the Gentile mission after his resurrection. Thus, Jesus Christ is the divine missionary, the suffering servant, the anointed leader, and the exalted sender (chap. 2). Christ's messianic kingdom continues to come while his people are being gathered from all nations through the agency of his Spirit and his church.

God the Holy Spirit was sent into the world, by the Father and the Son, to bear witness to Christ and to gather God's chosen people from all nations. The Spirit's ministry is the vital force of God's mission: he works for the salvation of God's people as the divine apologist, evangelist, and teacher; he works with God's church as the divine Helper, life-giver, anointing, and guide; and he works in God's history to accomplish God's cosmic plan (chap. 3). The Spirit empowers the church to bear witness to Christ, gifting God's people with spiritual abilities and sovereignly guiding all Christian witness. God's mission will be concluded when the Spirit has gathered the full number of God's people, when Christ returns at the end of this age, and when the Father's plan of redemption has been fully accomplished.

The *witness of the church* is subordinate to and flows from the triune mission. The church is firstly an object of God's mission, gathered throughout redemptive history, "a great multitude that no one could number, from every nation, from all tribes and peoples and languages" (Rev. 7:9). Yet God's purpose from the beginning was to sovereignly select his covenant people to be the human agency through which he accomplishes his mission in the world. The church collectively is God's human agency, witnesses of Christ who witness with the Spirit, testifying before the world that the only true God sincerely offers remission and reconciliation to rebelling sinners. The witness of God's people before Pentecost (chap. 1) laid the groundwork for the intensified and expanded witness of God's people after Pentecost (chaps. 4–6). As God's witness in the world, the church witnesses by means of its gospel presence, evangelistic message, apologetic response, and loving community within society (chaps. 7–10).

Christian witness is the public activity of the church in the world. We serve in God's mission by bearing witness to Christ. As God's people living within this un-Christian world, we serve in evangelism, apologetics, global gospel partnerships, church planting, compassion ministries, biblical counseling, cultural engagement, gospel worship, gospel suffering, and the many other activities that faithfully bear witness to Christ. There must always be new combinations of the church's time-tested methods of witness since local cultures and societies are constantly devolving and developing new mutations of Satan's lie. Our public task, guided and empowered by God's Spirit, is to study Scripture within our specific contexts in order to contextualize our approach and message, thereby engaging in faithful witness today.

The study of Christian witness requires the study of God's mission, traditionally called *missiology*, which includes the biblical theology of God's mission, traced throughout church history, with systematic explanation and reflection on contemporary themes. It also requires the study of the church's witness in the world, together with its many principles and methods, including the history of methodology, the theology of religion, and theories for faithful contextual communication and application.

Missional Hope

Having given extended attention in this book to the theology of mission and witness, we now end with the theme of missional motivation, an ideal case study for the experience and practice of Christian witness. By faith, God's people anticipate the conclusion of God's mission with missional hope. This hopeful faith engenders expressions of missional piety, which is often used by God to produce missional reform. Each of these terms—hope, piety, and reform—can be qualified with the term *missional*,[1] since all three are part of a faithful church's response to the story of God's mission. Our theology of missional hope, therefore, should lead to an experience of missional piety, which often motivates the missional reform of God's people.

What is missional hope?[2] In short, it is a joyful anticipation of the future success of God's mission. By faith, God's people in all ages anticipate the completed revelation of God's glory. From ancient times, the

---

1   Due to its present ambiguity, I have carefully avoided using the adjective *missional* in relation to the church and *Christian witness*. But in this chapter it is used in relation to the broader concept of *God's mission*, not merely as the essence or activity of the church.

2   The reader may be tempted to equate my views in this closing section to all the themes of Puritan eschatology as explained in Iain H. Murray, *The Puritan Hope: Revival and the Interpretation of Prophecy* (Carlisle, PA: Banner of Truth, 1971). While there are similarities, I have intentionally avoided the classic positions of millennial eschatology. This section on *missional hope* focuses only on the undeniable fact of unfulfilled prophecy, not on further developments that attempt to describe how these prophecies will be fulfilled in the present age and/or after Christ returns. My personal opinion aligns with Augustinian eschatology that views the millennial reign of Christ as inaugurated at his resurrection and extending until his return at the end of the world. See Augustine, *The City of God*, especially 20.9.

Old Testament church celebrated what God was doing and planning to do in the world, and they longed to see its success: the wolf dwelling with the lamb (Ps. 22:27–28; Isa. 11:6–9). The New Testament church also longs for the fullness of Christ's messianic kingdom, and they rejoice to see the Lord's redeemed people being gathered in from all lands (Ps. 107:2–3; Titus 2:13; Rev. 22:20). God's people have always longed for God's name to be hallowed, for his kingdom to come, and for his will to be done on earth as it is in heaven. Our theology of mission is not complete until we are stirred up with this same hope and the piety it produces. Consider several points for clarification.

Missional hope must be *built exclusively upon God's promises* as revealed in his word. This point is crucial: our hope is based on God's word, not on any external factors or the present social status of the church. Our hope is not a reaction to or affirmation of current political ideologies within society, nor is it derived from any millennial fantasies that have left behind Scripture's sufficiency and infallibility. Our hope is derived exclusively from the fact that God's word contains unfulfilled promises about the success of God's mission and his future universal glory.

As we observed in chapter 1, God's Old Testament people anticipated the coming of God's future kingdom and the fulfillment of God's global purpose:

In you all the families of the earth shall be blessed. (Gen. 12:3; cf. Ps. 67:1–3)

May he have dominion from sea to sea,
    and from the River to the ends of the earth! . . .
May all kings fall down before him,
    all nations serve him! . . .
May his name endure forever,
    his fame continue as long as the sun!

May people be blessed in him,
    all nations call him blessed! . . .
Blessed be his glorious name forever;
    may the whole earth be filled with his glory! (Ps. 72:8, 11, 17, 19)

And in the days of those kings the God of heaven will set up a kingdom that shall never be destroyed, nor shall the kingdom be left to
another people. It shall break in pieces all these kingdoms and bring
them to an end, and it shall stand forever. (Dan. 2:44; cf. 7:14; Zech.
14:9; Rev. 11:15)

For the earth will be filled
    with the knowledge of the glory of the LORD
    as the waters cover the sea. (Hab. 2:14; cf. Num. 14:21;
        Ps. 22:27; Isa. 11:9)

For from the rising of the sun to its setting my name will be great
among the nations, and in every place incense will be offered to my
name, and a pure offering. For my name will be great among the
nations, says the LORD of hosts. (Mal. 1:11; cf. Mic. 4:1)

The New Testament echoes these Old Testament predictions, showing how Christ's mission and the church's witness have begun to fulfill
them:

My house shall be called a house of prayer for all the nations. (Mark
11:17; cf. Isa. 56:6–8; Mal. 1:11)

You will be my witnesses . . . to the end of the earth. (Acts 1:8; cf.
Ps. 2:8; Isa. 44:6–8; Matt. 24:14;)

For so the Lord has commanded us, saying,

"I have made you a light for the Gentiles,
> that you may bring salvation to the ends of the earth."
>> (Acts 13:47; cf. Isa. 42:6; 49:6; Luke 2:32)

So that at the name of Jesus every knee should bow, in heaven and on earth and under the earth, and every tongue confess that Jesus Christ is Lord, to the glory of God the Father. (Phil. 2:10–11; cf. Isa. 45:22–23; Rev. 5:13)

In Romans, Paul teaches how Christ's first coming fulfilled many promises while also inaugurating a Gentile mission that began to fulfill ancient expectations for God's global kingdom and universal glory (Rom. 15:8–12; cf. 16:25–27). Paul sees his own ministry to the Gentiles as a localized fulfillment of Old Testament prophecies (Rom. 15:14–21). Precisely at this point in his teaching—between missional hope and ministry practice—Paul prays that "the God of hope" will fill the church with joy and peace, "so that by the power of the Holy Spirit [we] may abound in hope" (Rom. 15:13; cf. 15:14–21).

How and when will God fulfill these promises? There are conflicting explanations about their future fulfillment, whether historically in this present age or spiritually in the future age.[3] It is indisputable, however, that we have not yet seen a full and final fulfillment—every knee is not yet bowing to King Christ, and God's supreme glory does not yet fill the earth completely. So while avoiding distractions, we all should "abound in hope" as we together meditate upon God's unfulfilled promises. We trust unwaveringly that God's word is true, so we wait with joyful anticipation to see how God will use us and other means to accomplish his perfect plan.

Missional hope is *anchored in the unchangeable character of God's purpose.* Our hope, derived exclusively from God's promises, is even more

---

3   There is a sense in which the future is already present now, so already now in this age we enjoy foretastes of Christ's glorious kingdom, though God's universal glory will be fully realized only in the coming age. George E. Ladd, *The Presence of the Future* (Grand Rapids, MI: Eerdmans, 1974), 337–39.

certain because we know God the Father's eternal decree of redemptive mission must be accomplished. God's own character and reputation would be compromised if his mission were to fail (Ex. 32:11–14). God has guaranteed his promise to Abraham with an unbreakable oath, based on both his word and his character, which gives us double "encouragement to hold fast to the hope set before us" (Heb. 6:18). God's redemptive purpose includes not only the sovereign selection of his covenant people and the particular election of individual sinners, but also, more comprehensively, the whole mystery of redemption now revealed: the manifold wisdom of God made known through his people to the praise of his glorious grace (Eph. 1:5–6; 3:10–11; cf. Rom. 11:32–33).

With this strong encouragement, we hope with full assurance for the unstoppable completion of the triune mission.[4] The Spirit's sovereign work is effectual and irresistible; his mission of gathering the whole church will be successful despite all forms of demonic deception and human opposition. Christ's kingdom will triumph, and the Father's eternal purpose will be realized. This assured confidence drives us forward, out across all lands, for the cause of Christ our King.

Missional hope *produces assured confidence to follow God fully* in self-denial and suffering. Allow several faithful witnesses from the past to speak for themselves.

- Martin Luther (1483–1546): "Christians must have the vision which enables them to disregard the terrible spectacle and outward appearance, the devil and the guns of the whole world,

---

4 As John Calvin wrote, "But our chief consolation is that this is the cause of God and that he will take it in hand to bring it to a happy issue. Even though all the princes of the earth were to unite for the maintenance of our Gospel, still we must not make that the foundation of our hope. So, likewise, whatever resistance we see today offered by almost all the world to the progress of the truth, we must not doubt that our Lord will come at last to break through all the undertakings of men and make a passage for his word. Let us hope boldly, then, more than we can understand; he will still surpass our opinion and our hope." Quoted in Murray, *Puritan Hope*, xii.

and to see him who sits on high and says: 'I am the One who spoke to you' [John 16:33]."[5]

- David Brainerd (1718–1747): "I was constrained, and yet chose, to say, Farewell, Friends and earthly Comforts, the dearest of them all, the very dearest, if the Lord calls for it; Adieu, Adieu; I'll spend my Life, to my latest Moments, in Caves and Dens of the Earth, if the Kingdom of Christ may thereby be advanced. I found extraordinary Freedom at this Time in pouring out my Soul to God, for his Cause; and especially that his Kingdom might be extended among the Indians, far remote; and I had a great and strong Hope, that God would do it. I continued wrestling with God in Prayer . . . I longed to be as a Flame of Fire, continually glowing in the divine Service, preaching and building up Christ's Kingdom, to my latest, my dying Moment."[6]

- William Carey (1761–1834): "When I left England, my hope of India's conversion was very strong; but amongst so many obstacles, it would die, unless upheld by God. Well, I have God, and his Word is true. Though the superstitions of the heathen were a thousand times stronger than they are, and the example of the Europeans a thousand times worse; though I were deserted by all and persecuted by all, yet my faith, fixed on that sure Word, would rise above all obstructions and overcome every trial. God's cause will triumph."[7]

- David Livingstone (1813–1873): "We can afford to work in faith, for Omnipotence is pledged to fulfill the promise. . . . Missionaries in the midst of masses of heathenism seem like voices crying in the wilderness Reformers before the Reformation. . . . We work for a glorious future which we are not

5 Martin Luther, "Sermons on the Gospel of St. John" in *Luther's Works*, vol. 24 (Saint Louis, MO: Concordia, 1961), 417.

6 Written on May 22, 1745; see Jonathan Edwards, *An Account of the Life of the Late Reverend Mr. David Brainerd* (Boston, MA: Henchman, 1749), 186.

7 S. Pearce Carey, *William Carey* (London: Hodder & Stoughton, 1923), 326.

destined to see. We are only morning-stars shining in the dark, but the glorious morn will break."[8]

Missional hope is *best explained within the biblical vision of God's redemptive mission.* The Father's plan continues to unfold with unfailing progression. Christ has already now begun to reign, though his kingdom has not yet fully come (Matt. 28:18; 1 Cor. 15:24–25). The state of the church in different times and places, however, often oscillates between seasons of renewal and seasons of decline. Sometimes the Spirit works great public revivals in specific places; most often he works more silently behind the scenes. Yet Christ's kingdom continues to come.[9] Our hope, however, is not focused on the physical church or what Christians might do;[10] rather, it is anchored in God and in what he has done, is doing, and will do. So the church today, anticipating God's final goal and participating in Christ's ongoing mission, waits in joyful anticipation while being divinely aided by Christ's Spirit for the work of Christian witness.

Missional hope *draws us upward by faith and forward with spiritual endurance.* It repeatedly directs our attention to the joy set before us. Like John's vision in Revelation, it raises our gaze from the earthly realm with the chaotic devolution of society to the spiritual realm and the glorious triumph of Christ. We are not distracted by the present state of the world, whether cause for optimism or pessimism, or by the present state of the church, whether evidence of renewal or decline. What

---

8   William G. Blaikie, T*he Preachers of Scotland* (Edinburgh: T. & T. Clark, 1888), 142, 162.

9   Augustinian eschatology sees the coming of the kingdom in history as cumulative, never fully defined by a particular time or place. As David Livingstone wrote: "Our work and its fruits are cumulative. We work towards another state of things" (Blaikie, *Preachers of Scotland,* 143). We may be tempted to measure success (numerically or otherwise) at a specific snapshot of time, but God waits until the end when the full number of the elect will have been gathered and the renewed creation made ready for perfected worship (Rev. 7). Surely the stone, prepared without human intervention, is still growing into a great mountain that will soon fill the whole earth (Dan. 2:34–35; Isa. 2:2).

10 We must be careful to interpret unfulfilled prophecy within the historical-redemptive framework of biblical theology and in a way consistent with God's revealed purpose and plan. There is a long history of missionary motivation based on questionable eschatology. For careful discussion in this area, see C. J. Moore, "Can We Hasten the Parousia?" in *Themelios* 44, no. 2 (2019): 291–311.

is presently happening within the earthly realm cannot alter or thwart God's plan. Our hope includes both the certainty of its consummation and the sureness of its progress despite apparent setbacks in the present state of things, either locally or globally, since our hope is in God who has ordained both the means and the end. So we march forward with a spiritual endurance that is constantly replenished by the God of hope who gives us joyful anticipation of future glory.

Missional Piety

It is delightful to envision the glorious object of our missional hope: the coming fullness of the glory of the triune God. However, it is necessary to keep our hope grounded in Scripture and to exercise it consistently within a biblical theology of God's mission, which is a goal of this book. Moreover, properly defined theology is not enough; it must be experienced personally and become the heartbeat of our life and ministry. Our theology of missional hope should lead to missional piety and motivate missional reform.

What is missional piety? The concept of *piety* encapsulates many biblical virtues: spiritual godliness, loving submission and devotion to God, holy reverence and adoration of Christ, and a filial fear of the Lord.[11] Missional piety, a central aspect of spiritual godliness, flows from biblical knowledge of God's mission joined with joyful anticipation for the increase of Christ's kingdom and the fullness of God's glory. It is intellectual (head), rooted in biblical theology; it is emotional (heart), stirring up holy passions; and it is practical (hands), expressed in love and good works. It is also mystical, a sharing in Christ's suffering and victory, as well as communal, since the fellowship of the saints is itself the greatest witness in the world of God's triune love. In short, missional piety *spontaneously overflows* from a biblical vision of God's mission and an earnest missional hope for its success.

---

11   John Calvin connects theology and piety: "I call 'piety' that reverence joined with love of God which the knowledge of his benefits induces." Calvin, *Institutes of the Christian Religion*, ed. John T. McNeill, trans. Ford Lewis Battles (Philadelphia: Westminster Press, 1960), 1.2.1. The Puritans specialized in this area; see Lewis Bayly, *The Practice of Piety: Directing a Christian How to Walk, That He May Please God* (London, 1611).

Missional piety is *expressed in joyful celebration* of what God has done
and will do. Declaring God's glory among the nations has been the song
of the church in all ages. These songs were sung in ancient times by the
prophets and women of God, and compiled in the inspired Psalter (Ex.
15:20–21; Isa. 42:10; 54:1–3). The New Testament church expressed
hope in God with psalms, hymns, and spiritual songs (Acts 4:25–26;
16:25; Phil. 2:6–12). Likewise, the church during the past two millennia has continued this celebration, as we also do today.[12] The church
in heaven also continues to celebrate God's sovereign glory and the
success of his mission (Rev. 5:9). These songs of the church highlight
the communal aspect of missional piety; our collective joy is amplified
as we all celebrate together, joining in an unbroken chorus of praise
that continues to echo around the whole creation from ancient times,
across all lands, and for eternity. God's witnesses may appear to be suffering alone in some desolate prison, but by faith they join in chorus
with Paul and Silas (Acts 16:25) and with the innumerable multitude
of the redeemed to celebrate the triumph of the Lamb (Rev. 15:3–4).[13]

Missional piety *produces passionate prayer* for the success of God's
mission. In his high priestly prayer, Christ promises to continue making
known God's name in the world (John 17:26). This prayer and promise
is still being answered by the Father today as the church, united by this
prayer, echoes Christ's desires for God's name to be glorified in all the
earth.[14] As observed in chapter 6, spiritual awakenings and the subsequent

12 Famous examples are Isaac Watts's hymn, "Jesus Shall Reign Where'er the Sun" (1719), originally
titled "Christ's Kingdom among the Gentiles" based loosely on Psalm 72:12–19, and Edward Perronet's hymn "All Hail the Power of Jesus' Name" (1780), both written before nineteenth-century
Western missionary expansion.

13 This piety is expressed in both gospel celebration and gospel suffering; while the circumstances are
very different, the spiritual qualities of both are harmonious and flow together from a common
missional hope. John Piper highlights this harmony of missional piety in worship, prayer, and
suffering in *Let the Nations Be Glad* (Grand Rapids, MI: Baker, 1993).

14 Puritan George Newton (1602–1681) compels us to pray: "Let us strive with Christ in prayer
that he would make good the word that he hath spoken to the Father before so many witnesses."
Newton, quoted in Murray, *Puritan Hope*, 91.

progress of the gospel have often been preceded by times of earnest prayer for the success of God's mission.[15] Missional hope unites the church to pray in missional piety that God would continue to bless faithful gospel witness and to work again in the world with great power (Ps. 44:23; Isa. 51:9–11; Acts 4:31). In view of God's unfulfilled promises and the history of spiritual revival in past generations, we are encouraged to pray for future times of spiritual awakening.[16] Throughout the centuries, God has used the passionate prayers of his people to stir up faithful Christian witnesses and to send them forth into full-time gospel ministry.

Oh! Spirit of God, bring back thy Church to a belief in the gospel! Bring back her ministries to preach it once again with the Holy Ghost, and not striving after wit and learning. Then shall we see thine arm made bare, O God, in the eyes of all the people, and the myriads shall be brought to rally round the throne of God and the Lamb. The Gospel must succeed; it shall succeed; it cannot be prevented from succeeding; a multitude that no man can number must be saved.[17]

Missional piety *motivates evangelistic zeal* in Christian witness. This gospel zeal is holy passion, boldness, and confidence for gospel ministry.[18] The Spirit gives and matures evangelistic zeal within believers

---

15 Jonathan Edwards's *A Humble Attempt* (1747) is a famous example of a "concert in prayer" for the "advancement of Christ's kingdom." In his narrative on revival, Edwards writes: "The Scriptures give us great reason to think, that when once there comes to appear much of a spirit of prayer in the church of God for this mercy, then it will soon be accomplished." Edwards, *The Works of Jonathan Edwards* (New Haven, CT: Yale University, 1977), 4:350.

16 Many faithful church leaders in previous centuries have also prayed passionately for a Jewish revival. Regardless of one's position on this matter, we should not lightly dismiss the hopeful possibility of a future Jewish revival without also considering the missional piety undergirding these strong hopes. On this possibility, Jonathan Edwards writes, "Though we do not know the time in which this conversion of Israel will come to pass, yet thus much we may determine by Scripture, that it will be before the glory of the Gentile part of the church shall be fully accomplished, because it is said that their coming in shall be life from the dead to the Gentiles." Edwards, *Works*, 1:607.

17 Charles Spurgeon's prayer in sermon #3403 on Revelation 7:9–10 in *The Metropolitan Tabernacle Pulpit Sermons*, vol. 60 (London: Passmore & Alabaster, 1914), 198.

18 J. C. Ryle (1816–1900) writes that the zealous Christian "burns for one thing: . . . to advance God's glory. If he is consumed in the very burning, he cares not for it—he is content. He feels

individually and in the church collectively, especially as they faithfully use Christ's means of grace and obediently witness to others. Gospel zeal, especially when joined with gospel knowledge and practically expressed in gospel action, is often used by the Spirit for powerful witness in the world. Expressions of gospel zeal have been contextualized throughout church history in countless forms: self-denial for the cause of Christ, selfless acts of loving hospitality, financial support of global witness, and gospel suffering to defend the faith, just to name a few. All contextualized forms of gospel witness should be tangible expressions of the spiritual piety that motivates them (2 Cor. 8:7–8; Titus 2:14; Heb. 10:24).[19]

Missional piety is *documented in missionary biography*, the indelible testimony of a great cloud of witnesses who were compelled forward by a robust and undying missional hope. Some purely academic studies of church history fail by overlooking the spiritual passion that motivated millions of faithful men and women to selflessly offer themselves for the cause of Christ's kingdom. The life stories of most spiritual heroes of faith were never chronicled or have long been forgotten by the world. The stories we still know, however, are most valuable for their accounts of genuine missional piety, often in the face of many obstacles and much opposition. Truly, David's mighty men have slain their thousands, but with the gospel sword and in the strength of the Spirit, the mighty witnesses of Christ have won their ten thousands.

Missional piety is the *heartbeat* of Reformed experiential witness. Christian witness is not merely the repeating of certain facts to others or the presenting of various data publicly. To be a witness is to testify what we ourselves have seen and heard to be true, to share from personal

---

that, like a lamp, he is made to burn; and if consumed in burning he has but done the work for which God appointed him." Ryle, *Practical Religion* (London: Charles Murray, 1900), 185.

19 For example, Robert Findlater, a Christian businessman in 1800, bequeathed a large gift in his will to support mission, testifying that he was "viewing with joy the spreading glory of Immanuel's kingdom, when all His people's prayers, and all His Father's promises for the glory of His kingdom, shall be fulfilled. . . . O Lord, hasten the glory of the cross of Christ among all lands, that He may see of the travail of His soul, and be satisfied." Murray, *Puritan Hope*, 163.

experience, as noted in chapter 4. Bearing witness to Christ must begin with an experiential knowledge of Christ and his salvation. As Christ's witnesses, we tell others what we know is true, and we want everyone to experience the same truth for themselves (1 John 1:2–3; 4:14). Our hearts "burn within us" as we run to tell others that Jesus is alive (Luke 24:32). This experiential knowledge and burning passion for gospel witness is the missional piety that gives life and power and boldness and endurance to our witness of Christ. The personal questions asked at the end of the introduction drive home this point.

What is the best way to motivate Christian witness? It is not by evoking human pity with examples of dreadful suffering, or by overwhelming people with data about urgent needs in our dying world. It is certainly not by rebuking churches for their failure to obey the Great Commission.[20] Missional hope that has produced missional piety is the best motive for gospel ministry. A vision of God's mission and his ultimate glory, grounded in a faithful understanding of God's word, will resonate within the hearts of God's people to motivate experiential witness. This is the best and purest form of motivation for Christian witness.

Missional Reform

What should we do to motivate our churches to become better Christian witnesses? We have defined the biblical foundation and framework for witness as the church's participation in God's mission. We have also described a number of faithful methods of witness and reflected on the contemporary witness of the church in the world. Finally, we have been stirred up to witness by a glorious vision of God's mission. So now it is time for action. It is time to attempt great things for God, as William Carey urged when preaching from Isaiah 54:2–3 about God's vision

---

20 Legalistic slavery to the Great Commission and feelings of guilt for the Great Omission are never lasting motivators for Christian witness. While some other forms of motivation have merit, the best motivator is a vision of God's glory. See Ronaldo Lidorio, *Theology, Piety, and Mission: The Influence of Gisbertus Voetius on Missiology and Church Planting* (Grand Rapids, MI: RHB, 2023), 53–55 and 76–78.

for his church.[21] We are called now, aroused by our hope in the triune God, to motivate our churches to faithful action.

What is missional reform? To reform something is to make changes in order to improve it. Hence *missional reform* is the activity of motivating change in the church—starting with your local church community—in order to improve its participation in God's mission. This kind of change requires the Spirit's sovereign *revival*, usually experienced like raindrops here and there, though on special occasions as a mighty downpour. Either way, we earnestly desire God to work and fervently pray for the Spirit to revive the witness of his church. This kind of change also requires *repentance* for past failures and the times we have been fickle or false witnesses of Christ. It may involve the *restoration* of sound doctrine and it will involve spiritual *renewal* for faithful witness. Often it also requires *revitalization* and *rehabilitation* of churches that have become unhealthy or unfaithful witnesses. Missional reform will hopefully result in *transformation*, a significant improvement in the collective witness of our church community.

How might God use us to reform our church communities so that they will become more faithful witnesses of Christ? While God could change us all *immediately* with a new Great Awakening tomorrow, he normally works *mediately*, more progressively through the means he has appointed. So most likely the Spirit of God will use us as we wisely use biblical means to reform our churches. It will probably require much costly effort, both prayer work and reform work. As John Eliot wrote, "We must not sit still, and look for miracles: Up, and be doing, and the Lord will be with thee. Prayer and Pains, through faith in Christ Jesus will do anything."[22] We conclude this book, therefore, by considering

---

21 William Carey famously said, "Expect great things from God, attempt great things for God." See J. W. Morris, "Narrative of the First Establishment of This Society," in *Periodical Accounts Relative to the Baptist Missionary Society*, vol. 1 (London: J. W. Morris, 1800), 3.

22 John Eliot, *The Indian Grammar Begun; or, an Essay to Bring the Indian Language into Rules* (Cambridge: M. Johnson, 1669), 65. This same phrase, taken from 1 Chronicles 22:16, is repeated by Eliot's personal friend, Richard Baxter: "Let us, then, be up and doing, with all our might;

several actions for reform and features of reform for improved witness. As we reflect on these practical activities, you must ask how the Lord might employ you and others in this process to reform your church community. Prayerfully consider following these four actions as we seek to reform the witness of our churches. These are practical steps, explained here in logical order, which could in some cases be pursued simultaneously.

Table 6. Church witness assessment scorecard

Method of Witness	Present State	What to Stop	What to Start
Witness as showcase community			
Witness as loving confrontation			
Witness as expectant worship			
Witness as discipleship training			
Witness as showing compassion			
Witness as gospel living			
Witness as gospel speaking			
Witness as gospel defense			
Witness as gospel increase			
Witness as gospel suffering			

difficulties must quicken, not discourage us in so necessary a work. If we cannot do all, let us do what we can; for, if we neglect it, woe to us, and to the souls committed to our care!" Baxter, *The Reformed Pastor* (Carlisle, PA: Banner of Truth, 1974), 126.

First, missional reform begins with an *honest assessment* of the church's present state of witness, ideally done by or involving local church leadership. For this assessment we can use a scorecard approach (table 6) that assesses our own churches with the ten methods of witness highlighted in our biblical theology of God's mission (chaps. 1–4). Discuss with others in your church the present state of your witness in each of these ten areas, giving yourself a score of 0 to 4 for each, ranging from non-existent (0), to weak (1), to average (2), to improving (3), to mature (4). While discussing each area, list several suggested activities that should be stopped or started to improve your church's witness. These suggestions can later be used as points of departure when developing plans for going forward. For further assessment, you can also conduct a more in-depth study of your church's present witness in light of our theological reflection (chaps. 7–10).[23]

As we conduct an honest assessment of our church's witness, we should remember that Scripture is the perfect standard for measuring God's church. God's word is like a mirror; we look into it with our churches in order to view ourselves in relation to God's perfect standard. In fact, we must avoid the temptation to measure ourselves by a standard other than God's word. While there is much value in learn-

---

23 Perhaps a church elder could lead a small group discussion for several weeks using the questions at the end of each chapter in this book. Or your church leaders could spend time discussing the following summary questions:

  1. How is your church community called to follow Christ as his prophets, priests, and princes? Describe several other ways in which your church can show forth the truth and character of Christ in your local context and society.
  2. In what ways should your church communicate the gospel together with the Spirit? How can you contextualize your evangelistic methods in order to more effectively communicate the gospel to people in your community?
  3. How should your church respond to the idolatry and opposition in your society in a way that defends God's truth and declares Christ's gracious compassion? How can your church engage the local culture in a winsome way?
  4. How can your church, as part of Christ's new humanity, intentionally promote gospel reconciliation in your local region? Which two models of the church's posture in the world best describe your church community?

ing from the example of other mature churches, we do not measure ourselves by them or other human standards (2 Cor. 9:2; 10:12–18; cf. 1 Thess. 1:7–8). We also remember that even mature churches are not strong in all areas, and each church usually develops over time with different strengths and weaknesses. The scorecard approach is merely a practical tool to help us objectively identify the areas that need more attention.

Second, missional reform requires *spiritual renewal*. While earnestly praying for the Spirit to work revival among us, we actively work for a renewal of our churches that will motivate believers to faithful Christian witness. This renewing work requires several actions. We must repent of the idolatries that keep us from faithful witness—perhaps our sinful selfishness that hinders brotherly love, perhaps our myopic partiality for church traditions that hinder gospel fellowship, or perhaps our lack of self-denial and aversion to suffer for Christ's cause (Gal. 2:11–14; 1 John 3:13–18). We must remember our identity as God's people serving in God's mission, and we need to reaffirm our calling to be Christ's witnesses as his prophets, priests, and princes in society. We must refocus our gospel vision by returning to the foundation of biblical theology and the public confession of sound doctrine and gospel compassion. We should work to revitalize our first love for Christ and his kingdom, seeking with ardent desire to be "eminently holy" at all times, and sharing the gospel in passionate zeal to all people.[24]

Third, missional reform requires *practical guidance*. Each church community is unique, so this area of reform action will vary greatly; yet the following suggestions may provoke further ideas and growth. Ideally, the church leadership will initiate and guide the church's discussion about how to grow in these practical ways.

---

24 In 1662, Thomas Brooks wrote, "Now, Christians, the more great and glorious things you expect from God . . . the more eminently holy in all your ways and actings it becomes you to be." Brooks, "The Crown and Glory of Christianity" in *Complete Works* (1867), 444, quoted in Murray, *Puritan Hope*, 84.

- Affirm and encourage church members who already are examples of faithful witness.
- Create safe opportunities for church members to practice several methods of witness in order to disciple them and build their confidence in Christ.
- Discuss specific ways in which the church can become a better witness as well as the areas in which the church presently hinders its witness in society.[25]
- Promote opportunities for demonstrating gospel compassion, since the faithfulness of one member often contagiously motivates other members.
- Work together to upgrade organizational structures that frustrate faithful members, causing them to serve in ministries parallel to the local church.[26]
- Identify and mentor future leaders who already are faithful Christian witnesses.

Fourth, missional reform is directed by a *missional vision* of God's church. The church is the human agency, commissioned by Christ and empowered by the Spirit, which God is using to fill the earth with his glory. Alexander Duff passionately reminds us of this fact: "Never for a moment lose sight of the grand ulterior object for which the church was originally constituted, and spiritual rights and privileges conferred,

---

25 Be realistic in discussions about your church's specific calling and opportunities. For example, your church is not called to do campus ministry if it is located in a rural farming community far from academic institutions. Instead, you may be called to minister to migrant workers and lower income families nearby. Pray for wisdom to invest the means that God has provided your unique church in its specific time and place.

26 For example, denominational mission committees have rarely worked well for extended periods in the past centuries. While their leadership and goals were usually admirable, the structures themselves often caused much frustration. Is it not time to develop better structures for Christian witness within contemporary contexts? God has appointed his church to be his human agency for mission. But God's word does not require his church to continue using structures developed in Western societies largely under the influence of Christendom.

viz. the conversion of the world."[27] Many churches today, however, have lost sight of their place in God's purpose and plan of mission. So we must regularly teach this vision from Scripture. We should also constantly communicate the glorious vision of the success of the Spirit's ministry, the triumph of Christ's kingdom, and the ultimate glory of God. This vision guards us from becoming myopic or tribalistic, focused only on preserving our own families and our own traditions. This vision also guides us as we prayerfully develop strategies for faithful Christian witness.

Figure 13. Actions and features of missional reform.

What are the features of missional reform that we desire and work toward together? As we engage in these four actions for reform, we should also prayerfully consider five features of the transformation that we seek (fig. 13). These features guide us as the framework in which we work for reform.

Scriptural: We must ground our reform efforts in God's word. Too much evangelistic effort today is simply pragmatic practice that is not

---

27 Spoken at the ordination of Thomas Smith, missionary for twenty years in Calcutta, India. See Alexander Duff, *Missions the Chief End of the Christian Church* (Edinburgh: John Johnstone, 1839), 8.

aligned with the teaching of Scripture. Thus we need to return to a definition of witness that is developed from and operates within the biblical theology of God's mission, and that is shaped by systematic reflection on how biblical truths should be wisely applied in our world today.

Historical: The many methods of witness in the history of God's people must continue to guide the church today. It is very foolish to ignore the example and teaching of so great a cloud of faithful witnesses who have gone before us (Heb. 11:2; 11:39–12:1). Therefore, let us be stirred up to love and good works by their enduring witness.

Experiential: We who have seen God's glory and tasted his grace cannot hold back since we are filled with missional piety and abounding hope in God who does not lie. So we try to keep in step with the Spirit as he continues to tirelessly witness of Christ in our society and to the ends of the earth. Therefore, our Reformed experiential witness is heartfelt, gospel-centered, Christ-exalting, Spirit-filled, and God-glorifying.

Communal: The whole church together rejoices to witness of Christ in their culture and society as a public display of the communion of saints. We are not working alone as individuals or denominations, each with its own calling and areas of ministry. We have one calling by virtue of our union with Christ (Eph. 4:1–6), so we stand together, in Spirit and truth, as one spiritual community, both locally and globally, to serve as Christ's prophets, priests, and princes in the world.

Educational: We as God's church are commissioned to go and make disciples of all nations, starting with our own members and extending to believers from all nations. The preaching and teaching ministries of the church must never be minimized. Discipleship has always been a primary method of church reform.

Now therefore, let us not linger any longer: "Arise and work!" and "The LORD be with you!" (1 Chron. 22:16; cf. 2 Cor. 8:11; 2 Thess. 3:13). We have a rich spiritual identity and a great responsibility (1 Pet. 2:9; cf. Ex. 19:6), and we worship a great God. So let us in faith expect "great things" from "the LORD" (Ps. 126:1–6; cf. Gal. 6:9–10)! Every knee will soon bow before Christ, and our triune God will be glorified in all the earth. It is our great privilege, therefore, to continue pursuing this glorious vision, until Christ returns. The church must continue serving in God's mission by means of Christian witness.

Discussion Questions

1. What is God's mission, the witness of the church, and Christian witness? Briefly define these three terms and explain how they work together.

2. Explain how our missional hope is doubly encouraged by God's word and God's purpose, and why it produces spiritual boldness and endurance in Christian witness.

3. How is missional piety the heartbeat of Reformed experiential witness?

4. Describe the four actions and five features of missional reform.

5. How is God calling you and others to reform your church community?

General Index

Abraham, 29, 30, 77, 250
accommodation, 137
accountability, 140
activity, 63, 99
Adam, 2, 72, 190, 202–5, 206, 207n8, 215, 217
adoption, 168–69
adultery, 34
African culture, 49
Algonquin Bible, 135
Allen, Roland, 104n10, 114n1, 119n6
already and not yet, 232
ambassadors, 171, 211, 238–39
Ambrose, 143n24
Amos, 166
ancillary witnesses, 197, 215–17, 218
anointing, 84, 85, 186
antichrists, 148
antithesis, 210n17
Apollos, 100, 121, 143
apologetics, xviii, 1, 18, 103, 114, 149, 198, 201, 206, 211
apologetic strategy, 90
apostasy, 34, 148
apostles, 17, 50, 67, 74, 210
Apostles' Creed, 53
apostolic age, 117–22
apostolic church, 148
applied apologetics, 212n20
Aquila, 100, 121, 143
Asa, 137
assessment, 260

assurance, 250–52
atonement, 55, 230
Augustine of Hippo, 9, 136
Augustinian eschatology, 246n2, 252n9
authenticity, 227
authority, 51, 63

Babel, 30, 77, 87, 134, 193
Babylon, 239
baptism, 57
Baptist Faith and Message (2000), 20n30
Barnabas, 100, 143
Basil of Caesarea, 146
Bavinck, Herman, 216n32
Bavinck, J. H., 10–11, 27n1, 32n9, 81, 87n23, 106n12, 124–25, 189, 202n2, 207n8, 210n16, 212–13, 215, 219n37
Baxter, Richard, 145, 258–59n22
bearing false witness, 102, 109, 121
Belgic Confession of Faith, 19n27
believers, 95, 116
Bellarmine, Robert, 138n14
benediction, 168
Bible education, 143
"Bible experts," 164n10
Bible translation, 135–37
biblical counseling, xviii
biblical history, 124
biblical interpretation, 196

biblical theology, xix, xx, 7n3, 12, 27, 28,
    39, 114, 208n10, 219n36, 243, 246,
    252n10, 253, 260
biographies, xix, 21, 123, 126, 256
biology, 216
Blauw, Johannes, 114n1
blindness, 207, 209n13
Boa, Kenneth D., 212n20
Boer, Harry R., 78n11, 86n21
boldness, 221
Bosch, David, 10n10, 53n5, 123n11,
    131n1, 157n2
Bowman, Robert M., Jr., 212n20
Brainerd, David, 138, 251
Brakel, Wilhelmus à, 163n9
Brazil, 140n18
Brooks, Thomas, 261n24
Buddhism, 207n10
Buganda Martyrs, 149

Calvin, John, 82n15, 125n14, 143n24,
    161n6, 163n8, 167n12, 205n6,
    209n14, 215, 232n8, 253n11
canon, of Scripture, 74, 211
Canons of Dort, 19, 184n9, 214
Carey, William, xix, 132, 251, 257–58
Carson, D. A., 197n28, 217n33
Cassiodorus, 143n24
centrifugal force, 44n17
centripetal force, 44n17
cessationism, 74n7
Chalmers, Thomas, 145
charity, 146, 226
Christendom, 133, 143n23, 233, 262n26
Christianity, translatability of, 136
Christian (social label), 159
Christian witness, xv, 16–17, 245
Christian worldview, 16n22, 144, 217
Christological missiology, 122
Christology, 49n1
church
    apologetic response of, 204, 210–13
    calling of, 176
    as Christ's new humanity, 230–31
    as city on a hill, 165
    concept of, 115

as community, 120, 228–30
doctrine of, 173
in God's mission, 11–14
as God's temple, 32n8
gospel presence of, 174–76
as in the world but not of it, 235–40
missionary nature of, 116n3
mission of, 113–17
as object and agent, 6n2, 13–14
preservation of, 150–51, 173–74
and promotion of the gospel, 174
public testimony of, 98
purpose in society, 223–24
renewed calling of, 171–74
role of, 117
as a school, 237–38
social status of, 233, 240, 247
spiritual identity of, 158–63
as a temple, 232, 239
unity of, 91, 225
upbuilding of, 104
witness of, 17, 156–58, 245
church formation, 105
Church Growth Movement, 104n9
church history, xx, 124, 142, 148, 157
church planting, xviii, 18, 105, 114, 155,
    198
church revitalization, 105
city on a hill, 165
Clement of Alexandria, 230n5
cloud of witnesses, 21
Coillard, François, 19n25
colonialism, 15, 141
communalism, 231
communication words, 121n8, 179n1
communion of saints, 224–28
community outreach, 155
compassion, xviii, 69, 103, 145–47, 167,
    190, 219, 226, 229, 241, 261
condemnation, 87
confidence, 250–52
conflict, 231
confrontation, 35–40, 190, 220
consecration, 167, 174
consequences, of sin, 3, 203
consummation, 183, 235, 237, 253

context, of mission, 3
contextualization, 136n10, 174n18, 183, 196–98, 218
continuationism, 74n7
conviction, 3, 81, 86–87, 189, 190, 219
coram Deo, 176
Cornelius, 124, 180, 215n31
counseling, 198
counterantithesis, 210
countercultural examples, 170, 234
courtroom, 38–39, 102, 193
covenant, 226
covenant people, 32
covenant promise, 30
covenant unfaithfulness, 38
cowitnessing, 213–18
coworkers, 88, 106, 142
creation, 84
Crusades, 133
cults of personality, 164n10
cultural engagement, xviii, 226
culture, 174n18, 190n16, 196, 197, 218, 234
Cyril (Saint), 135n7

Daniel, 166, 174, 239, 240
deacons, 141
denominational mission committees, 262n26
DeRidder, Richard R., 27–28n1
DeYoung, Kevin, 15n18, 114n2, 157–58n2
dialogue, 101, 186, 214, 218, 220
direct fulfillment, 76
disaster relief, 147
discipleship, 18, 68, 98, 100, 143–45, 155, 198, 227, 237–38, 241, 264
discipleship apologetics, 212
discrimination, 231
divine sovereignty, 90
doxology, 20–21
dreams, 215n31
dualism, 147n35
Duff, Alexander, 144, 262–63
Dutch East India Company, 141

ecclesiology, 79, 83–85, 173
education, 143–45
educational ministries, 143
educational reform, 264
Edwards, John, 225n2
Edwards, Jonathan, 83n17, 91n26, 139, 255n15, 255n16
effective communication, 185
effectual communication, 185
elders, 141, 260n23
election, 29n5
elenctics, 189–90, 219n37
Elijah, 35
Eliot, John, 135, 137, 258
Elwell, Walter A., 55n7
embassy, 238–39
endurance, 252
Epistle to Diognetus, 120n7, 159n4, 230n5
eschatology, 42, 58n11, 79, 85–88, 133, 246n2
ethnic Jews, 61n14
euaggelizo, 99
European Reformation, 15, 125n14, 135–36, 138, 144
Eusebius of Caesarea, 161n6
evangelism, xv, xviii, 1, 17, 81–82, 85, 99, 114, 176, 180, 190–91, 201
evangelistic apologetics, 211, 212
evangelistic communication theory, 90
evangelistic outreach, 226
evangelistic trialogue, 218
evangelists, 99
Eve, 2, 190, 203
exaltation, 53
exclusivity, 184, 209, 217
exiles, 134, 149, 169, 172, 231, 233, 234
experiential reform, 264
eyewitnesses, 17, 94–95
Ezekiel, 76, 166, 221

faithfulness, xv
false religions, 202, 204, 207–8, 214
false teachers, 148, 213, 238
false witness, 102, 109, 121
fear, 2–3

fear of the Lord, 253
federal headship, 203
Felix, 107
fellowship, 224, 225–26
filioque clause, 73–74n5
final judgment, 4
financial hypocrisy, 140
financial support, 226
fire, 77
Flemming, Dean, 53n5
foreigners, 169
fortress, 237, 240
Foxe's Book of Martyrs, 126
Frame, John M., 212n20
fulfillment, 249
fullness of time, 67
future age, 249

general revelation, 72n3, 187, 215–16, 235
Gentile mission, 8, 33, 34, 36n12, 59–60, 64, 78
gentleness, 104
genuineness, 167
genuine revival, 89
geographic expansion, 15
Gilbert, Greg, 15n18, 114n2, 157–58n2
globalism, 30, 232–35
global partnerships, 114, 226
God
   fear of, 253
   future kingdom of, 43–45
   global purpose of, 41
   glory of, 6n2, 192, 246
   gracious dealings of, 41–42
   international power of, 42
   kingship of, 54n6
   manifold wisdom of, 228–32
   mighty acts and gracious dealings, 124
   mission of, 244–45
   promises of, 247–49
   purpose and means of, 31, 249–50
   redemptive mission of, 252
   sovereignty of, 194, 209
   supreme being of, 40
Goheen, Michael W., 15n20
good works, 230

gospel
   communication of, 120–21, 185–91, 195–98
   concise message of, 180–84
   as exclusive and essential, 184
   mystery of, 191
   preached in advance, 29–32
   proclamation of, 191–95
   as singular and holistic, 182
   translation of, 134–37
   universal message of, 183–84
gospel community
   as covenantal, 226
   definition of, 224
   in God's mission, 1, 240–41
   as synergistic, 227
gospel confrontation, 220
gospel defense, 96, 101–4, 212
gospel globalism, 134, 232–35
gospel increase, 96, 104–6
gospel living, 96–98
gospel offense, 212
gospel partnerships, xviii, 18, 142, 155
gospel promise, 3
gospel speaking, 96, 98–101
gospel suffering, 96, 106–9, 226
grace, 174
Great Awakenings, 140, 258
Great Commission, 1, 4, 9, 34, 63–64, 68, 75n8, 76, 78, 82–83, 85, 116, 119, 145, 223, 227, 228, 257
Great Omission, 257n20
Greek dualism, 147n35
Green, Michael, 16n23, 99n3
growth, 104
Guder, Darrell L., 114n1
guilt, 2–3, 80, 206, 257n20
Gutenberg, Johannes, 143n24

Harnack, Adolf von, 99n3, 146n33
Hartenstein, Karl, 9n6
Haykin, Michal A. G., 125n14
healing, 236
Heidelberg Catechism, 64n17, 145n31, 160–62, 165, 169n13, 170n15, 208n11, 211n18

heresies, 148
hermeneutics, 183
Hexapla, 135
Hezekiah, 37n14, 137
Hiebert, Paul, 197n29
historical-redemptive framework, 252n10
historical reform, 264
holiness, 33–34, 167, 207
holistic Christian living, 162
Holy Spirit
    anointing of, 186
    of the church's witness, 88–92
    conviction of, 3, 8, 189, 214, 219
    dependence on, 221
    empowering of, xv
    filling of, 5
    gift of, 87
    in God's history, 85–88
    guidance of, 118–19, 198
    illumination of, 210
    indwelling of, 164
    keeping in step with, 242
    ministry with God's people, 83–85
    ministry of, 79–88, 126–27, 244–45
    mission of, 8–9, 71–75
    outpouring of, 75, 93
    at Pentecost, 75–79
hope, 246–53
hospitality, 1, 114, 236, 241
hospitals, 146, 236, 240
Hughes, R. Kent, 230n5
human agency, 76–77n9, 83, 191, 245
human flourishing, 237
humanism, 207–8n10
humanistic globalism, 30, 134, 193,
    232–35
human methodology, 105
human reason, 209n14, 215, 216
human responsibility, 90
human trafficking, 147
humiliation, 53
humility, 104, 213, 221
Hungarian Hussite Bible, 135
hymns, 21
hyperindividualism, 164n10
hypocrisy, 227

identity, 99, 173
ideologies, 234
idolatry, 22, 34, 36, 37, 81, 193, 201,
    204–10, 213, 214, 220, 234, 239, 261
illumination, 81, 189
image of God, 209n13
incarnation, 67, 68n21
indigenization, 136, 196
individualism, 116, 164n10, 231
intercession, 167
intolerance, 206
inward facing ministry, 158
Isaiah, 37n14
Islam, 215n31
Israel, restoration of, 60–61

Jehoiada, 137
Jehu, 137
Jeremiah, 36
Jeremias, Joachim, 60n13
Jerome, 135
Jesuits, 137
Jesus Christ
    as anointed leader, 56–61
    as apostle and witness, 67–69
    authority of, 51
    baptism of, 57
    centrality of, 49
    death of, 55, 110
    as divine missionary, 50–54
    as divine sender, 62
    earthly ministry of, 51–53, 56, 59, 67
    as exalted sender, 61–66
    as example, 67–68
    exclusivity of, 184, 209, 217
    human nature of, 73n4
    humiliation and exaltation of, 53
    as last Adam, 205
    as messianic shepherd, 58–59
    miracles of, 53–54
    mission of, 49–70
    parting instructions of, 76
    preservation of his church, 150–51
    vs. Satan's lie, 204
    as suffering servant, 54–56
    threefold office of, 161–63, 175
    triumphal procession of, 125

Jewish revival, 255n16
John the Baptist, 165
Jonah, 35–36, 124
Jones, Peter, 207n9
Josiah, 137
joy, 254
Judaism, 98
Jude, 121
Judeo-Christian worldview, 217
judgment, 4, 37, 38, 86–87, 101, 194
Julian the Apostate, 146n34
justice, 194, 229, 237, 241

Keller, Timothy, 114n2, 196n25
kerysso, 99
kingdom of God, 43–45, 58, 100, 180,
    183, 235, 252
kingdom of priests, 33
kingship, of God, 54n6
Knights Hospitaller, 146
koinonia, 225–26
Korean Christianity, 139
Köstenberger, Andreas J., 64n17
Kuyper, Abraham, 209n15

Latin Vulgate, 135
Lausanne Covenant, 20
Lawrence, John B., 86n22
Leeman, Jonathan, 114n2
legalism, 77n9, 257n20
Leithart, Peter, 114n2
Lewis, C. S., 68n21
liberation theology, 58n10, 236
Liddell, Eric, 108n16
light, 49
Lightfoot, Joseph Barber, 120n7
light of nature, 82n15, 214–15
Livingstone, David, 141n19, 251–52,
    252n9
Llull, Ramon, 149
local church, xv, 11, 127–28
location, 197
Log Colleges in New England, 144
Lord's Prayer, 20
love, 213, 226
Luther, Martin, 149n37, 238n15, 250–51

Malagasy Martyrs of Madagascar, 149
Manila Manifesto (1989), 20n31
Martyn, Henry, 160n5
martyrs, 107, 126, 149
means, 63
medium, 197
meekness, 103
Melanchthon, Philip, 143n24
mentorship, 68, 198
mercy, 194
merit, 29n6
Methodius of Moravia, 135n7
methodology, 90, 119n6, 179
Middle English, 135
militant mentality, 237
millennial eschatology, 246n2
miracles, 53–54
missio Dei, 9–11, 15n17
missiology, 15, 49n1, 122, 246
mission
    before Christ, 45–47
    of the church, 113–17
    committees of, 262n26
    comprehensive plan of, 4
    context of, 3
    definition of, xviii, 1–2, 10, 14, 115
    history of, 123–27
    methodology of, 90, 119n6
    objects of, 3
    and witness, 244–46
    wonder of, 3–4
    word and deed in, 12n15
missional, 15, 173n17, 246n1
missional ecclesiology, 173
missional hope, 246–53
missional piety, 253–57
missional reform, 257–65
missional vision, 262–63
missionaries, 15
missions, 15
monastic orders, 141, 143
monotheism, 208n10
Moravian movement, 141
Moreau, A. Scott, 15n17
motifs, 28
motivation, xvi, 179, 191–95, 243–65

Mukhanyo Theological College, xix
Muller, George, xxin3
Muller, Richard, 196n24
multiethnic church, 106, 231, 232
multiplication, 227
Murray, Andrew, 139
Murray, Iain H., 79n12
Muslims, 215n31
mystery, 65, 191

Nasmith, David, 145
Nathan, 220
nations, inclusion of, 36, 65–66
neighbors, love for, 69
Neill, Stephen, 10n12, 157n2
Netland, Harold A., 212n20
neutrality, 184, 209
new age, 93
Newbigin, Lesslie, 114n1, 182n7,
    218n35
new covenant, 88
New Testament
    apostles in, 121–22
    mission in, 44n17
    promises in, 248–49
Newton, George, 254n14
Nicene Creed (381), 72
noetic effects of sin, 209n13
North American Indians, 137, 138, 251
North Korea, 140n18

obedience, 184, 228
objects, of mission, 3
Old Testament
    church in, 52, 56
    Jesus on, 4–5
    mission in, 27–47, 44n17
    on outpouring of God's Spirit, 75
    promises of, 247–48
    prophets in, 121–22
    witness of, 12–13
online learning, 144
opposition, 148, 193, 201, 205–10, 213
oppression, 236
optimism, 252
organization, 140–42

Origen, 135
Ott, Craig, 114n2
outzward facing ministry, 158
overrealized eschatology, 237
Owen, John, 73n4, 84n19, 183n8

Packer, J. I., 66n20, 82n16, 90n25, 99n4,
    214n23
parachurch ministry, 114
paradigm shifts, 131
Paul
    calling of, 125
    on general revelation, 215–16
    teaching of, 100
Pentecost, 4–5, 73, 75–79, 93, 206
Perkins, William, 161n6
Perronet, Edward, 254n12
persecution, 96, 105, 108–9, 148–49,
    233
personal evangelism, 77n9
personality, cults of, 164n10
personal testimony, 181
persuasion, 212n20
pessimism, 252
Peter, 95–96, 109–10, 121, 122, 124,
    171–72, 180–81
Peters, George W., 11n13, 40n16
Philip, 121
piety, 246, 253–57
Pilate, Pontius, 17
pilgrims, 170, 234
Piper, John, 7n3, 107n14, 116n4,
    254n13
plethuno, 104
pluralism, 42, 143n23, 228
political ambitions, 133
polity, 140–42
Polycarp of Smyrna, 171
postmodernism, 194n22
poverty, 237
power, 63
power encounters, 91n26
practical guidance, 261–62
practical theology, 211n19
pragmatism, 133
praise, 232, 254

Pratt, Richard L., Jr., 220n39
prayer, 118, 224, 254–55
preaching, 17–18, 85, 99, 198, 264
present age, 86
priesthood of all believers, 229
priests, 166–68
princes, 168–71
Priscilla, 100, 121, 143
proclamation, 180
progress, 133
promises, 63, 247–49
Prophetic Literature, 35, 36
prophets, 55, 164–66
prostithemi, 104
Protestant Reformation, 138
Protestant theology, 9, 164
Psalms, 21, 40–45
public confession, 162
Puritans, 125n14, 162n7, 198, 246n2,
    254n14
Pyongyang Revival (1907), 139

Rabbula of Edessa, 146
racism, 231, 236
rebellion, 36, 37, 39, 80, 81, 166, 190,
    203, 204
reconciliation, 101, 160, 168, 188, 230,
    237
re-creation, 84
redemption, plan of, 3, 6
redemptive history, 78
redemptive mission, 182, 252
reform, 137–40, 246, 257–65
Reformation, 15, 125n14, 135–36, 138,
    144, 162n7
Reformed experiential witness, 18–22,
    184, 256–57, 264
refugees, 147, 169
regeneration, 81–82, 139, 212
rehabilitation, 258
religious pluralism, 42, 143n23, 228
remnant, 35
renewal, 258, 261
repentance, 258
restoration, 168, 236, 258
Revelation, 123

revitalization, 258
revival, xvi, 78, 79, 84, 85, 139, 255, 258
Robinson, C. Jeffrey, Sr., 125n14
Roman Catholic Church, 133, 138n14,
    146
Roman centurion, 59
Ryle, J. C., 255–56n18

sabbath rest, 237
salvation, 80–83, 180, 195
Samaritan woman, 59
sanctification, 81–82, 90, 212
Sanneh, Lamin, 136n8
Sargent, Leslie, 197n27
Satan, 148, 182, 195, 203, 204, 220,
    234
scope, 63, 64–65
scorecard, 259–60
Scripture
    canon of, 74, 211
    and reform efforts, 263–64
    sufficiency and infallibility of, 247
selection, 29n5
self-denial, 261
Sexton, Jason, 114n1
shalom, 10
shame, 2–3, 80
showcase community, 32–35, 157, 173,
    229
signs and wonders, 77, 91n26
Simeon, 61
Simeon, Charles, 169n13
sin
    consequences of, 3, 203
    conviction of, 190
    exposing and rebuking of, 38
    vs. grace, 174
    noetic effects of, 209n13
slavery, 140
small groups, 260n23
Smith, Thomas, 263n27
so-called gods, 37
social apostasy, 238n15
social communities, 97
social identity, 97, 159
social improvement, 236

social justice, 241
social reconciliation, 237
social status, 233, 240
social transformation, 140
society, 212, 218
sociocultural analysis, 218
sojourners, 149, 169, 172, 231, 234
soldiers, 170
songs, 254
soteriology, 79, 80–83
South Africa, 140n18
Southgate Fellowship, 20
speaking in other tongues, 77
special revelation, 72n3, 74, 216, 217,
    235
spiritual adultery, 34
spiritual ambassadors, 171
spiritual blindness, 207
spiritual communion, 225
spiritual endurance, 252
spiritual enmity, 206
spiritual exiles, 169
spiritual gifts, 77n10, 87
spiritual growth, xix
spiritual identity, 173, 230
spiritual pilgrims, 170
spiritual regeneration, 81–82
spiritual renewal, 261
spiritual soldiers, 170
spiritual warfare, 162, 182n6, 195
spontaneous witness, 119–20, 253
Sproul, R. C., 232n8
Spurgeon, Charles, 255n17
Stephen, 121, 125, 148
Stott, John R. W., 49n1, 157n2,
    220n38
strategies, 179
Stroope, Michael W., 15n19
substitutionary atonement, 55
success, 194
suffering, xviii, 105, 121, 134, 148–49,
    194, 237, 257
suffering servant, 54–56, 58n11
Sunday school ministries, 145, 238
Sundkler, Bengt, 44n17
Sun-Joo, Kil, 139

supernatural factor, 83–84n18
syncretism, 149
systematic theology, 7n3, 211n19

Table of Nations, 30
Taylor, Hudson, 89–90n24, 142
teaching ministries, 100, 264
team dynamics, 142
technology, 198
temptation, 203
Tennent, Timothy, 9n5
Tertullian, 109n17
testimony, 16, 181, 221
Theological Education by Extension
    (TEE), 144
theology, 253
theoretical apologetics, 212n20
therapy, 236
threefold office, of Christ, 161–63, 164,
    175
Timothy, 121
Titus, 121
Tower of Babel, 30, 77, 87, 134, 193
transformation, 127, 140, 182, 184, 258
translation, of the gospel, 134–37
trialogue, 186–88, 218
tribalism, 231
Trinity, 3, 7–11
triumphalism, 62n15, 134, 237
triumphal procession, 125
true religion, 207
truth, 102, 194, 206
Turretin, Francis, 161n6
Tyndale, William, 136
types, 56

unbelief, 35, 39, 80, 204–10, 219
unbelievers, 87n23, 166, 187, 215
unfulfilled prophecy, 252n10
ungodly society, 233–34
union with Christ, 162, 164, 166, 172,
    229
universal, gospel message as, 183–84
universal church, 116
universal story, of mission, 28
unlikely means, 191

Van Til, Cornelius, 202n2
Vicedom, Georg, 9n6, 11n13
victory, 62
visions, 215n31
Voetius, Gisbertus, 9–11, 192n20

Waldensian movement, 138
Warneck, Gustav, 138n14
Watson, Thomas, 188n12
Watts, Isaac, 254n12
weakness, 241
Western colonialism, 15
Western culture, 116, 133, 217, 218n35
Western philosophy, 90, 207n10
wind, 77
winsomeness, 227
wisdom, 215
witness
    of all believers, 163–71
    before Christ, 45–47
    as biblical, 16, 94–96
    definition of, xviii, 6, 113
    by discipleship, 143–45
    empowering of, 4–6
    expansion of, 132–34
    as expectant worship, 40–45
    as gospel defense, 96, 101–4
    as gospel increase, 104–6
    as gospel living, 96–98
    as gospel speaking, 98–101
    as gospel suffering, 106–9
    as loving confrontation, 35–40
    by kind acts, 145–47
    methods of, 117–22
    and mission, 244–46
    polity for, 140–42
    as showcase community, 32–35
    as spontaneous, 119
    in suffering, 148–49
    in the world, 14–18
wonder, of mission, 3–4
word of God, study of, xx
world, 14–18, 79–88
worldliness, 121, 167, 174
worldview, 16n22, 144, 190n16, 217, 218
worship, xviii, 20–21, 40–45, 116n4, 128, 157–58, 170, 224, 232, 239, 254
Wright, Christopher J. H., 114n2
Wycliffe, John, 135

xenophobia, 236

zeal, 98, 133, 255–56
Zwemer, Samuel, 170n14

Scripture Index

Genesis

1:2 72
1:28 30
2:7 72
2:15 158
3 . . . . 2, 3, 3n1, 13, 29, 46,
        80, 202, 217
3:1–7 . . . . 203, 221
3:1–21 . . . . 2, 6, 22
3:7–8 206
3:8 2
3:9 . . . . 2, 3, 192n20
3:9–13 190
3:9–15 xvii
3:11 3
3:13 3
3:15 . . . . 3, 4, 54, 206
4:25 206
8:17 30
8:21 167
9:1 30
10 30
10:8–10 30
11:1–9 . . . . 30, 193, 233
11:4 . . . . 30, 52, 165
11:6–9 134
11:7–9 77
12 . . . . 29, 30, 31
12:1 12
12:1–3 . . . . 1, 30, 52, 77, 193,
        233

12:2–3 . . . . 29, 134
12:3 . . . . xxii, 28n4, 36n12,
        65, 93, 247
18:18 65
22:18 65
26:4 65
28:14 64
50:20 108

Exodus

1:22 206
3:2–6 77
9:16 . . . . 38, 52
15:11 38
15:18 66
15:20–21 254
19:4–6 . . . . 32, 33, 98, 122
19:5 33
19:5–6 . . . . 1, 226, 229
19:6 . . . . 172, 264
29:45–46 73
31:2–5 73
31:13–17 237
32:11–14 250
34:6 53
34:6–8 52

Numbers

11:29 . . . . 84, 164
14:21 . . . . 132n4, 232, 248
14:21–23 31
33:4 38

Deuteronomy
3:24 33
4:5–8 33
7:6–8 .... 29n6
18:15 .... 56, 164
19:15–21 102
26:18–19 33
30:3–4 59
30:6 73
31:19 17
31:26 17
32:16–17 37
32:21 239

Joshua
20 237

2 Samuel
7:22–23 33
7:23 .... 30, 193, 228
12 220
12:7 220
12:13 220

1 Kings
8:41–43 34
19:12 134

2 Kings
2:3 68
2:3–5 143
5 34
17–19 .... 37n14
17:6–19:37 47
17:7–23 .... 34, 240
18:33–35 .... 37n14
19:15–19 .... 37n14, 47
19:21–28 .... 37n14
19:22 37

1 Chronicles
16:24–26 41
22:16 .... 258n22, 264

2 Chronicles
6:32–33 65

Ezra
6:10 167

Nehemiah
9:20 78

Esther
3:6 206

Job
1:6 37
34:14–15 72

Psalms
book of 40, 41, 42, 43, 44
2 .... 28n4, 42, 52
2:1–3 .... 36, 206
2:2 .... 30, 56
2:4–6 .... 38, 102
2:6–9 .... 11n14, 62
2:7–8 60
2:7–9 7
2:8 .... 4, 44, 65, 134, 248
2:9 54
2:9–10 211
9:8 42
11:4–7 43
14:1–3 208
14:4 206
18:50 56
19:1 .... 6n2
19:1–4 215
19:1–6 17
22:27 .... 41, 65, 248
22:27–28 .... 42, 247
22:27–31 44
33:12 41
44:23 255
45:7 56
46 237
46:4 76
47:1–9 44
47:9 42
51:1–4 220
51:11 78
53:1–3 208

58:1–11............43
59:5 42
59:8 42
67....................1
67:1–2 42
67:1–3 ....229, 247
67:3 ....20, 41, 65
68:18...............43
72....................43, 44n17
72:1 44
72:8 ....60, 248
72:8–11............44
72:11...............60, 65, 248
72:12–14 237
72:12–19 ....254n12
72:17...............60, 65, 248
72:17–19 44
72:19...............52, 60, 132n4, 232,
                   248
80....................137
82....................37
82:1–2 42
82:8 42
85:4 137
85:9–13............43
86:9 41
89:7 40
95:3 40
96....................40
96:3 ....12, 33, 65
96:3–5 41
96:10–13 43
98:2 41
98:3 42
98:9 42
105 41
105:1...............42
105:1–2............134
105:6...............41
106 42
106:5...............41
106:37 37
106:47 59
107:2...............20
107:2–3............247
110:1...............62

110:1–3............44
110:4...............56
110:5–6............43
115:4–8............37
117:1...............41, 65
118:22 55
126:1–6............264
135:4...............41
135:5...............40
137:1–4............240
137:4...............45, 170, 238
144:15 41
145:3...............40
145:4–6............134
145:10–13..........43

Proverbs
8:1...................216
8:1–4...............81

Isaiah
1:3...................216
1:8...................169
2:1–5...............129
2:2...................252n9
2:2–4...............44n17
2:2–5...............44, 65, 127
6:3...................52
6:8...................22
6:9–10 61
6:10 ....209n13
9:1–7...............132n3
10:20–23 169
11:2 ....57, 73
11:6 54
11:6–9 247
11:9 ....xvii, 132n4, 232, 248
11:12...............59
13–23 37
17:13...............38
24:14–16 44
26:11...............87
26:14...............37
26:15...............132n3
27:13...............65
32:15...............76, 86

34:1–2 38
34:8 38
37:19 37
40:11 59
40:18–26 37
41:21 37
41:21–24 37
41:29 37
42:1–7 55
42:1–9 8
42:6 .... 33, 65, 98, 249
42:10 254
43:8–12 .... xvi, 33, 37, 39, 102, 228
43:9–12 .... 191, 193
43:10 .... 16n23, 39
43:12 4
43:21 228
44:3 .... 76, 86
44:6–8 .... 228, 248
44:6–9 39
44:6–20 37
44:8 .... xvi, 4, 16n23, 17
44:18 .... 209n13
45:20 66
45:20–23 .... 39, 40, 102
45:21 28
45:22 1
45:22–23 .... 37, 86, 249
48:9–11 34
49:1–7 55
49:6 .... 4, 12, 28n4, 33, 60, 65, 98, 249
49:19 .... 132n3
50:4–9 55
51:4 98
51:9–11 255
52:7 100
52:10 65
52:13–53 55
53:10 51
54:1–3 254
54:2–3 .... 13, 64, 132n3, 257
55:3–4 56
55:3–5 .... 28n4
55:4 .... 39, 62, 67

56:6–8 .... 127, 248
56:7 .... 31, 65, 167
56:7–8 65
56:8 59
60:1–3 93
60:3–7 44
61:1–2 57
61:1–3 .... 1, 55, 78
61:1–4 .... 161n6, 163
61:6 166
63:10–11 73
63:11 78
65:17–25 168
66:15–16 38
66:18–20 128
66:18–21 129
66:19 .... 41, 232
66:20 .... 65, 66n19

Jeremiah
1:5 36
5:21 61
8:7 216
9:23–24 21
9:24 237
10:2–11 37
23:1–4 58
23:5 56
25:31 .... 37, 102, 211
29:4–7 .... 170, 238
29:7 .... 167, 229
30:9 56
31:31–34 78

Ezekiel
2:3–5 221
2:5 166
5:5–8 34
12:2 61
20 34
20:41 167
28:24–26 .... 36n12
33:11 .... 87, 194
34:11 59
34:11–24 58
34:15–16 59
34:23 56

34:26 76
36:22–24 34
36:26–27 78
37:1–14 77
37:11–14 137
37:24 56
47:1–12 . . . . 76, 86

Daniel
2:34–35 . . . . 252n9
2:44 . . . . 56, 66, 134, 248
6:10 174
7:13–14 62
7:14 . . . . 66, 248
7:18 169
9:4–19 240
9:25 56

Hosea
3:5 56

Joel
2:28 . . . . 75, 86
2:28–29 93
2:28–32 . . . . 28n4
3:2 37

Amos
3:2 . . . . 29n6, 34
5:23–24 166
9:11–12 . . . . 28, 61, 64, 137

Jonah
book of 36

Micah
2:12 59
3:8 73
4:1 248
4:1–5 . . . . 44, 127
5:1–2 56

Nahum
1:15 100

Habakkuk
2:14 . . . . 31, 132, 232, 248

Zephaniah
2:11 38

Haggai
2:5 73

Zechariah
3:1 37
4:6 134
9:9 56
12:10 86
13:7 . . . . 56, 59
14:9 . . . . 66, 132n4, 248

Malachi
1:11 . . . . 128, 166, 232, 248
3:1 56
3:3–4 138
3:4 . . . . 166, 167, 167n12
3:17 35
1:11 . . . . 13, 31

Matthew
1:20 73
1:22 56
2:5 56
2:6 56
2:17 56
3:15 56
3:16 57
4:1–11 . . . . 204, 221
4:23 . . . . 51, 183
5:10–12 148
5:13–16 165
5:14 . . . . 165, 237
5:14–16 . . . . 17, 65
5:16 . . . . 1, 98, 120, 146
5:44–48 146
6:33 . . . . 170, 229
8:5–13 59
8:11 . . . . 65, 127
8:11–12 65
8:23–27 xvii

8:29 54
9:35 183
9:36 .... 53, 146, 219
9:36–38 59
10:5 .... 5, 98
10:5–6 .... 51, 59
10:16 103
10:16–25 148
10:40 50
11:10 15
11:11 .... 79, 133
11:27 162
11:28 .... 194, 237
12:18 57
12:28 73
13:13–15 61
13:15 .... 209n13
13:17 55
13:33 165
14:14 53
15:24 .... 51, 59
15:24–26 59
15:32 53
16:16 109
16:18 .... 105, 150
16:19 211
16:21 51
16:24 108
20:1–16 235
20:6 192
20:28 .... 51, 55
20:34 .... 53, 219
21:12–14 138
21:13 65
21:43–45 65
22:10 59
23:15 98
23:37 59
23:37–38 61
24:14 .... 8, 67, 86, 94, 134,
                        183, 192, 195, 248
24:31 59
25:1–13 235
25:7 137
25:14–30 235
26:31 59

26:59–68 103
26:72 109
28 1
28:18 .... 62, 63, 100, 252
28:18–20 .... 4, 63
28:19 .... xvi, 1, 15, 63
28:19–20 .... 68, 143
28:20 .... 18, 63, 75, 82, 86,
                        238

Mark
1:10 57
1:14–15 .... 58, 183
1:15 .... 56, 67, 179
1:38 51
1:41 53
5:7 54
6:7 5
6:34 53
8:2 53
8:31 .... 51, 55
8:35 194
9:37 50
10:45 .... 8, 51
11:17 .... 65, 128, 248
13:10 134
16:15 .... 63, 184, 192
16:15–18 .... 4, 63
16:16 63
16:17 .... 63, 121
16:20 .... 121, 168

Luke
1:33 66
1:69 56
1:78–79 53
2:31–32 61
2:32 .... 33, 65, 249
2:34 61
3:22 57
4:18 .... 50, 73, 236
4:18–19 .... 51, 57, 58n10,
                        161n6, 163, 185
4:19 168
4:21 56
4:43 .... 50–51, 51
5:32 52

7:2–10 59
7:13 53
7:22 53
8:1 51
8:28 54
9:1 5
9:22 51
9:48 50–51
10:1 5
10:2 192
10:16 50–51
10:18 62
10:20 104
10:33 .... 53, 219
11:49–51 51
12:11–12 165
12:35 137
13:28–30 65
13:33 195
13:34 51
14:23 65
15:4 52
15:20 .... 53, 219
17:25 51
19:10 .... 2, 8, 52, 59
19:14 51
19:41 192
19:46 65
20:10 51
20:16–18 61
20:17 55
22:19–20 55
24:7 51
24:26 .... 51, 55, 108
24:27 28
24:32 257
24:44–49 28
24:45 .... 82, 162
24:46 .... 51, 55, 63
24:46–48 .... 56, 121
24:46–49 .... 4, 63
24:47 63
24:48 .... 63, 93
24:48–49 8
24:49 .... 63, 76, 84, 89, 163

John
book of 94
1:9 .... 51, 65, 81
1:14 162
1:18 .... 52, 164
1:29 .... 52, 55
1:32 57
1:32–34 73
1:34 .... 16, 96
1:41 57
1:45 57
2:14–17 138
3:5 83
3:8 139
3:11 95
3:16 .... 8, 192
3:16–17 194
3:17 .... 50, 52
3:18 209
3:19 .... 51, 221
3:34 50
4:7–42 59
4:22 59
4:23–24 91
4:25 57
4:34 51
4:42 55
5:36 .... 50, 53
6:29 50
6:57 50
6:63 .... 72, 185
7:8 67
7:29 50
7:32–36 59
7:38 76
8:12 51
8:42 .... 50, 51
8:54 51
8:56 56
9:5 51
9:39 61
10:11 58
10:16 .... 59, 166
10:28 52
10:36 50
11:9 51

11:42...............50
12:20–26...........59
12:31...............52, 54, 62
12:36–40...........61
12:40...............209n13
12:41...............56
12:46...............51
12:49...............51
13:3................53
13:14–15...........69
13:15...............67
13:20...............62
14:6................217
14:10...............51
14:12...............79, 88
14:15–17...........76
14:16–17...........83
14:17...............82
14:24...............11n14
14:26...............11n14, 73, 76
15:18–20...........148
15:26...............11n14, 73, 76, 82
15:26–27...........5, 16, 62, 83, 94, 96,
                   188
16:7................76, 79
16:8................3, 8, 40, 76, 80, 86,
                   189
16:13...............9, 76, 85
16:16...............16, 94
16:28...............53
16:33...............251
17..................51
17:2................52, 55
17:3................50
17:4................51
17:6................52
17:8................50, 51
17:9................66, 162
17:14–18...........169, 235
17:14–19...........68n21, 90
17:15–19...........174n18
17:18...............50, 62
17:20...............66, 166
17:20–21...........59
17:21...............50, 69, 85, 91, 97,
                   159, 225, 231

17:23...............50
17:25...............50
17:26...............52, 254
18:36...............170
18:37–38...........103
19:19–20...........135n7
19:30...............108n15
20:21...............8, 9, 15, 50, 62, 63,
                   68n21, 73n5
20:21–22...........4
20:21–23...........63
20:22...............63
20:23...............63, 211
20:31...............179

Acts
book of.............4, 16, 74, 76, 77, 78,
                   85, 87, 94, 104, 105,
                   106n12, 107, 113,
                   118, 121n8, 123,
                   124–25, 132, 179,
                   206
1–2................118
1:1................179
1:1–11.............2, 4, 6, 22, 93
1:2................64
1:4................76, 84, 89
1:4–8..............63
1:5................63, 76, 79
1:7................63
1:8................xvi, 1, 4, 5, 16,
                   16n23, 42, 63, 65,
                   84, 132, 160, 248
1:14...............77
2..................77n10, 79, 98n2
2:1................77
2:8–10.............134
2:11...............136
2:17..............86, 163
2:17–18............164
2:17–20............84
2:17–21............28n4, 75
2:32...............96, 160
2:32–36............100
2:33...............62, 73, 75, 76, 78, 87
2:38...............87

2:40 96
2:41 104
2:42–47 .... 97, 120, 224
2:44–47 92
2:47 .... 104, 105, 225
3 97
3:12 211
3:14–15 62
3:15 .... 96, 160
3:20 51
3:22 56
3:22–26 164
3:25 .... 28n4
3:25–26 .... 44n17
3:26 51
4 .... 139, 140, 148
4:5–7 102
4:7 140
4:10 140
4:11 55
4:12 .... 103, 217
4:19–20 140
4:20 191
4:21 .... 106, 159
4:23–31 118
4:24–26 42
4:24–30 148
4:24–31 .... 28n4, 221
4:25–26 254
4:26–27 56
4:27 30
4:28 108
4:29–31 xx
4:31 .... 79, 117, 118, 188,
                       255
4:32–33 .... 92, 96, 160
4:32–34 224
4:32–35 97
4:32–37 120
4:33 96
5 140
5–6 142
5:3–4 140
5:12–13 97
5:12–14 120
5:13 159

5:13–14 92
5:14 .... 104, 225
5:17–33 102
5:29 140
5:31 56
5:32 .... 96, 160, 188
5:39 140
5:41 .... 96, 109
5:42 .... 117, 143
6 140
6:1 104
6:1–7 140
6:7 .... xx, 69, 104, 143,
                       225
7:1–53 34
7:51–54 61
7:52 .... 56, 148
8 121
8:1–4 108
8:4 117
8:4–5 96
8:12 100
8:25 96
8:29 85
9:4 108
9:10–19 110
9:15 102
9:15–16 124
9:31 .... 104, 105n11, 225
10 .... 215n31
10:1–11:18 119
10:34–35 184
10:34–43 .... 121, 180
10:38 .... 57, 73, 84, 146
10:39 .... 96, 160
10:40 96
10:42 .... 64, 96, 103, 119
10:45 79
11:5 118
11:15–16 76
11:15–18 97
11:19 .... 99, 117
11:19–21 119
11:24 .... 104, 225
11:25–26 .... 100, 143
11:26 .... 69, 97, 159, 230

11:29–30 141
12:24 .... xx, 104, 225
13:1–2 97
13:1–3 .... 118, 141
13:16 196
13:23–41 56
13:31 96
13:32–33 42
13:34 .... 28n4
13:41 12
13:46–47 60
13:47 .... 12, 28n4, 33, 65, 98,
          249
13:49 104
14:15 220
14:17 .... 17, 216
14:21 .... 69, 143
14:22 108
14:23 105
14:26–28 106
14:27 117
15 .... 136, 142
15:1 136
15:7–9 119
15:8 17
15:16–17 61
15:16–18 28
15:19 136
15:28 .... 85, 119, 140
15:30–35 97
16:6 9
16:6–10 .... 85, 118
16:14 81
16:25 .... 118, 254, 254
17:2 .... 103, 186n10, 212
17:2–3 96
17:6 .... 210n17
17:17 .... 96, 103, 186n10,
          212
17:22 196
17:22–31 216
17:30 198
17:31 .... 42, 100, 103, 194,
          211
18:4 .... 103, 186n10, 212
18:6 60

18:19 .... 103, 186n10, 212
18:23 .... 69, 143
18:24–28 .... 18, 68, 100, 143,
          238
18:26 .... 69, 121
19 142
19:6 79
19:8 .... 100, 186n10
19:8–9 .... 103, 212
19:9 .... 69, 143, 159,
          186n10
19:20 .... xx, 104, 225
19:23 159
20:7 .... 117, 186n10
20:9 .... 186n10
20:18–38 97
20:24 17
21:8 .... 99n5
21:16 .... 69, 143
21:27–28:31 107
22:1 .... 103, 196, 212
22:15 96
22:17–21 118
22:21 60
23:11 .... 16, 66, 96
24:12 .... 186n10
24:14 159
24:22 159
24:24–25 107
24:25 .... 186n10
26:1 196
26:16 96
26:23 98
28:23 .... 16, 96, 100
28:23–24 .... 103, 212
28:25–27 61
28:26–28 12
28:28 .... 60, 219
28:31 100

Romans
1:4 73
1:5 .... 15, 65, 66n19, 119,
          129
1:16 .... 60, 184, 191
1:16–17 .... 43, 101, 110

1:17 194
1:18 .... 2, 206
1:18–20 214
1:18–32 81
1:19–20 81
1:19–25 187
1:20 .... 87, 209
1:21 .... 209n13
1:21–32 207
1:25 203
1:26–27 216
1:28–32 206
2:9–10 60
2:14–15 214
2:15 81
2:16 182
3:10–12 208
3:19 86
3:20 .... 183n8
3:20–26 204
3:26 194
4:16 30
5:3 .... 109, 149
5:12 .... 2, 203
5:12–21 .... 203n5
8:7 206
8:9–11 76
8:11 .... 72, 73, 82
8:14 85
8:14–18 169
8:14–27 188
8:16 17
8:19–22 184
8:23 .... 88, 168
8:28–30 .... 29n5
8:31–38 150
8:35 108
8:35–37 133
8:37 .... 62n15, 162
9:2–3 61
9:6 .... 35, 29n5
9:17 124
10:1 .... 61n14
10:9–13 42
10:14 .... 147, 166, 191
10:14–15 195

10:14–18 100
10:15 15
10:17 196
11:1–5 134
11:7–10 61
11:11–12 61
11:15 .... 61n14
11:23 .... 61n14
11:25 61
11:31–32 .... 61n14
11:32–33 250
11:36 8
12:1–2 .... 158, 232
12:4–6 116
12:18 229
12:21 168
14:17 .... 98, 100
14:19 104
15:8 .... 51, 52
15:8–9 .... 8, 60, 204
15:8–12 .... 28, 44n17, 249
15:8–13 .... 12, 122
15:8–16 129
15:9–11 41
15:9–12 .... 8, 93
15:11 65
15:13 .... 88, 249
15:14–21 249
15:16 .... 66, 66n19, 128, 166
15:18 .... 66n19, 69
15:19 121
15:22–23 .... 16n22
15:22–29 120
15:27 .... 66n19
15:30 xx
16 106
16:3–16 142
16:25 182
16:25–26 .... 65, 128
16:25–27 249
16:26 .... 66n19, 119, 129

1 Corinthians
2:1–5 .... 107, 196
2:14 .... 209n13
3:6–8 .... 105n11

3:7 105
3:10–15 105
5:7 167
6:9–10 100
9:16 192
9:19–23 . . . . 103, 199
9:22 218
10:14–22 239
10:19–22 . . . . 208n12
10:20 37
10:33 218
11:1 . . . . 18, 67, 166
12:4–11 . . . . 83, 87
12:11 . . . . 9, 83, 127
12:11–14 116
12:12–13 163
12:13 119
13:1–3 147
14:4 . . . . 105n11
14:12 242
14:26 104
15:15 102
15:22 204
15:24–25 252
15:24–28 . . . . 8, 100
15:45 . . . . 3, 72, 204
15:57 . . . . 62n15
16:1–2 141

2 Corinthians
1:21 163
1:21–22 84
2:14 125
2:14–16 165
2:15–16 126
2:16 . . . . 184, 194
2:17 211
3:4–6 . . . . 9, 84
3:4–12 90
3:5–9 96
3:6 72
3:7–9 87
3:7–18 127
3:9 87
4:1 88
4:4 . . . . 209n13, 218

4:6 81
4:7–11 107
4:18 88
5:5 88
5:14 . . . . 90, 192
5:14–20 171
5:17–20 168
5:18–6:1 . . . . 96, 110, 229, 231
5:20 . . . . 100, 211, 214, 219
5:20–6:1 . . . . 184, 188
6:1 . . . . 88, 106, 214
6:14–7:1 . . . . 92, 138, 167, 239
7:10 . . . . 190n18
8–9 141
8:4 226
8:7–8 256
8:11 264
8:23 106
9:2 261
10–13 . . . . 104, 105
10:1 219
10:3–4 85
10:3–6 170
10:4 . . . . 9, 81
10:4–6 . . . . 18, 103, 204, 211, 212
10:5 1
10:5–6 229
10:8 104
10:12–18 261
10:13–18 21
12:10 107
12:12 121
12:19 . . . . 103, 212
13:11 229

Galatians
2:8 15
2.11–14 261
3:2 81
3:8 . . . . 8, 13, 30, 44n17, 46, 73
3:14 46
3:27 136
3:28 119
3:28–29 . . . . 230, 231

4:4 .... 56, 67
4:4–5 51
5:16–25 90
5:17 85
5:18 85
5:25 91
6:9–10 .... 168, 264

Ephesians
1:3–14 .... xviin1, 163
1:4 .... 29n5
1:4–6 7
1:5–6 250
1:5–10 244
1:6 .... 6n2, 232
1:9–10 228
1:10 .... 56, 67
1:12 .... 6n2
1:14 .... 6n2, 32, 67, 75, 76
1:18 81
1:21 62
2:1–10 230
2:3 8
2:4 2
2:5 82
2:8–9 8
2:10 166
2:11–22 97
2:13–17 160
2:14 231
2:14–15 230
2:15 106
2:17 231
2:18 119
2:19 .... 159, 231
2:19–20 228
2:21–22 232
2:22 .... 127, 241
3 228
3:1–13 65
3:3–11 46
3:6 .... 65, 128
3:10 .... 171, 191, 228
3:10–11 250
3:18 .... xxi, 128
4:1–6 264

4:3 .... 9, 85, 91
4:7–12 87
4:8 .... 39, 62, 125
4:11 .... 15, 99n5, 141
4:11–12 100
4:11–16 .... 117, 238
4:12 .... 68, 104
4:12–16 232
4:17–24 230
4:18 .... 209n13
5:1 146
5:1–2 168
5:8 120
5:8–15 98
5:11 .... 81, 103, 212
6:18 225
6:18–20 118
6:19–20 108
6:20 171

Philippians
1:5 .... 18, 106, 142, 226
1:7 .... 103, 212
1:12–18 108
1:16 .... 103, 212
2:6–11 53
2:6–12 254
2:9–11 .... 30, 62, 193
2:10–11 .... 86, 192n20, 249
2:15 .... 98, 120, 165, 167, 221, 227, 229
2:15–16 148
2:15–16a 192
3:2–3 92
3:10 226
4:3 106
4:15 142

Colossians
1:10 166
1:13 170
1:14 55
1:15–20 67
1:24 108
1:26–27 65
2:7 105

2:15 ....39, 52, 54, 62, 125
2:19 91
3:11 231
3:14 91
4:2–3............xx
4:3............118
4:3–4............65
4:5............103
4:5–6............103, 212
4:6............165
4:16 101

1 Thessalonians
1:7–8............120, 165, 261
2:1–12............103, 103n8
2:12............101
4:1–12............120
5:11 104
5:15 168

2 Thessalonians
1:5............100
1:5–8............87
1:8............66, 184
3:1–5............xx
3:13 264

1 Timothy
2:1–4............229
2:1–8............42
2:1–10............167
2:4............198
2:5............217
2:6............51
3:1–13............141
4:1............92
4:7............145, 238
4:10 55
5:20 ....103, 212
6:12–13............103
6:13 ....17, 67

2 Timothy
1:6............138
1:8............18, 226, 238
1:8–9............19

1:14 82
2:2............18, 68, 143, 238
2:3............109, 226
2:9............107
4:5............1, 99n5
4:16–18............133
4:17 ....66, 108

Titus
1:14 ....145, 238
2:7–8............166, 168
2:11 ....42, 229
2:12............227
2:13 247
2:14............32, 256
2:15 ....103, 212
3:1............238

Philemon
11............124

Hebrews
book of............121
1:1–2............51
1:2............164, 183
1:3–4............53
1:5............42
1:9............56, 57
1:13 62
2:4............81, 83
2:10 169
2:14 ....39, 52, 54, 204
2:14–15............162
2:15 125
3–4............35
3:1............8, 15, 50, 54
3:1–6............68
4:2............184
4:8–9............237
6:4............81
6:18 250
6:20 169
7............166
7:3............56
7:25 ....66, 162, 166
9:11–12............55

9:14 73
9:24–28 55
10:20 56
10:24 256
10:29 92
10:30 66
10:32 81
10:32–36 149
11:2 264
11:4 xx
11:9–10 195
11:10 170
11:13 56
11:13–16 170
11:32 121
11:39–12:1 264
12:1 21
12:1–3 126
12:2 ....169, 194
12:28 ....100, 169
13:1–3 18
13:2 ....1, 236n14
13:16 167

James
2:5 100
2:14–17 69
2:14–26 167
2:17 238
2:26 147
4:4 206

1 Peter
book of 173
1:10–11 13
1:10–12 ....28, 44n17, 55, 73,
                     182
1:11 61
1:12 75
1:25 136
2:4–5 232
2:5 ....105n11, 127
2:6–7 55
2:8 184
2:9 ....32, 122, 172, 173,
                     264

2:9–10 ....98, 226, 229
2:9–12 ....28, 33, 34, 171
2:10 ....159, 230
2:11 ....85, 167, 169, 231,
                     234
2:11–12 120
2:12 ....1, 16, 18, 96, 98,
                     146, 166, 167, 227,
                     238
2:15 168
2:20 ....107n14
2:20–21 204
2:21 ....67, 108
2:24 ....52, 55
3:13–15 219
3:13–17 ....18, 103, 212
3:14–17 204
3:15 ....1, 17, 96, 149, 201,
                     219
3:18 ....108n15
4:1 17
4:6 184
4:12–16 169
4:13 109
4:13–14 84

2 Peter
1:18–19 164
2:5 13
2:9 150
3:1 101
3:9 87
3:16 101

1 John
1:1–4 182
1:2 ....16, 95
1:2–3 257
1:3 225
2:1 ....56, 83
2:2 55
2:18 148
2:20 84
2:27 ....76, 84, 163
3:5 ....52, 55
3:8 ....52, 54

3:13–18 261
3:16–18 .... 147n36, 226
3:17 167
4:1–6 92
4:9–10 50
4:14 .... 15, 50, 55, 95, 257
4:20–21 .... 69, 227
5:6–12 .... 17, 86
5:21 167

2 John
7 148

3 John
1:5–12 142
7 121

Jude
1:3 103
3 .... 212, 219
22–23 .... 192, 229, 236

Revelation
book of. 94, 123, 133, 134, 137
1:1 123
1:5 .... 39, 67, 84n19, 94
1:6 .... 163n8, 166
2:7 133
2:11 133
2:13 .... 16, 68, 96
2:17 133
2:26 133
2:27 42
3:5 133
3:12 133
3:14 67
3:21 133
4:8 52
5 62
5:9 .... 128, 129, 254
5:10 166
5:13 249

6:1 131
6:2 133
6:9–11 149
7 .... 252n9
7:9 .... 66, 117, 129, 245
7:9–10 .... 30, 193, 231, 232, 255n17
7:16–17 237
7:17 66
11 193
11:3 .... 16, 96
11:3–7 101
11:8 148
11:15 .... 66, 248
12 54
12:5 .... 42, 54
12:6 169
12:9–10 62
12:13–17 233
12:17 206
13:2 37
14:6 .... 135, 136, 184
15:3–4 254
16:13 148
17:6 .... 16, 96, 148
17:14 62
19:10 86
19:11 67
19:11–21 8
19:15 .... 42, 54, 211
19:16 62
20:6 166
21:10 165
21:23–24 65
21:24–26 .... 128, 129
22:1 76
22:5 169
22:17 .... 72, 75, 89
22:18–19 .... 74, 164n11
22:20 247